3/6 nett.

D Sealey

yours as ever
Geo Heath

MEMORIAL EDITION.

THE POEMS

OF

GEORGE HEATH,

THE MOORLAND POET.

With an Introduction, by

THE REV. JAMES BADNALL, B.A.,

VICAR OF ENDON.

Memoir,

BY FRANCIS REDFERN,

AUTHOR OF THE "HISTORY OF UTTOXETER," &C., &C.

Portrait and Illustrations,

BY HERBERT WILSON FOSTER.

LONDON :
SIMPKIN, MARSHALL, & CO.

HANLEY :
ALLBUT AND DANIEL, PERCY STREET PRINTING WORKS.

1880.

The Invalid poet
Bradstown Etc
Dunwood
Rudeset Lake   view from
                    his cottage
Henyro Gap
Erador Valley
The Ranches

"from inhibited in wildly
beautiful dream to the
curl of the shining
and the rise of the sun"

as an
appetite

        I have committed
        to the flames a batch of
        letters that I received
        from a love, that one
        or like to me.
        Such letters — but yet
Love   the writing in the
loft   end deserted me.

                    "The Doom of Babylon"

CONTENTS.

———o———

PREFACE.

OUR pleasant task is over. Our labour of love is
finished. It remains for the public now to appre-
ciate the genius of our Poet. A few words,
perhaps, are necessary in explanation of raising the price
of the present volume, which originally was intended to
cost 3s. 6d. At that price it was found that many pieces
must have been omitted, which, for their own intrinsic
merits, it was desirable should be included in the volume.
As it is, we have been obliged to curtail several of
the lengthy pieces, viz.—"A Country Woman's Tale,"
" Icarus," and the " Doom of Babylon." Sufficient, however,
it is presumed, has been given of these to enable the reader
to form a tolerably good idea of the drift and style of the
whole. As regards myself, I can only say that I have con-
sidered it the greatest privilege of my life to have been

B

allowed to help a little in arranging and bringing out the present volume. And any one (and I feel sure my fellow-labourers, who have so materially assisted me in this work, participate in my feelings) who knew the late lamented George Heath as well as we did, would envy us the privilege. I take this opportunity of most thankfully acknowledging the valuable assistance I have received from my friend and parishioner, Mr. George Foster, in all the details incident to this publication ; also to Mr. Francis Redfern and Mr. H. W. Foster, for their valuable departments of service, which are before the reader to speak for themselves. And I may also here, on behalf of the Poet's family, sincerely thank those ladies and gentlemen who have so kindly subscribed towards the erection of a Memorial Cross to his memory, in Horton Church-yard. By the time this volume is in the hands of the subscribers, it is hoped that the monument also will be over the place

"Where our friend sleepeth."

JAMES BADNALL.

Endon, June 20th, 1870.

PREFACE TO THE SECOND EDITION.

N issuing a second edition of the poetical works of George Heath, it appears essential to take advantage of the custom, when publishing a book, of making a few prefatory remarks. In doing this it is proper to state that the friends of the deceased Poet have been prompted to the undertaking partly to meet a demand for copies of the poems, and also from a laudable desire to preserve in a printed form other poetical writings from the manuscripts of the Author. In the latter respect this volume will be found to contain an addition of nearly eighty pages of hitherto unpublished poetry, which every one who can appreciate the struggling efforts of genius in most unpromising conditions, will be glad to possess. The erasions, which, much to the regret of many, and without my knowledge, were made from "Icarus," have been restored in this issue, and the other poems which are added, are entitled "The Invalid Poet," "Found Dead," and many lengthy fragments surpassing, in some instances, in power and beauty many of his other efforts, and evidently intended for an extension of "The Invalid Poet," and not as I had previously believed for the "Country Woman's Tale." The volume now comprises all that the public will most admire from the pen of George Heath, or that can conduce to the esteem in which the memory of

the extraordinary young man is held.   No further ap-
propriation has been made from the "Doom of Babylon,"
for although he thought so much of that performance,
which he wrote under the feverish influence of reading
Dante, he was not titanic and desperate enough to deal
with such heavy moral subjects.   He was rather the poetic
child of nature, from whose brighter aspects as well as
from her more secret recesses of meaning, his fancy and
feeling might have drawn out many more shades of delicate
beauty had he been spared to have lingered long and
lovingly over them.

It is not necessary to make any further remarks with
regard to the additions made to this volume, but before
dismissing this preface, it will be well to refer to the highly
appreciative terms in which the first edition of the poems
was received.   The notices of them in literary journals
and in the press generally were accompanied by remarks
expressive of great surprise at the unexpected evidences
they bore of unmistakable poetic merit, and of equally
undoubted promise of greater achievement.   But it was
especially gratifying to find that a most interesting paper
of some fourteen columns in length, from the pen of
Robert Buchanan, the Poet, was thought worthy of a place
in *Good Words* for March, 1871, with the addition of
two engravings on wood representing himself and his birth-
place.   From this excellent and discriminating essay liberty
is taken to make a few brief extracts which place George
Heath, for his peculiar poetical gifts and manliness of mind,
in a very marked position.   Speaking of the young man
from a look at the portrait prefixed to the poems,

Mr. Buchanan remarks as follows :—" The portrait struck me first, for about the lips and chin there was a weird reminiscence ; and on the whole face there was a look seen only on the features of certain women, and of those of poets that die young—a look unknown to the face of Milton, or of Wordsworth, or of Byron, but faintly traceable in every likeness of Shelley that I have seen, and almost obtrusive in the one existing portrait of Keats.   This look is scarcely describable—it may even be a flash from one's own imagination ; but it seems there, painful, spiritual, a light that was never on sea and land, quite as unmistakable in poor Kirk White's face as on the mightier lineaments of Freidrich Von Hardinburg."   Speaking of the poem entitled " The Discarded," and especially of the passage beginning with " Ah ! but think not, haughty maiden," the writer observes :—" These were the lofty utterances of a lofty nature, capable of becoming a poet sooner or later ; already a poet in soul, but lacking as yet the poetic voice.   That voice never came in full strength, but it was gathering, and the world would have heard it if God had not chosen to reserve it for his own ears.   The stateliness of character shown in this little love affair was never lost from that moment, and is in itself enough to awaken our deepest respect and sympathy."   Again—" The poem " Icarus " or " The Singer's Tale," though only a fragment, is more remarkably original than any published poem of Gray's, and in grasp and scope of idea it is worthy of any writer." The productions now restored to this poem will give it a more complete appearance to readers.   " Of the same character," Mr. Buchanan says, " strong, simple, and original, are the love poem 'Edith,' and the wonderful little idyl called 'How is Celia to-day?'" One other passage must conclude the extracts from the notice by Mr. Buchanan: "What struck me at first when I read the little book of remains was the remarkable fortitude of style fearlessly developed in treating most unpromising material, and the occasional intensity of the flash of lyrical emotion."

Perhaps I ought to add in conclusion that I copied for the press nearly the whole of the poems for the first edition, and that they were printed as I arranged them; and that I have performed a similar duty for this edition.

FRANCIS REDFERN.

Uttoxeter, March 1st, 1880.

MEMOIR OF GEORGE HEATH.

" Read from some humble poet,
    Whose songs gushed from his heart
  As showers from the clouds of summer,
    Or tears from the eyelids start.

Who, through long days of labour,
    And nights devoid of ease,
  Still heard in his soul the music
    Of wonderful melodies."—*Longfellow.*

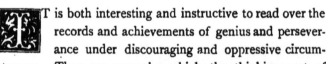T is both interesting and instructive to read over the records and achievements of genius and perseverance under discouraging and oppressive circumstances. They are examples which the thinking part of mankind are ever ready to admire, and which form incentives to others to exertion in future times. A large proportion of British biography is occupied with showing how poverty—a meagre education—the obstructions of friends—enfeebled health—and often unmerited frowns and cold neglect—have failed to prevent Worth rising by its native force to win admiration and renown. In the lives of inventors, men of science, or students of literature, art, or poetry, all do not

attain a degree of lofty eminence; neither, perhaps, is it
desirable they should.   Diversity in degree is as much a law
of Mind as it is a law of Nature; when, however, we do
observe some peculiar bent of mind breaking through the
bars of hindrance, whether of poverty or sickness, and, laying
at our feet the varied fruits of its endowments, even though
they be but a little bunch of sweet poetic flowers—tinted it
may be with many plaintive hues—it becomes a pleasure, if
not a duty, to add their names to the list of those who, having
toiled hard, have won a place amongst the world's worthy
ones.   There is much interest attaching to the story of the
brief, sad life of the late George Heath, the Invalid Poet.
Warmhearted, deeply-feeling, of many moods, and as a
student earnest and hardworking, it seems incumbent on his
friends, in justice to his memory and merits, to undertake
the task necessary for the preservation of his works, and of
a knowledge of the incidents of his life.

His published poems, entitled, "Rudyard at Sunset,"
"The Pauper's Child," and "Heart Strains," are productions
which boded considerable promise.   They were read on
their first appearance with much delight, and yet remain a
surprise as from an author so young, so unfavourably situ-
ated, and so very severely afflicted, and whose future was shaded
in utter gloom.   The poems which he published comprise,
however, but a small proportion of those he wrote.   Many
are left in manuscript, evincing great advancement and
poetic insight; some of these are in a finished state, and
several to all appearance (although of considerable length)
have not been carried to completion.   In this condition are
found his two most ambitious attempts, named respectively,

"The Doom of Babylon," and "The Country Woman's Tale." It is evident he intended most of these poems for the press; and their publication, with those which appeared in his lifetime, would be a consummation of his fondly-cherished hopes; indeed, were they not published, the poetic literature of our county would sustain the loss of a most interesting chapter by one of her truest and most earnest children.

The present "Memorial Edition" of a *selection* from his writings (suggested by myself) has been partly undertaken to meet this object, and partly with the hope that some profit may accrue to benefit his worthy parents, whose difficulties, though cheerfully borne, must have been seriously augmented by the protracted illness of the author of these poems. The invalid Poet has left a "Diary," extending from January 1st, 1866, to the day preceding his death. It is a curious record of his moods and feelings, of the almost daily aspect of Nature, which he loved so much to contemplate, and as seen by an ardent and imaginative person; of the visits and kindness of his friends, of his reading, his books and his studies; it affords a characteristic picture of its recorder, but not many details for a "Memoir." It is most touching to trace his lingering hopes of life and amended health running through this "Diary;" to see how they gradually faded out, and then arising over those "hopes" the grander light of fortitude and submission to the will of God. His literary career was a short one, and not crowded with many incidents or great events. His time passed quietly on, alternating between bodily sufferings, producing at times sad melancholy and gloom; at others keen visual and mental enjoyment from the beautiful works of creation, and the pursuit of knowledge, in acquainting himself with English authors, and in giving form to his own poetic conceptions and feelings. Such facts, however, as the " Diary " affords, with a few from other sources, and in particular from our mutual friend, Mr. Foster, of Endon, who knew him intimately, may be woven into the best account of him it is in our power to prefix to his poems.

George Heath was born at Gratton, a hamlet in the moorlands, about midway between Endon and Horton, in the latter parish, on the 9th of March, 1844. The house in which he died has been occupied by his parents for many years, and is just such a humble time-worn cottage one loves to associate with the name of a lowly-born poet. It is in a romantic part of the moorlands. The views therefrom, of Bradshaw Edge, the heights of Dunwood, the hills overlooking Rudyard Lake, Harper's Gap, the Endon Valley, and the Roaches, with their clustering associations, are well calculated to nurture the ideas of a poet. He was the eldest son of a large family; two of his married sisters died during his own sickness. His parents—to use his own words,

> " The toiling ones who gave him birth,
> Whose influence strewed his way with joys,
> Whose care had shared and soothed his many woes,
> Whose overburdened shoulders had sustained
> His tottering footsteps on the path of life,"—

are small farmers, worthy and industrious people, whose lot has been one of difficulty and toil with a numerous family and humble means. He received the merest elements of reading and writing at the National School, at Horton, with religious instruction subsequently obtained at the Endon Wesleyan Sunday School, under the superintendence of his relative and namesake, George Heath. He was taken early to farm labour, at which he toiled early and late for several years. These rustic employments, however, were exchanged for another calling. He was apprenticed to Mr. Samuel Heath, of Gratton, joiner and builder. Soon after this, his mind become more thoroughly awake and active ; he acquired a thirst for knowledge ; " fancy (he states) indulged in wildly beautiful dreams to the curl of the shavings and rasp of the saw :" imagination began to jingle poetic lines that were never written down ; afterwards the poor joiners' apprentice boy felt his first pulsations of ambition. Strange feelings moved in his breast, and as novel conceptions flitted through his brain. A chord had by some means been struck, which awoke his whole being to a new life and purpose. He felt that he must be a poet. Following this instinct, he formed the resolution to make the cultivation of poetry his chosen pursuit. His inward teachings seem to have intimated that there was room in the large human world even for him to utter a few thoughts, and that there were some in it, he felt persuaded, who would listen to, and remember the revealings which swelled upwards from his heart for expression.

There were few at Gratton who could sympathize with George Heath in his new dawnings. The means of improvement were far away, and books of the right sort were not at hand, and certainly had not before fallen in his way. He did, however, meet with a young friend of like mind with himself, one who had received a good education at the old Grammar

School of Alleyne's, at Uttoxeter, and to whom a well-stocked library at home had always been accessible. This young friend was Mr. H. W. Foster, son of Mr. Foster, of Endon. Their natural tastes drew them together : they both loved the beauties of the woods and fields, and delighted to converse on intellectual subjects. They both formed their resolutions at the same time as to their future pursuits in accordance with their individual taste and talents, H. W. Foster choosing to pursue the study of art. I find this interesting circumstance referred to by poor George Heath in an isolated note in his " Diary," written a few months before his death, thus—" My dear old friend and fellow toiler, Herbert Foster, came up for just an hour. He is still as earnest and persevering as ever. He and I started together in the life struggle. We have gone on both of us undeviatingly in the path we first chose. We cannot be said to have fought shoulder to shoulder, for our paths have lain apart, and he, I believe, has through my ill health and one thing or other, gained upon me. But we have always been one in heart, and still we are agreed our motto must be *steadily onward.*" The further success of his friend, in securing a National Art Scholarship at South Kensington, is referred to with great elation at a subsequent date.

But in the height of his newly-formed plans and brilliant dreams

> " All woven in gorgeous tissues,
>   Flaunting gaily in the golden light ;
> Large desires, with most uncertain issues,
>   Tender wishes, blossoming at night."

George Heath was unfortunately seized with a sad

affliction. He took cold whilst assisting at the restoration of Horton Church, just before the close of his apprenticeship in 1864 (with the sorrow of a broken *first love*, following in its train). This cold brought on the insidious disease of consumption, to which, after years of suffering, he ultimately fell a victim.

Being entirely laid aside from work, he began, after the suspension of his first prostrating attack, to read, to write, and study in earnest, although quite uncertain of the use of doing so. He had written some verses before this, early in the year of 1863. To this period belongs a lengthy rhyme, an earnest of something better, having the title of "The Churchyard," and also another shorter one of a more pretentious character. His first published Poems appeared in 1865 under the title "Preludes," afterwards altered to "Simple Poems," including "Rudyard," "The Pauper's Child," and a few others. A second edition was called for in 1866, and the reading of these for the first time, makes one feel as if wrapt round with the spell of a wonderful singer. In January of this year he speaks of thinking over the past, and trying to plan a poem which should excel all his previous efforts, and to weave into the narrative characters whom he had known. The "Discarded," a Reverie, was finished by the 9th of this month, and this (his then longest poem) he thought would be his last. The Volume entitled "Heart Strains," which included "The Discarded," was ready for the press by the 19th of June, and the first instalment of 50 copies came to his hands from Mr. Hallowes, of Leek, in September following. His direct profits from the sale of this small volume did not amount to much, but if it

did not yield great pecuniary benefit, it was an advance in
the right direction, and increased the number and deepened
the sympathy of his friends.   These poems were very
favourably reviewed by the press at the time of their issue.
They were also honoured with Public Readings, both at
Stafford and Leek.   And falling into the hands of Walter
Montgomery, Esq., who felt much interest in them, that
gentleman also gave Readings from them, which was pro-
perly regarded by the poor invalid as a great honour.   He
contributed a number of poems to the *Staffordshire
Advertiser*, and several were accepted for Literary Journals.
The *first* money, however, he received direct from a Publisher,
was from Messrs. Walker and Son, York, for the use of a
"School Dialogue" in verse, but very superior to the
general run of such kind of compositions.   There were
1500 copies printed, and his fee was very small, but he
received that which was equally dear to him—usually the
poet's only meed—"the tribute of a smile."   To many,
"The Discarded" may seem a production of some mystery,
but careful readers will perceive, from its warm and indignant
outburst of feeling, that it is no mere work of art or imagin-
ation, only, but "an o'er true tale," and such it really is—
it is a "heart strain."   His Jenny had proved unfaithful.
This cruelly broken first love, caused many an after-bitterness
to George Heath, and appears to have followed and haunted
him through many of his lines.   This entry in his "Diary"
will throw some light upon it.

"February 26th, 1868.—To-day I have brought down and
committed to the flames a batch of letters that I received
from a love, that was once as life to me—such letters—yet

the writer in the end deserted me. · O, the anguish I
suffered ! I had not looked at them for three years, and
even to-day, when I came and fingered them, and opened
the portrait of the woman I loved so much, I could scarcely
keep back the bitter tears. O, Jenny, the bitterness you
caused me will never be obliterated from my heart." We
will let the spell lie lightly on the " Deserted One," and only
say, that although he loved her so intensely, he fully forgave
the object that left him, and breathed that forgiveness in
lines at the close of the following poem, entitled " True to
the Last."

" Prop me up with my pillows, sweet sister, and then
　　Just open the casement, and close the room door,
And let me look out on the landscape again,
　　And breathe the pure air of the summer once more,

Then twine your arm round me to comfort and stay,
　　And wipe the big tears from these deep mournful eyes,
And listen awhile ; I have something to say
　　Ere I pass from this world to my home in the skies.

'T was summer, sweet sister, bright summer, as now,
　　And earth wore a mantle of radiant sheen ;
A wreath of pure roses encircled the brow
　　Of the queen of my bosom—you know who I mean.

At twilight, we met, 'neath the sycamore's shade,
　　And there 't was she whispered those words, ' Ever thine ;'
Her beautiful head on my bosom was laid,
　　And her lily-white hand was clasped fondly in mine.

O God ! how intensely and madly I loved !
　　How wildly I worshipped that beautiful one.
You know how inconstant and faithless she proved,
　　How basely she left me when summer was gone.

You'll see her perchance when affliction hath chased
  The bloom from her cheek and the light from her eye ;
When sorrow's dark signet hath silently traced
  Deep lines on her forehead, once noble and high.

Then tell her, sweet sister, that all was forgiven,
  And all was forgot, but the bliss of the past,
And tell her I wish her to meet me in heaven,
  Where all who have loved are united at last."

Amongst the loose papers of George Heath, I have met with upwards of fifty more lines to be added to the "Discarded," and which have, therefore, been placed in connection with that poem. They commence with

    " Ah ! but think not, haughty maiden ;"

and conclude with

    " Make me sadder, more forlorn."

Nearly the whole of the unpublished poems which he left in manuscript were written after the spring of 1867. From that date till towards the autumn of the succeeding year, his pen must have been almost incessantly at work ; after that the strains he did write were few and plaintive. In March, he had put together about three hundred lines of " The Countrywoman's Tale," which was extended to more than nine hundred. This poem is no doubt the one he was planning before he published his " Heart Strains," and some of the incidents in it are actually taken from his mother's personal history. As a tale it is very interesting and affecting, and some parts, especially the latter, are highly poetical.

Of the " Doom of Babylon " its author made much account, more than of any of his other poems, and he mentions it often. It is certainly his most ambitious endeavour; it displays much power of imagination and grasp of mind, and evinces, as much as anything, his real strength, and of what he might have been capable. Whilst engaged upon it he wrote, " I know not whether it will reflect me much credit, but I will do my best." Again, " I often wonder if it possesses any sterling merit, yet I am determined to persevere, and trust my efforts will not be fruitless." About this period he was likewise engaged in one way or another upon the poems under the name of "Songs of the Shadows," a title which he adopted on account of his own shadowed life. He says of them, as if in anticipation of some one undertaking the publication of his poems, "This has struck me as being the most likely title for my little things, as they are what my life has been, a series of shadowed scenes." Amongst these will be found some of his choicest productions, including "The Single Grave," and " The Old Blind Man," a picture. The poem, "Icarus," which was left on a number of loose sheets, purports to be an extract from an imaginary journal, and to give an obituary notice of a fictitious Thomas String, who had suffered neglect, became lorn, and hid himself from public gaze, his poor wailing harp, sadly shattered and beaten, still remaining his only companion and solace. The poor Poet was lost sight of, and one Sir Hodge Poyson, who had been deeply touched by a knowledge of his troubles, is represented as going on an expedition in quest of the scene of his conflict.

> " To search out and know
> The deep yearnings, the sorrows, and all that befel
> The true bard of the sad, and his merits as well."

c

The worthy Baronet is represented as being successful in his enquiries, and the scenes he describes are very touching, and have been often repeated in the history of friendless poets, artists, and authors in their life struggles.

> "In a hole where he crept, in his pain and his pride,
> Mournful song-scraps were scattered on every side;
> I read the damp slips, till my eyes were tear-blind.
> 'Neath a couch where he nestled with hunger, and died,
> In a dirty damp litter of mouldering straw
> Stood a rude alder box, which when opened, supplied
> Such proofs of a vastly superior mind,
> That filled me with anguish, and wonder, and awe."

Further pictures of the scene are given, interspersed with "The Singer's Tale" and other "Song-Scraps," assumed to have been found about the poor Singer—

> " Rumpled and creased,
> Long lines all awry, blotted, jumbled, and stark."

This is a remarkable poem, and sufficient of itself to make its author remembered, if he had written nothing else. Alas! the poor desponding poet had *himself* in view when he wrote " Icarus." It was finished in February, 1869, as is evident from an entry in his Diary over the two pieces found there, " Enamoured " and " Yearnings," and attached to which is this remark, " To be added to ' Icarus.' "

The names and titles, belonging to several poems, not specified here, but which will be found in the volume, are sweet poetic names borne by children, ladies and friends, who visited him. Prominently amongst these are " Edith," " Minnie," " Lizzie," " Mademoiselle Ida Ratchez," a Swiss

lady, living near, and on her removal from the neighbour-
hood, his lamentation, " Now thou art gone," was dedicated
to her.

After October, 1868, he used the pen less frequently, and
the few after-strains which did flow from his harp, as the
" September," " The Poet's Monument," " Tired out," and
" December," which is probably about the last he wrote,
are very plaintive. His prospects of life were growing
perceptibly short, and his songs woefully melancholy, and
gradually but surely he begins bravely to face his inevitable
destiny.

During the whole of the time George Heath was embody-
ing his thoughts in verse, and thereby trying to fulfil the
only sacred duty of productive labour in his power, he was
engaged with equal earnestness in cultivating his mind by
special educational studies. There was a charm in earnest
endeavour to him ; and consequently he had set times in
each day which he devoted to study, except when he was
too ill to make any mental exertion. During his long ill-
ness he strove to gain a good knowledge of his own language,
making at the same time highly satisfactory advancement
in Latin and Greek. The study of these languages he
prosecuted under the kind direction of the Rev. J. Badnall,
M.A., Vicar of Endon, who also presented him with Greek
and Latin books. He felt much the kindness of this gentle-
man, and amongst the many expressions of it, there are these
two, " 1866, January 7th—my esteemed friend, the Rev. J.
Badnall came to see me. He has acted a noble part by me
in giving all the instruction possible in my attempts to master
Latin." On the 1st of March, 1868, he likewise observes,

" The Rev. Mr. Badnall, my dear old tutor, has paid me a
visit, has spoken many kind encouraging words, and has
spoken very graciously of the progress I have made : I am
much cheered though sorely afflicted." The following trans-
lation, the result of this instruction in Latin, is from Virgil's
Æneid, and does not read amiss.

> " I sing of grand exploits and martial might,
> Of Rome's great hero, valiant in the fight !
> Whose fame, like incense, floats, from clime to clime,
> And sweeps re-echoing down the stream of time ;
> Who, first cast out by fate, unknown to fame,
> From mighty Troy to fair Italia came,
> Paused in his wanderings and his heavy toil,
> And pitched his tent on rich Lavinium's soil.
> Plagued by the Gods above, on sea and shore,
> With sorrow, suffering, and misfortune dire,
> On Juno's count, and Juno's 'vengeful ire,
> And bloody war by Demon Passion waged
> With horrors fraught around him madly raged ;
> Whilst he, with dauntless hand, the city wrought,
> And th' household Deities to Latium brought ;
> The source from which in widening streams we trace
> The Albanian fathers, and the Latin race ;
> And Rome's magnific walls that proudly rise
> In cloud-capped spires and turrets to the skies. "

He made an effort to read himself up in Ancient and also
in English History, and his Saturdays were exclusively de-
voted to the study of Arithmetic. His ardent thirst for
knowledge also led him to seek acquaintance with "Flowers,"
" Those loving faces which looked up to him from the earth,"
and on this delightful subject he oftentimes sought informa-
tion from his botanical friend, Mr. G. Foster, of Endon, the

friend and coadjutor of Richard Buxton, the Lancashire Botanist.

On one occasion, in March, 1868, he sent to Mr. Foster a collection of flowers, gathered within the narrow range of his walks round Gratton, for description, etc., accompanied with a note so *modest*, that I am tempted to give this extract from it. "There is a great change just beginning to creep over our surroundings now : the earth is about to trap herself out in her holiday attire, and ripple out her tresses to the sunshine, and the sky is about to take on a new and marvellous splendour. This, if we are spared, I know we shall both enjoy. I am a true lover of Nature ; and I think that the more prominent features of her scenery are quite familiar to me. But I am miserably deficient in the *minutia*. I know nothing of Botany, Natural History, or anything of that stamp, and have no chance of knowing much, for there is not one in my neighbourhood who seems to have the least taste in that line. The flowers are all of them beautiful faces looking up at me ; but though familiar to me in one sense, they are not familiar, inasmuch as I do not even know *their names*. On this account, as well as on others, I often wish I were nearer to you, because I know you possess some knowledge on the above subjects, and believe it would be a pastime and a pleasure to communicate it. I have no doubt that I should lay myself open to your just ridicule, on account of my ignorance, but am quite willing to make a good many concessions in the pursuit of knowledge, and would consider a lowering of my dignity a cheap exchange for *real* information. I now send you a few little things I have met with in my rambles. One of them is but in leaf. I would be glad to know *their*

names if you will be kind enough to explain, as I shall look
upon you from this time, as a sort of travelling dictionary, to
which I may refer at pleasure." It is scarcely necessary to
add that the information thus so nicely requested, was ever
after cheerfully afforded him. He was far from being ignor-
ant of Literature and writers in general. He had means,
through the kindness of his friends, of thoroughly imbuing
himself with the spirit of some of the most genial authors of
the age, especially of those who were so much to his taste.
He read with admiration Buchanan's London Poems, and
those of George Mc'Donald, Alexander Smith, and Gerald
Massey; also several of the works of Thackeray, Dickens,
and Tom Hood. "Ecce Homo" and Mr. Gladstone's
Essay upon it interested him much. He was delighted with
the writings of Wordsworth, and carefully read all the poems
of Tennyson. Dante he made a study in a translation by
Thomas. He read Byron with much delight for his Poetry,
but thoroughly guarded himself against his voluptuousness
and irreligion. The works of Scott, Shakspeare, and Living-
stone's Travels fell into his hands—and pithy quotations
from these are found in his Diary. His favourite Burns he
read with pride, but the story of this bard—" The loved of
Scotia's heart," set him thinking some sad, but withal, needful
thoughts. His taste for literary gossip was supplied by a
kind friend in the "Bookseller." He was also fairly read in
several of the high-class "Monthlies," American and English,
but the "Argosy" appears to have been a special favourite
with him. Thus it will be seen, from the completest lack
at the _outset_, he ultimately revelled in a feast of intellectual
things of the first order.

He was highly fortunate in the class of friends who gathered round, and showed great kindness towards him during his long wasting away of life; all being of kindly dispositions, cultivated habits, and appreciative of real merit and noble struggles. Those ladies and gentlemen who so expressed their sympathy towards him, will, I am persuaded, continue to feel that it was one of the greatest pleasures of their life. He, in particular, makes mention in his " Diary " of Matthew Gaunt, Esq., of Rudyard; Mr., Mrs., and Miss Pender, of Endon; W. Challinor, Esq., of Leek; J. E. Davis, Esq., the late learned Stipendiary Magistrate of the Potteries; Mrs. J. Bailey; Miss Cleminson, of Sheffield; the Vicar of Horton; Mr. W. Brough, of Leek; Mrs. Brindley, of London; Mr. and Mrs. Foster, of Endon; Mdlle. Ida Ratchez, a Swiss lady; Mr. Hall of Stafford, now of Derby; Miss Charlesworth; Mr. Hancock, of Mow-Cop; and Mr. B. Barlow, junr., of Leek. Some of these ladies and gentlemen presented him with some very choice books, lent him others, sent him periodicals and newspapers, contributed materially to his comfort, paid him visits, and used their endeavours to circulate his poems, Mr. Hall selling for him fifty copies of "Heart Strains." He particularly esteemed the visits of his friends, and the letters which they frequently wrote him. The visits were always made, and the letters written in a way to relieve his sadness, which they invariably did. They acted as charms to him. He often relates in his Diary the purport of the letters he received, and the turn conversation took when his friends called upon him, as, " My dear neighbour, Mrs. Bailey, has been over and spent something like an hour with me ; to illustrate perseverance, she has been telling me of Professor Simpson, of Edinburgh, who, by his own exertions, has risen from a baker's boy to receive the honour of knighthood."

Two gentlemen, above-named, Matthew Gaunt and J. E. Davies, Esqrs., made a special call, to consult him about his being sent to the seaside ; a kind proposal, which his fears of immediate consequences of such a course disposed him to decline.   He felt deeply all this kindness, and frequently expressed hopes that he should eventfully be enabled to prove himself worthy of it.   It is feelingly referred to in the following lines, extracted from a poetical " Dedication," but of which he did not make any use in connection with the poems he printed.

> " To those who in days of anguish and despair
>   Came unto me with tender words and smiles,
>   Who from the goodness of their own true hearts
>   Shed over mine a stream of light and hope,
>   Whose sympathy was bread of life to me ;
>   To all who, though perchance unknown to me,
>   Or in the greatness of their noble hearts
>   Have truly wished their fellow-pilgrim well ;
>   To all who in my secret soul are shrined,
>   All who are dear to me, with earnest love
>   I dedicate this little work of mine."

From the same dedication, which has supplied previous quotations, it would appear that his affliction was the means of rousing him to think about practical religion ; it also indicates his entire submission under it to the will of God, as instance the following—

> " To Him, the High, the Mighty, and the Good,
>   Prompter of all that in my calmer hours,

When passion slept, dawned on my being, and
Suffused my thought of beautiful or good ;
The great Upholder of the universe,
Whose power created, and Whose blood redeemed
A 'fallen world ; Whose tender mercies are
O'er all His works ; Whose sweet compassion bore
With all my wayward and rebellious youth ;
Whose chastening rod but checked my downward course ;
Whose light shone round me 'mid the dark ;
Whose loving hand, though oftentimes concealed,
Has led me safely through the wilderness ;
Whose voice, in all His works, has cheered me on :
To Him, the First, the Dearest, Best of all."

It should be stated that although the subject of this memoir was on terms of friendship with the Rev. James Badnall, that he had attended the Wesleyan Sunday School, at Endon, and like his father and mother was a member of the Wesleyan Society there. His Sunday Diary attests his Wesleyan principles and his love for its ministers, but at the same time it evinces a catholicity of spirit which made him in sympathy with what was good in other religious bodies.

As before observed, the complaint of George Heath assumed a more decided and alarming form towards the latter end of 1868. Indeed, his medical attendant, Dr. Heaton, never entertained any hope of his recovery. His cough become more incessant, and his throat and mouth painfully affected, and greater debility ensued. His beloved books lay around him unread, and all his high designs apparently broken and vanished. He began to see " the restless march of the boundless eyes,' and underneath, a little grave,' with no inscription, beneath the awfully constant stars." " All

things seemed fading down into the dim obscurity of non-
entity—gliding away from the busy world, and entering the
valley of shadows, where the circle of interest narrows down
to a point ;" " drifting further and further down," " and him-
self feeling the cold hand of fate crushing off the flowers of
his promise." Yet at times he was not all lethargy ; he had
some remarkably strange feelings within. " The din and fret
of outward things passed before him as a dream, and he
seemed to have such a wide sweeping of spirit—such a power
to conjure up strange imaginations, that startled him." The
bitterness passed, and he could trust in God, and indulge in
"the beautiful thought of that *far-off Home*—that home whose
wonders none may guess, shining through the glory of the
sun radiance coming through the windows." So he wrote
with such delightful prospects, of the house of many mansions,
on the 29th of April.   He witnessed, as he lay almost help-
less, the dawn of beautiful May, which he always notes in
his Diary with such pleasure as the harbinger of Summer's
many charming scenes, of verdure and flowers.   On the
fourth of May he was but just able to scrawl in his Diary,
" his thanks to God for one more day," acknowledge the
receipt of " such a kind letter from Mrs. Brindley," and in the
evening he dictated a few farewell lines to his young com-
panion and friend, H. W. Foster ; on the morning of the
following day he peacefully passed away from the scenes of
his earnest struggles, his painful affliction, and blighted
hopes, " to his far-off home of perfection and peace."

All will regret that so hopeful a beginning was so soon
closed ; that the brief space in which so much had been
bravely done, was so mournfully and prematurely terminated.

It may be long ere we are called upon to listen to another such singer as George Heath, amidst the bleak hills of the Staffordshire moorlands, where fancy will continue to picture him in association with the scenes and objects in which he delighted.

A memorial was suggested by his kind friend and tutor, the Rev. J. Badnall, of Endon, to be erected over his grave in Horton churchyard, and by the aid of numerous subscribers, it was successfully carried into effect. It is cheering, therefore, that he does not lie " forsaken and forgotten"— a cold fate he seems to have apprehended—" beneath some tiny dot of earth," with only " a rude slab " (if even that) reared at its head, but at the foot of a beautiful Runic Cross, raised by the affection of many, after a design by his friend, H. W. Foster, for the respect he bore him, with the following inscription :—

Erected in Memory
Of GEORGE HEATH, of Gratton,
Who, with few aids,
Developed in these Moorlands
Poetic powers of great promise,
But who, stricken by consumption,
After five years suffering,
Fell a victim to that disease,
May 5, 1869, aged 25 years.

" His life is a fragment—a broken clue—
His harp had a musical string or two,
The tension was great, and they sprang and flew,
And a few brief strains—a scattered few—
Are all that remain to mortal view
Of the marvellous song the young man knew.'

The above lines are a quotation from an epitaph found amongst his papers, entitled " Inscription on a Rude Stone." It seems intended to fit himself, with the date, Nov. 10, 1868, at the foot.   The whole epitaph runs as follows :—

" A quiet youth in the valleys grew,
And thought o'er his being a mantle threw,
And dawned on his spirit a meaning new,
And he dreamed of a mission great and true ;
But God, in His infinite wisdom, drew
A severing finger his projects through.
His life is a fragment—a broken clue—
His harp had a musical string or two,
The tension was great, and they sprang and flew,
And a few brief strains—a scattered few—
Are all that remain to mortal view
Of the marvellous song the young man knew.
O, ye who have feeling ! a tear from you !
Rest, saddest of singers, in peace—adieu !"

F.   REDFERN

Uttoxeter, Dec., 1869.

THE POET'S HOME

SONGS OF THE SHADOWS.

THE OLD BLIND MAN.

THE summer's day lies sickening in the west
   Upon a citrine couch of melting blooms ;
   No breath of air, or fringe of cloud upheaves
One long-line ripple on the ether calm.
The heat is sobering, mellowing ; and the cool
Comes filtering o'er the eastern mountains, from
The balmy breathings of the dawning eve.
The tingling mists, dissolving, mingling, deepening,
Rise up—like blushes on a maiden's face,
Upturned amid the moonlight, glowing with
Her lover's parting kiss : whose form she sees,
With something of a sadness, fading in
The dusk—amid the vales, to bid the sun,
Earth's lover-face, good-night.
             A murmurous sound
Of eddying voices, and the rumbling roll
Of toil and traffic from the city world

Float up, and clamour lazily amid
The thickening air.
                      A plastic form, with eye
Of slumberous fire, and broad and brooding brow, ·
And floating webs of brown and glossy curls,˙
Strolls 'neath dim cypress-shaded avenues,
And twines among grey monuments and tombs,
·And enters through a grand cathedral door ;
And pauses reverently, and gazes long,
Awe-wrapt, upon the vast, magnific pile ;
Around the cavernous nave, adown the long
Dim-lustred, chancel, where a mystic flush
Of variegated light pervades, cast through
The Saviour, saint, and scene-limned glass, that fills
The web-arched, scalloped, many-mullioned windows,
And wanders with a step subdued adown
The grey-'lumed aisles, beneath huge canopies,
Agape to catch and toss from nook to nook
The faintest sound ; climbs lightly to the grand
High-vaulted choir, and sinks from sight beyond
A crimson curtain, crown and cross emblazed.
    Anon, a sound—a breath—a sob— a strain—
Soft as the dawn-sigh on the coppice leaves
Breaks forth and trembles like a distant moan,
And swells into a gush of tremulous jets
Like to the sear-wind 'mongst the autumn days,
And bursts at length in one harmonic roll
Like to the storm-wind wrestling with the waves—
A throbbing tide that fills the echoing choir,
And sweeps its bounds, and leaps in billows huge

Along the dusky cavities and domes,
Till all the hungry space is thrilled and gorged
With one weird, frantic torrent-tide of sound.
　　Outside, a wan, decrepit, blind, bowed man
Sits shaking on an almost sunken mound,
Deep in the shadow of a flaunting tomb.
All suddenly a wee wind-mercury
Wafts to his ears a rumour of the sound ;
He lifts his thin white head and hearkens, still,
Then gathers up his form and totters forth,
And with his iron-shod staff creeps feeling up
The gravelled path, beneath the vestibule,
And thence into the huge-ribbed tenement,
Where throbs the music like a mighty soul
Apant for immortality, and drops
Upon an oaken bench that skirts the wall,
Shrinks softly farther, farther, from the draught,
Slopes dreamily his staff, and piles his hands
Atop, and droops his furrowed cheek thereon,
And listens, listens.
　　　　　　And now the prelude ends ;
And from the massy pipes the master-hand
Draws forth the occult power and wonderment,
The madness and the mystery of music ;
At first, a soft, sweet quivering of weak
And infant tones, and then a turbulent gush
Like glorious youth wind-beating on the hills ;
Anon, a strong calm roll of dauntless might
Like manhood majesty ; a throb of pain,
Of desolation, hunger, grief, despair,

A home-sick murmuring of weariness,
A brief temptation, struggle, feverish,
A holy swell of firm, heroic will,
A passionate burst of lofty eloquence,
A grieved complaint, a yearning humanness,
A pleading moan, a wailing trouble-prayer,
A storm of passion wrestling terrible,
A cry of agony, intense and wild,
A gasp of pitifulness, a sob of death,
A trumpet-crash of triumph-ecstasy !
The master-soul has burst the manacles
Of its long incarnation, and has leaped
With falcon-wing to its own element,
And revels there exultant ; even as
A bird escaped anew the fancier's toils ;
Thought, memory, are carried off and lost
In the storm-harmony ; while on and on
The tempest sweeps, till all the depths and heights
And torrent-rolls of fever-life have found
An utterance.
                    Incessantly the rush,
The panting, fluctuating cataract
Sweeps through the thrilling minster, vault, and dome ;
And twists and doubles 'neath the gothic spans,
And twirls and eddies round and round, and up
The many-pillared piers and pedestals,
And tall and massy columns ; chuckling wild
In echoing crypt and niche, recess and nook ; .
And leaps and dances through the clamouring space ;
Into the dusky transepts, everywhere ;

Rushes and meets, and clashing, twirls along ;
And wriggles up the zigzag architraves
The fluted buttresses, and pilasters ;
Among rare ornament and tracery ;
And swarms along the transoms huge and carved,
And plays upon the sculptured draperies,
The statues, worship-faces, finials,
The spiral volutes, scrolls, and mimic urns ;
And touches lightly, still recumbent forms,
White marble hands clasped over marble breasts ;
And kisses fearfully white lips and eyes,
And throbless brows that sleeps unconsciously
In all the rigid peace of sepulture :
And breaks away and skims along the aisles,
As sensible unto the ear as is
The street-lights lingering quiver to the eye !
The old man listens, and the shrivelled face
Grows strangely fresh again : the cold hard lines
Depart : a nervous tremor runs around
The thin seared lips ; the sightless balls roll up
And round, e'en as the eye-balls work beneath
The half-closed lids of one a-dream ; and great
White globes of tears slide off and dash upon
The bony fingers, all a-twitch with nerve.
But suddenly the chant is hush'd ; and through
The vacuous pause the echoes rush and clasp
And wild and frantic-eyed swoop here and there
Sink down to faint vociferations ; melt,
Dissolve, and swooping, die away, away !
The old man lifts his white head with a start,
And, sighing low, sings in his soul a song :—

"O! wherefore pauseth the lofty strain,
The triumph and ecstasy?
Why sinketh my spirit to bonds again
From the transport of liberty?
My soul is a-weary of waking gloom,
My limbs are with pain a-wrack:
O waft me away on that strain once more,
Ah! tenderly waft me back!

For I am a desolate, sear'd old man,
And dark as a dawnless sea;
A stranger man in the world of men:
Alone in my misery!
The scourge of care and the tooth of age
Have wrought on me many a track;
I stand in the mirk of a vanished day,
O tenderly waft me back!

The pure I loved, and the base I scorned
Have passed from the world and me;
And I long for my home with a longing strange-
My home o'er the darkest sea:
The further I go the sadder I am,
And the more I find I lack;
My sun hath gone down on a northern night;
O tenderly waft me back!

Away from the cold and the shadow'd now—
The nothingness, hunger, woe;
Away from the weakness that rains with tears,
. From all that 'tis pain to know :—

Away to the haunts of the glorious hills
  Where the winds of the roses smack,
And the earth lies glad in a noontide glow ;
  O tenderly waft me back !

Away to the time of my youth and might—
  Of rapture and liberty,
When the voices of nature were tropes of fun,
  And the wild winds spirits of glee ;
When I breasted the trees and vanquished the nuts
  In a brief and a bloodless strife ;
Imprisoned the bee in the foxglove bell,
  And laugh'd in the face of life ;

When health gave my footsteps a lithesome ring,
  My features a lustre bright ;
And the poet Hope gave my eyes and ears,
  And loving—a bosom light :
When life was the glimpse of a joy-wing'd hour,
  The world—all I hoped or dream'd ;
When faces were minds ; appearances, truths,
  And dewdrops the gems they seem'd.

Away to the scene of my fair lad-love,
  Whose features I most forget ;
But whose goodness and worth lay sweet on the years,
  And gladden my memory yet.
When my eyes were awake, and could drink the sky
  And the grandeur-world's great dower ;
When music to me was a worship-breath
  A rapture, a tongue, a power !

They say I'm a child, and I feel like a child,
    Am weak as a child, ah me !
O waft me away, to the brief bright sky
    Of the life that I dream'd might be :
There let me close up the weary lids,
    Forgetting the now and then,
And pass to the birth of a deathless life
    From the sorrowful world of men."

The old man listens, but no more, no more
The wonder-spirit flutters to his ear ;
Comes but the sound, by echo multiplied
Into a troop of footsteps in the aisle,
ꞌHe drops his head, and, for a moment, sobs
In quiet helplessness ; then draws once, twice,
His russet sleeve across his darkened eyes,
And, rising, gropes his way and totters out
· Into the wide, cold world, beneath the night
That melteth into dawn for him no more.

EDITH.

"What happy moments did I count !
    Blessed was I then, all bliss above !
Now, for this consecrated fount
    Of murmuring, sparkling, living love,
What have I ? shall I dare to tell ?
    A comfortless and hidden WELL."—*Wordsworth.*

HE came amid the calm of Autumn days,
    Came from her distant home among the hills,
    To spend a tiny sheaf of days with us.

Her parents and our parents, in the day
When they were young and newly gone to house,
Had been near neighbours, and the closet friends;
Had parted later, where their roads diverged,
In mutual confidence, esteem, regret.
And now she came with kindly messages
And warm remembrances from them to us,
In token that the past was unforgot.
'Twas many a day since we had met; and each
Was changed.   We scarce were more than children then,
And now, well, we were changed: the world was changed.
We each had grown into another sphere,
Bounded by other skies and lit by suns
Of different hues; and life had changed its shape.
She had grown beautiful; her woman-form
Was rounded into perfect symmetry.
Her face was soft, and fair, and delicate,
And constantly reminded one of music;
For ever as the eye gazed, on the heart
Arose a sense of harmonies; a swell
Of soft refrains, that thrilled one as they died.
But oh! her glory was the flood of hair
That gushing o'er her shoulders, shrouded her.
No line was on her forehead, and no shade
Touched with a saddening, sobering influence
The laughter of her life; so far, indeed,
As human eye might penetrate the show.

   We liked her from the first, and those to me
Were blessed days.   The intercourse with true
And tender womanhood has been the one

Green grove of palms in all my desert life !
 One other round of hours remained to us
Yet, ere the confluence of our lives and thoughts
Should separate and grow distinct again ;
When on an afternoon we sallied out
Among the browning fields, adown dim lines,
Beneath the ragged shade of chastened trees,
To view the scenery, and drink into
Our hearts the Nature-spirit *felt* o'er all :
For we were kindred in our Nature-love.
It was a calm ; the winds were bridled up.
A film of mistiness, indefinite,
Paled the wide azure of the strandless heavens.
The sun, enthroned amid a cloudless sphere,
Trailed o'er the western heights his regal robe.
A valley lay before us, prone and mute,
Too happy in the luxury of peace
For voice or breath, or music's gayer charm :
A valley fair, with outlets 'mongst the hills,
Sun-touched, and flushed with amber radiance,
Caught from the flood of yellow, glamouring
The blenching sycamores, and tempered with
The wild black lustreing of Bradshaw Edge.
Beyond a solemn wave of shaggy heights,
Crowned with the tuft of Roches, glimmered red.
 We talked of all the wonder of the world :
Bewailed the narrowness of human ken ;
Pictured the might-be from the known-to-be ;
Pushed off Conjecture's shallop on the surge—
The vast, dumb, unrevealed that round us lies

Clomb from the inanimate far up the scale
To the Divine ; and felt a lifting up
To God.

    I spoke of all the undertones
Of sad humanity ; the current-beats
That underlie the surface, bland and calm.
I said, " No home arises 'mid these vales,
No hearth gleams brightly ; but around it grow
Romances strange, that interweave and mix
Like circles on a pond beneath the rain,
And yet are separate, and spread distinct,
And die away, as they had never been :
In these is much of joy, and much of good,
An under-shade of wrong, and sin, and blame,
And much of voiceless sorrow nobly borne."

    " Ah, painful is the school of discipline !"
She answered with a sudden change of tone ;
" Yet sorrow is a tutor wonderful !
Our life is like a tiny shallow stream,
Until the storm-rack wear it deeper, wider.
We know not life, nor aught of human nature
Until the probe has pierced our heart of hearts,
And then we come to know what living means :
Our view is circumscribed, until the winds
Roll off the morning mists that hide the heavens :
Ah, sorrow is a blessing in disguise !"

    I stared into the chaste, unfurrowed face
In utter wonderment ; and silently
We sauntered back into the house again.
But when the light lay swimming, mantling on

The margins of the hills, and o'er the pond
The swallow glided with a homeward wing;
When all the air was quivering with the chant
Of vesper bells; and the wild melody
Was dying out serenely towards the west;
We sat beside the window.
                              I had read
One of Buchanan's thrilling melodies;
And while its flood of lofty tenderness,
Its soul of pitying, sorrowing sympathy,
Its plaintive cry of human pathos, knit
Our spirits in a strange affinity,
I said, " You spoke of sorrow; you, so fresh,
And erst so buoyant; from whose life, I dreamed,
No shadow-hand, as yet, had snatched the charm,
The fond illusive phantasy of youth,
That fades too soon! Dare you not trust me then?
Won't you believe me true, and open up
That hidden chamber of your heart to me?"
She paused a moment, and the hot pink blood
Ran up her temples, dyed her cheeks and neck,
Then answered meekly, looking down the while:
" Three years gone by, a cousin came to us.
His health was shaken by the years of stern,
Unflinching study he had passed; and he
Had fled the city world, to search among
Our Hebe-haunted hills for vigour new.
He was a noble, manly youth; had all
The attributes of woman's hero-dreams.
His lofty intellect unveiled for me

The world whose name was wonder, and the sky
That domed the flight of mind ; a realm, to me,
Of utter glory, dreamed of—never seen.
We were together much ; were friends at first :
And, last, were more.

                  Ah ! I was very young ;
I should not be, I think, so foolish now.
Well, it is past and gone ;

               He went away,
To mix again with college life and scenes.
As time went on, I knew and felt the change.
I never blamed him once ; 'twas all my fault,
I owned it in my deepest bitterness !
He was ambitious ; full of lofty aims ;
I, but a simple girl ; I should have known
' The eagle mates not with the dove.'

                 He toiled ;
Came off with honours manifold ; is now
A clergyman.   He writes to me, and we
Are friends, are friends," she echoed ; paused and dropped
Her hands, that trembled o'er the embroidery
(Until the needle-point had pierced the skin)
Upon her lap.   Her face sank lower and lower,
And such a storm of agonizing sobs
Burst from the heavings of the o'ercharged breast
As I had never witnessed ; have not since
Through all the bitter scenes my eyes have met.
" Ah !" thought I, " never bosom shrined a heart
More true and tender."

                              Silently I laid
My two warm hands on hers, and held them there
Till she had grown more calm ; then, bending, said,
" I, too, have suffered much ; I feel for you."
She raised her head, and for a moment each
Looked through the sense of seeing to the heart.
She went her way, back to the old, brown hills.
The days went on ; but, often as we met,
There was a something in the clasp of hands,
A quiver in the cadence of the voice,
A language in the motion of the lip
The world could not discern ; tacit bond
Our souls could feel, but never comprehend ;
A deeper looking through the upper show
Into the heart.
                      We knew not how or why,
But we were kin for ever after that.

HOW IS CELIA TO-DAY?

 MAIDEN in the first warm, tender flush
        Of holy womanhood ; a sprightly thing,
        With gaily fashioned robes of choicest hues,
Rich artificial buds, long ribbon-ends,
And loops of beads a-tremble in the wind ;
Warm, honey-eyed, and fresh, and country-faced ;
Plump, luscious cherry-lips, apart ; a chin
A-sly with dimples, touching lightly now,

Now dropping lovingly upon a brooch
That clasps the shawl around her spotless throat,
Where smiles always a shy, but sturdy swain.
A careless thing, with quick and jaunty step,
A tiny reticule looped on an arm, and in
One dimpled rosebud hand a parasol.

A thin and battered woman, who has braved
The frosts and blasts of many winter-times,
And borne the heat of many suns ; a grey,
A worn, subdued, and spirit-softened thing,
Wrapt in a suit of unimpressive black,
Twitched up before, behind, for fear the dust
Should fleck its rusty hue beyond redemption,
And then, where must the next come from ?
                              A thing
With features drawn, and mute, and sharp ; and brow
Of many creases, all surrounded by
A widow's frill, and bonnet-rim of crape.
A stooping form, with bent and shrunken neck,
A limping gait, and short and heavy stride,
A basket linked upon the long, numbed arm,
A pair of slippers, dangling at the side.

These meet amid the fields, beneath the noon,
Upon a footpath, on a market day.
The light of welcome recognition shines
Upon the face and in the eyes of each.
The rosebud hand, the brown and bony hand
Are clasped a moment closely, while the lips
Speak quiet words of greeting, and the like.
At length, the maiden lays her hand upon

The woman's arm, and looks into her face,
And with a sudden tenderness breaks out :

   " How is Celia to-day ?
     Is she going as I hear ?
   There's a shadow on your face,
     Gathering in your eye a tear !
   When I saw her last, I knew
     Something dark had cross'd her skies,
   By the whiteness of her lips,
     And the rings around her eyes.
   How is Celia to-day ?
     Is she fading as I hear ?
   There's a pathos on your face,
     Trembling on each lid, a tear.

   What a girl she was, for sure,
     In the days I knew her best !
   Gayer, blither, as in sooth
     She was fairer than the rest :
   She,—the idols of the lads,
     Envy of us maidens all.
   Is there then no hope ? no hope ?
     Is she sped beyond recall ?
   How is Celia to-day ?
     Is it truthful that I hear ?
   There's a sorrow on your face,
     On your cheek a bitter tear.

   Yester-e'en I watch'd poor Fred
     Mope an hour and never stir ;

And he sobbed like any child
   When I spoke to him of her.
Every topic we discuss'd
   Brought us round to that at last :
Never saw I such a blank
   As the trouble on him cast.
How's your Celia to-day ?
   Must we lose her then, poor dear ?
Ah, the anguish on your face ?
   I will weep you tear for tear !"

The shadow of the older, darker nature,
Sinks on the brighter for a moment, as
The shadow of a thin wool-cloud falls on
The brightness of a May-day upland side.
They cry together on the lonely path,
Then part with just a little shake of hands ;
And each goes on her several way, with head
Bent lower, and wet, and solemn softened eyes.

———

THE SINGLE GRAVE.

UPON a wild, wild ridge that bristled up
   From the white surf-lip of the garrulous shore,
   Like some long sloping front of knaggled cloud
Seen over the east i'th' dawning dusk of eve ;
There stood a dwelling, with a ledge of rock
Rising above the northward gable in rude
Irregular grandeur like a pyramid :

A rustic cottage, quaint, yet pleasing, with
A certain fragrant beauty, not in art,
With tiny vestibule, where, in the time
Of flowers, gay wreaths of honey-suckles came
From the long wiry snakes that clasped it round
And bloomed and shed a perfume on the wind,
That blew up rough and nauseous from the brine.
Long leafless parasites webbed o'er the front,
And fell around the windows and the doors,
A cozy covert, where a skilful hand
Had realized the shapings of a mind
And thought refined, and warm with nature-love.
Behind it rose a crooked mountain-ash,
And hung its long loose tresses o'er the roof.
About the front, that faced the tremulous sea,
And all the thousand sunsets that were strung
Upon the brow of ocean, like a wreath
Of flashing topazes, along the course
Of the departed gladiator years,
Were slips of garden beds, and strings of walks,
And gleaming rockeries, on terraces
Amid the boulders, gay with unhewn slips
Of many-coloured, half-transparent stones,
Rude blocks of blue-lined quartz, and drift, and grit,
And lumps of granulated dark conglomerate,
And chips of marble clogged with fossil stems,
And shards of porphyry, calcareous shale,
And tall white spires of rock-salt crystalline ;
And squares of felspar, studding round the top,
Like some embattled tower in miniature ;

And scatter'd all among, were curious waifs
Washed up from ocean in his younger days :
Smooth pied-ringed pebbles ; crystals, where the sun
Became an hundred stars ; and shoals of shells
Of every hue, and every shape and size ;
And straggling o'er and round about, thin strands
Of creepers grew ; and moss and lichen clung
About the rugged bases of the stones ;
Ragg'd shrĕds of tangled sea-wood lay along,
Coquetting with the amours of the breeze ;
And from the fissures, feathery fronds of ferns
Streamed, dark and withered ; and among the rocks
That heaved above, great, gaunt, and ran out far,
Uprose grey clumps of shrubs, with festooned webs
Of dark green matted ivy, interwoven.
Inside the cottage was a cozy room,
Neat as a finch's nest with feathers lined ;
Along the floor a spongy carpet lay ;
A fire glow'd brightly in the polish'd grate,
And saw its flickering dance an hundred-fold
In burnish'd rosewood, plate, and lacquered glass.
A carved piano, with a gilded volume
Upon its wreath-wrought rack, wide open braced
On " Waves, be calm !" stood in an arched recess ;
And round the walls, in massy ebon frames,
Were 'gravings from the marvellous picturings
Of the old Masters !—saints, and martyr-scenes,
Strange attitudes, and weird effects that strike
The spirit dumb with awe ; and everything
Spoke but of comfort, peace, and competence.

Beside the window looking towards the sea,
A woman sat upon an afternoon
Amid the flitting of the by-gone years.
She gazed not on the fire or furniture,
Not on the picturings, but far away ;
Away along the shimmering of the sea.
Her hair, 'mid which still sprays of rose-light broke.
Was coil'd and twisted deftly o'er her ears,
And plaited in a little boss behind.
Her lips were delicate as dew-dipp'd rose-leaves ;
Her face was round, and every lineament,
Tho' sharpen'd, was a slumbering beauty-line ;
A blue transparency lay on her brow ;
Her cheeks were white and saintly as the hue
Of lilies drooping in the heat ; and 'neath
The arching of the eyebrows, slumber'd shades
Of purple pencilings ; within the wide,
Brown, lash-laden eyes, the lustrous orange-light
Lay soften'd, dusk'd, and solemnized, much like
The twilight of a dim-glazed sanctuary ;
But sparkled in the upper rim of tears,
That lay beneath the orbings of the eyes,
And press'd to gather up and shed themselves :
Soft, tender eyes, beneath whose tremulous gaze
There was the undershade of suffering ;
Of plaintive helplessness, and hope, and dread,
That haunts one like a mournful questioning
When delicate women have, when cherishing
Within their inner life a second life.
Beside her, on a velvet-cushion'd couch,

Lay scattered, long white linen baby-robes,
Lace-fringed, be-stringed, and 'broidered up the front.
One finger like a gnomon, marked a spot
Upon a map spread loosely o'er a stand,
On which she leant her elbow.
　　　　　　　Silently
Still gazed she o'er the shimmering of the sea.
North-west, a great grey shank of piled-up rocks,
Immense, irregular, and here and there
Snow-mottled 'mongst the shadows of the cliffs,
And flanked with tufts of broom, whose fibrous claws
Clasped tightly round the rifted blocks, leaned out
Like the enormous shoulder of the land
Down bent in muscular attitude to meet
The feverish pushing of the imperious sea,
Afar into the wildly lungeing waves.
Away to southward bent the freckled coast
Its corrugated forehead to the waves,
Who kissed it now,—now spat upon it in wrath.
And by the sinuous shore where villages
Of low white cottages, and masts, and nets,
And groups of children racing on the sands ;
And quaint, grey fishermen, straggling to and fro,
Or baling boats that grated on the strand,
Or floating far along the shivering light.
The sun poured o'er the southern occident
A yellow, dense, mist-mingled lake of flame ;
Soft clouds above broke up and widened out
To south and north in tattered demi-rings,
That caught and held the light in nets of fringe.

E

The long, still stretch stooped sloping to the beach,
Whose thin white line ran stark and bald before
The molten roll of liquid brass beyond.
The scattered groups of grim and naked trees
Furred with a flossy shag of spangled rime,
Stood up like rabbled cordage 'gainst the sky ;
And low in mouths of grots, and at the foot
Of jutting crags, lay little rims of lakes,
Frost-bound, opaque, and stony-browed ; while wide
Along the still horizon heaved the grand,
Sublime, un-iced, untrammelled ocean-soul
Beneath the fondling of the mirrored heavens.
Even thus like little lakes are little minds,
Numbed into stony-death by frost-tongued woe ;
While mighty minds roll on for ever, calm,
Unchilled, unshackled, by an adverse fate,
Reflecting evermore the light of God—
The soul's unchangeable, eternal sky !
The woman dropped her cheek upon her palm
And gazed along the shimmering of the sea.
Twelve moons and eight had run their orbits round
Since she had sauntered up a winding path
That wriggled 'mongst the hillocks and the rocks,
Through rude ravines a mile or so, and came
At length unto an inland village, with a Church,
A dialled steeple, and a chime of bells ;—
Since she had sauntered by the side of one
Erect and firm, and glorious in the strength
Of manhood—pure, developed, and complete ;
And leaned upon an arm that well might bear ;

And looked upon a forehead and a face
Serene and noble as the brow of faith ;
And seen the wonder through the eyes of one
Who loved the very ground she trod upon.
Her brow had on a wreath of blossoms then,
And moved she in a cloud of snowy silk,
Like to a star amid a vapour-flake ;
And down behind her to the puny feet,
Yclad in softest velvet, hung a veil ;
And fluttered in the breeze that laughed along
The dancing plumage of the sea.   Anon
In little pauses, when the breeze had wrought
Itself into a breathless ecstasy
Of mirth, and e'en perforce must stop for breath,
Came to their ears a stanza of the bells ;
And there had been a scattering of flowers,
And grey old clouts thrown loose along their wake ;
A tingling finger wore a new donned ring,
And they had kissed her much and named her " bride."
He led her to his cottage home ; and there
A grey-hair'd woman, beautiful in age,
With eyes of peace—the outlets of a soul
Whose every base inclining was subdued,
With many thousand mingling autographs
Of holy thoughts and doings on her brow ;
A woman eager-lipped came to the door—
The bridegroom called her " mother,"—came and stood
And gazed upon the rose-faced bride a bit,
Then took her in her arms and to her heart,
And kissed her everywhere about her face,

And loosed her arms, and strained her close again.
And called her " child ; " and said, 'twixt little sobs,
" She had a daughter now to bless her age,
Who never had one of her own, except——"
And here she stopped and sobbed, " for just one day ;
Her only solace hitherto had been
That great rough boy," and here she glanced aside
With sly content, and wept for love or joy,
Or in remembrance of her own young days.
And joy was in that cottage ; day, without
One softening night ; calm sunshine and no cloud.
Old haggard Time put off his seams, and took
A youthful semblance ; and with ringling locks
Down with the golden sunsets ran, and brow
Fair as the sunrise on the morning hills,
When May-day garlands tremble ; and with eyes
Struck dim-bright with an inward, untold bliss,
Told out the tale of days that round the year
With youth's impetuous haste ; slipping the hours
Swift through his limber fingers, as a maid
Bent 'fore the Virgin's shrine, slips rosary beads
While dreaming of a young-browed masculine saint.
It happened that there came a certain day when he,
The husband of a twelvemonth, bade farewell
To those he cherished ; and, with eyes tear-dewed,
But purpose-strong and resolute of will,
And firm of soul to follow Duty's lead,
Went with the Bible in his hand, which oft
He oped and read for strengthening the words,
" Go ye into all the world and preach the Gospel."

And with a comrade, who had none to leave
Behind to mourn him dearer than a friend,
Sailed from the shadows of the rocks, and passed,
And died away into the mists, where stoops
The sky to kiss the ocean's pouting lip.
The ship sailed on, nor met with one mishap.
The ocean glided from beneath ; the sky
And sun rose hotter o'er their heads.
One day while drifting o'er the line, they stood
Upon the rifted deck and, dazzled, watched
The burning incandescence lie along
The vast profound of waters.   Not one throb
Of air broke up the surface into waves ;
Only a solemn heaving, and a low,
Strange, moaning sound ; the great white sheet of fire
Lay prone along, unbroken, like a sea
Of crystal oil.   Strange fishes glided slow,
With great grey sides, and dazed and dreamy eyes,
Beneath the surface radiance, and at times
Upheaved a sluggish eddy 'neath the keel.
The laggard sails hung idly round the masts ;
The sailors lounged half-roasted in the shade.
Around the ringed base of blazoned sky
A purple circle, like a nimbus, glowed.
The comrade from beneath the awning stepped.
'Twas but a moment, yet the sun looked down
With awful eye upon his upraised brow,
And smote him to the planks.
                              One day and night
He raved and writhed in frenzied agony,

And knew not of his pain, and never spake
Coherently again, but sank and died.
And o'er the shrouded form, low words of hope
And prayer were uttered in the cool of day;
And bald old ocean tomb'd another form
Amid the caverns of his treasured waifs—
'Neath coral eaves where sea-nymphs twist their hair.
The ship sailed on: the missionary mourned
In ten-fold loneliness his comrade's fate.
'There came a day, swift dawning, when they dropp'd
The intrepid wanderer and his little all
Upon an inland in the southern seas,
And sailed the ship into the mist again.
The lonely being on the untried shore
Stood still with hands clasp'd, sending o'er the surge
The sadness of his eyes, until the ship
Sank into a speck of rising cloud; and then
Low bent him by the juggling surf, and prayed
Until the sweat dropped from his eyebrows' fringe:
Then rose and passed among the torrent wilds;
And found an uncouth horde of naked men,
Who formed a circle round, and yelled, and leaped,
Now closed, now menaced; and at last, in awe,
Came kneeling down and grovelling at his feet;
And on them like a fascination fell
The influence of his loftier intellect,
His breadth of soul; the exaltion of
His great humanity imbued with truth.
Expanded, knowledge-deepened, God-impressed.
He knelt, bare-browed, and raised his hands towards
         heaven;

Then passed among them fearless for himself.
With simple remedies he soothed their sick,
And taught them how to hide their nakedness ;
Began to gather symbols for the sounds
They uttered ; and to build a hut of stakes.
But thirty days since first he trod the shore,
When came a dark malaria, and he fell
Exceeding sick, and lay three days and nights
Amid the heats and damps, and sank and died—
Died with his clothes on, and his long hands locked
Across the Bible spread upon his breast.
The wild dark forms pressed round him silently,
And while he suffered brought him shreds of flesh,
Wild fruits, and draughts of lymph in cocoa-nut shells ;
And watched his spirit leap from out his eyes
In brilliant flashes in the dawn of eve ;
And stood around, stone-still, for many an hour
Amid the gloom-light, deeming that he slept,
Till one stole up and touched the set, cold cheek,
And tossed his arms and shrieked the fearfullest shriek,
Caught up and echoed by an hundred throats,
What time the sun blazed through the forest boughs.
One day they danced the death-dance round the hut ;
Then in the sunset raised the unbending corse
And bore it to the hoarsely-babbling shore,
Far looking to the north, and found a spot
Where, stealing from them in the twilight hours,
In secret oft they watched him stand or kneel
With quivering hands outstretched, and mournful eyes
Wedged 'twist the sky and ocean : while his lips

Moved fitfully, but shaped no words in voice—
And scooped a shallow grave, and laid him there,
Hair loose and flowing, hands clasped, as he died ;
And heaped the dust that filled the mouth and eyes ;
And shrieked one wild, wild shriek, that smote the air,
And woke the ravings of the rocks, and skimmed
Along the terror-bristling waves, and died
In one long lingering wail, and went their way.
   The days seemed longer as they gathered o'er
The cottage-dwelling by the mournful sea,
The young wife grew to wander on the beach,
Or by the window sit and watch the sea,
And lose herself in dreamings of the time
When she should dare the treacherous deep, and go
Through storm and danger to the man she loved.
One midnight, being restless, up she got
And drew the curtain half-aside, and leaned
Her head against the icy glass, and gazed
Along the mummery of the solemn sea.
The moon-white radiance sheeted all the stretch ;
The sky was cloudless, vacant-hued, and vast ;
Ten thousand million stars were on the sea.
The moaning trouble of a restless wind
Rose o'er the staring bluff, and came and went,
And chafed the waters into crimp-line gleams
Of quivering waves, that flattered in the light
Like plumage of a swan, when, in the sun,
She shakes the April shower-drops from her down ;
A misty yellow splendour rose and fell
Now mixing with the moon-sheen, fading now.

And silently lower her forehead slid
  Down the glaze of the dew-damp pane,
And heavier still on her arm she leant,
And lower and lower her shoulders bent,
  And rose on her features a shadow of pain.
And deepened the strangeness the cliffs amid,
  And softened the gloom round the ring of the main ;
And ever the radiance came and went,
And lay on the moon-mist mingled and blent ;
  And ever the sobbings did burst and flit,
And came o'er the waters a marvellous stir
Of funeral music, that rose and fell
Like the saddening thrill of a muffled bell,
    Or mournfully sweet,
    Low, distant beat
Of a vast-stringed dulcimer ;
And died up the sky with a passionate swell
That troubled the midnight, till it was spent ;
And her features worked as if anguish smit,
  And she stood as if ringed in the thrall of a spell.
Anon, a mystic, tall, colossal form,
Snow-sheeted, foam-draped, marvellously still,
Seethed, like a spray-white fountain, slowly, slowly
From the hushed awe-calm ocean, with the face
And eyes of him she loved—a moment paused—
Threw up long jets of arms, and swooned down back,
And misted out along the lunar ridge.
She started backward, deeming she had dozed,
But in her heart there grew a bitter dread.
The days went on, and sailed the swift-winged ships ;

And now she gazed along the sun-gleamed sea,
And with a world of anguish sang a song :—
Sobbing down 'mongst the tears she sang this song :—

"O would that I were there,
    Away beyond the sea,
Among the hills of the summer isle
    Where sleepeth he lonelily !
Ah, me ! but one hour, one hour
    To sit on that one dear mound,
Where the note of the mocking-bird
    Awakens the echoes round,
Like the muttering in a dream
    Of the slumbering Oread-sound.

"To dream on that wee ridge,
    By wild bloomed weed o'er-topped,
Where never a sigh was heaved,
    And never a tear was dropped ;
Where standeth a tamarind tree
    That watches alone, alone,
And the shadows broken lie
    On a grave without a stone ;
And the wild beasts prowl and lurk
    Where sleepeth my own, my own ;

"Ah, God ! my heart is sad
    To think on that lone grave,
Where roameth the savage horde,
    And the waters sob and lave ;
Where lieth the long, cragged shore,

And flitteth the swift sea-mew
O'er billows alight with foam,
  Not changing, but ever new ;
And the breath of a breeze is fanning
  A sky that is ever blue.

" To think that never a word
  From Christian lips should fall,
That never a heart should stoop
  O'er the grave at his funeral ;
And never a kindred foot
  By the rude-cast heap should stand,
And never a love should breathe a prayer,
  And never a fond white hand
Should plant a flower, and never a tear
  Make spot on the loamy sand.

" I dream when I would not dream ;
  I weep though I know 'tis wrong,
To picture that single grave
  The desolate lands among.
I know not if the pangs
  Of death were agony :
If his faith was firm ; or if he yearned
  For a grave in his own country ;
Or if he wept for the love I gave,
  And hungered in heart for me.

" He seems so utterly severed
  From all he loved the best !
O tender, tender showers,

And balm-winged winds and flowers
   Sweet, soothe him in his rest.
Could I only lie and kiss
   That desolate grave unkissed,
The savage might come in his wrath
   And do me to death if he list,
If he only would bury me there,
   Though none in the nations wist."

The darkness gathered, and the woman toiled,
And cried in woman's bitterest agony.
The midnight came ; she tossed her arms and moaned
And turned her head about and babbled much
In low delirium of " the lonely grave."
Those round her looked on one another pained,
And held their hearts, and uttered 'neath their breath,
" Poor thing she rambles !" ·
                              Darkly dawned the morn :
The lovely limbs round-modelled, beautiful,
And eloquent as heart-full tears on cheeks
Of Virgin youth—lay straight beneath the sheet,
That settled silently, and out-lined forth
Their marble fulness and exquisite curves.
And fair, limp hands were on her bosom crossed :
The light stole up, and looked about the eyes
For its old mirror ; but the blue-shot lids   ·
Were hooded down ; the long brown lashes made
Dark raylings on her cheeks.   The lips were close,
The long hair lay about the pillow loose,
All o'er her shoulders, down each side her face,

About her breast. A woman wrung her hands,
And swayed her form—tear-dry, without a moan.
Two days stole on ; and then a shrouded mite—
Soft, bald, white head, blue face, faint lines of eyes,
Shut-up, wee dot of mouth drawn close, like faint,
Pink-petalled daisy when the dews have fallen—
They brought and laid beside the woman form ;
And over them the huge Eternity,
Broken for a moment by the bubble, Time,
Stretched its infinitude of firmament,
Horizonless for evermore for them :
And Silence, hand-in-hand with heaven-eyed Peace,
Knelt by the shrine of Innocence in death.
A week : and 'neath the shadow of the Church
Another grave had risen ; where careless feet
Would tread unthinkingly on summer eves.
A weakly woman went in dawn of spring,
And bent above the grave—veil-screened, and wept ;
And sowed a ring of seeds about its head.
But when the seeds had grown a crown of flowers
There rose another grave beside the first ;
The bells chimed sadly and the day went out.
Another fond romance had dropped from earth ;
Tossed down among the myriad faded wreaths,
And bays, and garlands of the time complete.
Another circle clasped—a bond complete
In that calm region some folks deem so far,
But which, methinks at times, is very near ;
Where desert wastes, or sweeps of angry seas
Can separate no more the vital loves—

For soul is love in essence—of the true.
And other feet were on the rock-fringed path,
And other voices in the trellised cot,
And other eyes upon the crimson wave ;
And other objects gathered on the shore,
And laughed, and wept, and died ; and others came
And still the surge of being swept, altho'
The generations rose and seared and dropped,
Like leaves about an hundred-summered oak.
And nature aye completed and renewed
Herself. The sky was changing, yet for aye
Unchanged, and still the glory lay upon
The world in wonder, music, mystery—
Sealed symbols ! 'gainst which many a spirit beat
Its frail life out, vain-striving to unlock
And let the revelation in upon
The insatiate soul, and barely struck one clue !
The ocean fell to wrath and calmed again ;
And tossed its surf-white wrinkles up the shore
What time the moon was circled in its noon.
The days came up the east and so the nights :
And time went on and evermore went on,
And notched his progress on the western line
In golden sunsets down behind the wave.

THE SHADOW OF DEATH.

 HEAR strange music in the trees ;
I see the mild melodious stir
Of clouds and corn ; can almost feel the breeze

That waves the long bright films of gossamer,
Running in tissue-strands from tree to tree ;
And the wild joy of living and expanding
  Comes from the outer-world to me ;
And all the radiance and the melody
    Upon me lying,
Moveth my spirit (as a summer wind
  Troubleth a weeping willow tress)
    Unto a soft strange kind
Of sadness, gladness, pain, and silentness,
    Vague, mingled, undefined.
For here I lie amid the stranding
Of my life-hope ; must leave behind
    All that I see
Of beautiful and grand ; no more to be
A portion of their life and poesy—
    I am dying !
  O wonderful Light ! O Music marvellous !
    My soul hath dwelt with you.
  O beauty, heavenly beauty ! is it thus
    That I must fade and pass away,
      While thou art ever new,
      Fresh-born, and sparkling as the dew ?
  O, I have felt a kinship with the grand,
    The tender, the magnificent ;
      Is 't possible the hand
That once hath swept the mystic under-keys
      Of this vast instrument,
      Can perish utterly ?
      Is 't possible the night

On which I enter now
Will know no day?
Can that, that feels and utters all decay?
O spirit, bend thy brow!
O soul, sink on thy knees!
Wait calmly till the light
Break on thy trembling, deep anxiety.
Far, hid eternity!
What is thy shadow? what thy mystery?
Most holy Book!
To which great earnest men have come
Through the long ages with their agonies
Of dark implorings, doubts, uncertainties,
And fierce upreachings of the spirit dumb,
I cling to thee.
O spirit! dawn on me;
Unseal my inward seeing while I look!
My hands are clasped before me, and my eyes
Are dim with prayer.
Thou man of Calvary!
Thou of the fairest fair!
With the atoning blood on brow and side,
Come near, and let me kiss Thy feet,
Receive Thy holy chrism, and rise complete
Serene of soul, and pure, and pacified.
Smile on me till these achings feel Thy balm,
And my rocked soul is strong to wait
Amid the darkness, and
Be calm.

THE MISSED BUTT.

A SUPERSTITION.

There is a superstition current in North Staffordshire (if elsewhere, I am unacquainted with the fact) which holds—or did hold a generation back—that if a farmer, in sowing his yearly breadth, accidentally misses or overlooks one of the "butts," a circumstance which occasionally happens, and does not perceive the omission till the absence of the green blade discovers the fact, it is a sure *sign* of a death in his household.

The "butts," in the North Staffordshire vernacular, are the long narrow ridges, or beds, thrown together by the plough, with separating furrows for the drainage on which the seed is sown.

WAS Teamsman for that year
   Tho' but slim and over-grown :
   Father did the sowing then.
All the yearly breadth was sown,

Save an angle of a field,
   Lately broken up from lea—
That where stood the old sheepcote
   By the lightning-splintered tree.

Night was down upon us ; yet
   Father coughed and firked his beard ;
'Twas not much—the mould was dry—
   Seed was down—the team was geared.

Then he skyward looked, where winds,
   Clouds, and rain were gathering might—
" Up, my lads !" he said ; " we'll do't
   Ere we stable for the night :

F

" 'Tis over late a week or more
　　Now—and every sign of rain ;
We may wish it done i'th' morn,"
　　So we slapped to work again.

Flew the harrows o'er the loam ;
　　Flew the seed from flying fist,
But when springing blades showed green
　　Then 'twas found a butt was missed !

" I have farmed for forty year,
　　Sown my seed myself a score,"
Said my father ; " but I never,
　　Never played this game afore."

Then up spake a wrinkled crone,
　　" 'Tis a deadly certain sign ;
There will be a death i'th' house
　　Ere the Christmas berries shine."

Then the household laughed aloud,
　　Lightly chode the dame, and said
" 'Twas a weak old woman's tale :"
　　But the woman shook her head.

All the family after that
　　Scanned the butt with dubious eye,
Felt a sinking at their hearts,
　　Probing not for reason why.

Came disease when fields had flowers,
　　Breathed upon a lassie fair,

Stole her music, laid her dead—
  Dead among her glory hair !

Bare and barren stretched the butt
  Just as if the need were less ;
Dead and still our darling lay
  With no want we might redress.

Dropped the silence on the earth,
  Came the ripeness to the corn ;
And the reapers went about,
  And the crowded fields were shorn.

Sadly eyed we all the butt,
  Hinting never aught ; and yet
Through the years that barren butt
  No one of us may e'er forget.

ASSOCIATION.

A REVERIE.

'TIS an early spring-time ramble,
  Where the lambs on hillocks gambol,
  And the blackbird in the bramble
    Tells its dream of brighter skies.

'Tis a noontide dusked and stilly,
And the wind comes low and chilly
From the northern, wild and hilly,
    Where the snow in patches lies.

'Tis a welkin dark and lowering,
Demon-pinions spread and soaring,
Craggy turrets grim and towering,
    Groaning beams and rafters under ;

Gorgon faces, foam exuding,
Double-chinned, and black and brooding,
Hateful serpent-eyes protruding,
    Languid bosoms ript asunder ;

Foaming seas and forms titanic,
Moping geryons, scaled, satanic.
Rabble-hordes in wildest panic,
    Bannered armies dim revealed.

Monsters doubling and disjointing,
Druids eld, white heads anointing,
Arms upraised and fingers pointing,
    Eldred fingers, half concealed ;

Heads in profile, bold, gigantic,
Pigmy forms with smirk and antic,
Ghostly shapes with aspect frantic,
    Forms on tiptoe upward reaching ;

Gaudy mimes with bow and caper,
Spiral stairways, statues taper,
Long dull lakes of moony vapour,
    Figures knelt, hands clasped, beseeching.

Here, a splintered column sleeping,
There, a woman bowed and weeping,

Close behind, a maiden peeping,
    There, a poet brooding lorn.

Snowhills yonder, seamed and drifted,
Here, a wind-blown garment lifted,
There, a fortress, shattered, rifted,
    'Neath a curtain rent and torn,

Through the which the sunlight flashes,
Out, in long and milky lashes,
And the sullen landscape dashes
    With a hundred burning dots,

With the clouds, dream-moving, veering,
Opening, closing, widening, nearing,
Fading, dying, re-appearing
    Everywhere in varying spots.

'Tis a land-stretch, villa-studded,
Here and there be-rocked and wooded,
Vales with April waters flooded ;
    Lofty spires in each direction.

Torpent hillocks bound the vision,
Height on height in rude precision,
Cleft with many a deep incision,
    Flanked with many a huge projection.

This the frame : the picture, nearer,
Lies in outline firmer, clearer,
Vision-swept and cherished dearer ;
    Memory haunts each feature doting !

Larch-serrated uplands sleeping,
Where a windmill watch is keeping ;
Up a gorge, a steam-horse creeping,
       Clouds a sluice and barges floating.

Hills 'mid valleys, scalloped, shaded,
Heath embrowned and hedgerow braided,
Furze be-ruffled, brook-cascaded,
       Mottled o'er with ivied dwellings ;

Shaded cots and fat farmhouses,
Steaming byres where Milcher drowses,
Pastures brown where Dobbin browses,
       Brambled hollows, hillock-swellings.

Nearer still—a sloping valley
Where the shadows longest dally,
And the mist-wraiths, still and palely,
       Linger over dell and gloom ;

Through the which a streamlet, brawling,
Shrieks when o'er the boulders falling,
Scrambling, hustling, whimpering, sprawling,
       Struggleth towards an old mill-flume.

Deep within—a marshy meadow,
Where the noonlight faints to shadows ;
Chilly now ; at midnight wed to
       Will-o'-th'-wisp and goblin chases.

Patrolled round with hedgerow marches,
Sentinelled with dragoon larches,

Flanked with oaks, whose branching arches
     Lift the shade in bridge-like spaces.

There a flock of rooks are vieing
With each other ; fiercely plying
For the acorns underlying,
     Hidden deep in autumn weather.

Some from far are hasting for them,
Some are circling, wheeling o'er them,
Some down-dropping swell the quorum,
     Swaying, mingling all together.

Some amid the shadows loiter,
Some where glows the linting brighter,
Some on outposts reconnoitre,
     Till relieved by sable brothers.

Some among the oaks are sitting,
Some are coming, some are quitting,
Ever restless, swaying, flitting—
     Stealing booty of each others.

Rubbing beaks with ancient armours,
Hailing friends with boisterous clamours
While the ether titters, stammers,
     With their ceaseless cawing, cawing.

But the vision dims before me,
And a haunting gathers o'er me ;
Comes a presence to restore me
     To the past—the veil withdrawing.

In the morning' glowing, golden,
Up a pathway, shaded, olden,
Satchel hung and tippet folden,
        Two fair sisters and a brother.

Burnished, ringlet-hung, are tripping,
Laughing gaily, jumping, skipping,
Now behind, and now outstr:pping
        In their joyance, one another.

Suddenly they pause and listen,
Upward glance with eyes that glisten,
For a bickering sound has risen
        Up the dawning red and cool.

Flocks of rooks are gliding, flowing
Through the dreaming and the glowing;
Say the children, " They are going
        Just as we are now, to school."

Hailing them, they kisses blow them,
And a low obeisance do them ;
Hope their dame is kindly to them,
        Bow again and say " good morning."

And to those who croak and linger
Talk they of the truant-stinger,
Deal with stern and upraised finger
        Many a grave and solemn warning.

Passing on, they quiz and wonder
If their school is where the thunder

Mutters awfully ; or under
        Forest roofs of leaves a-quiver.

If on clouds or branches perching,
Drone they 'neath great goggles, searching
Luckless trifler for a birching ;
        If they wear the dunce-cap ever.

And at night when home returning
Free from all the quags of learning,
Glancing upwards toward the burning,
        Once again they hear and see them.

Gathering o'er the sunset, swooping,
Chasing, wheeling, tumbling, whooping ;—
" Playing at tick," they say, " while trooping
        Home from school, rejoiced with freedom."

Crows across the valleys skimming,
Through the molten ether swimming ;
Children chasing—laughter-brimming,
        Flap their arms, and caw, and leap.

Ah ! the lane, the brook, the swelling
Upland side, and rustic dwelling !
But the music bears no telling :
        Chords of memory throb and weep !

O ye glories evanescent,
Sunrise dreamings passing pleasant,
Nothing had ye of the present :
        All of life hath changed its meaning.

Long the bitter tears have started ;
For the sisters, tender-hearted,
Both have sickened and departed,
　　　And I too am earthward leaning !

Gone for aye the glittering fancies,
Gone the visions and the chances,
Gone the weaving, the romances—
　　　Not a vestige lingers of them !

And the anguish lives unspoken,
Though the heart still beats unbroken—
Morn had many a promise token—
　　　Clods are cold and clouds above them.

Soon I too shall sleep serenely,
Where the grass grows wild and greenly,
And the frost-wind whistles keenly,
　　　And the night hath awful wings

O'er my grave the rooks will chatter,
Rain and hail will beat and patter,
And the gay foot tread—what matter ?
　　　'Tis the lot of men and things.

Peace, my soul ! the stars are throbbing,
And the winds and waves are sobbing,
Ever robing and disrobing
　　　Is the landscape as of yore :

Trust the good in meek contrition ;
Every shape hath one fixed mission ;
And the calm, serene volition ;
　　　Moves the same for evermore !

TO A THUNDERCLOUD.

LOVE AND ANXIETY.

H, black-browed, thunder-cloud, that broodest upon
The world that lies beyond yon distant peak—
Embodiment of vengeance, rapine, strife,
Whose murky vestments skirt the solemn pines
That crown the foreheads of the boundary hills ;
A faint streak of whose scowling front I see,
Crowned with a glory indescribable !—
A tumulous mass of bullion, height on height ;
A convex sea, with billows turbulent ;
A glacier amid a sunset tropical ;
A black and threatening providence beneath ;
Above—the glory of a paradise !
Oh, awful thunder-cloud, whose voice I hear
In half-breathed murmurs from the echoing crags ;
Whose lightning fury shocks the very heart
Of the iron world, and sends a flashing fear,
Like to the passage of a death-sprite, o'er
The blanching earth, and through the shuddering air ;—
Oh, fearful thunder-cloud, be pitiful·!
There is a valley where thou broodest now,
A quiet valley, garnitured with beech,
And meadow flowers, and twining eglantine :—
Be merciful, oh, dear, good thundercloud,
And spare that valley, for my love is there.
If thou hast now upraised thy murderous dart,
Oh ! pause a moment ; pause, and glance below ;
There stands a cottage which thou well may'st know,

Forsooth, it is the fairest in the lot ;
Around it creep the ivy and the vine,
And o'er the porch a bush of roses leans.
Peep in that cottage and behold my love.
My love is beautiful,—so beautiful !
In her chaste loveliness and innocence ;
Beyond all maids in feature and in form,
With the strange halo of her tenderness
Encircling her and glorifying her ;
With the great flood of tresses fluttering,
And trembling round the lily love of face,
Does not such beauty half unnerve thy arm ?
My love is graceful as a willow bough
Charmed by Æolian winds and moonlit dews,
And comely as the face of youthful hope.
And then my love is pure, so very pure !
I have not seen a day of virgin spring,
I have not seen a mountain stream, that through
Unnumbered labyrinths distilleth aye,
Nor winter snowflake half as pure as she.
Oh, spare my love, she never wronged a thing ;
She could not find at heart to crush a midge.
Oh, spare that cottage for the sake of her !
Oh, spare that valley for the sake of it !
Or if thou canst not curb thy demon will,
Then wreck thy rage upon the hills around ;
Tear up the rocks and cleave the giant oaks,
But do not miss, oh, do not miss thy mark,
Lest one stray shot should, glancing off, escape,
Blaze through the vale, and terrify my love !

Oh, spare my love, most mighty thunder-cloud,
Lest all my joy to sorrow should be turned,
My light to darkness—blackness such as thine.
And Thou, great God! all things are known to Thee :
Infinite, wonderful, beyond compare !
Embodiment of all things good and pure !
Whose power is manifest in all we see;
In every sound we hear, the breath we breathe ;
Oh ! guide Thy vassal thunder-cloud away—
Away beyond the valley ; for my love,
My beautiful is there, my better life,
The choicest of Thy choice create, O God.
I love her, Father, with all human love,
With that blessed instinct which we have from Thee.
'Tis not idolatry, not passion love ;
Not that high spirit-worship thou hast sown
And fostered in our nature's heart, in proof
That there's a subtle link that joins the weak
Humanity to Godhead, and asserts
The spirit's growing immortality ;
Not that pure glow of praise and wonder which
I owe to Thee.
     Thou hast created her
A simple part, to join another part
To make one whole, one soul to worship Thee.
And she is Thine : I see in her e'en more
Than all Thy glorious works, thy handiwork.
She is a step to lift me up to Thee,
A spirit-hand to lead me to Thy love ;
For, in her presence all things mean and base,

The envyings, hatings, strifes, and dreams of earth,
All sensual promptings, selfish ends and aims,
Depart, and leave me Christ-like, humble, meek.
She seems a link between my soul and Thee ;
For in her presence I am nearer Thee.
And when away, the halo of her charms,
Her love, her tenderness, enwalls me round ;
A charméd circle where no evil comes !
Protect her, Father ; give her unto me ;
And as one soul we'll yield ourselves to Thee.

A COUNTRY-WOMAN'S TALE.

Y, woman ! I had six as pretty bairns
        As any you could find, search th' country o'er ;
        Bright-eyed, an' golden-haired, and rosy-cheeked,
Well made and sprightly, sharp an' full of tricks,
As bonny a lot as e'er were born and reared !   ·

  Time after time they came, like gifts from God,
An' grew into my heart, an' blessed my sight ;
(I felt the proudest woman in the world ;)
An' all the pain I suffered for their sakes
Seemed nothing, when compared to th' joy I felt
At havin' them.
                Why, bless you, woman, you
Ne'er were plagued wit' children, as you say ;
Know naught o' th' love that tingles every nerve,
When lyin' on your lap, the bit, bright eyne
First looken up, an' gazin' into yours

Wi' such a look o' listless wonderment!
An' when the dimpled fingers claspin' yours,
An' the red ripe cherry lips part open, buzz   -
And pout—
O think what clinging, helpless things they are ;
The hardest heart grows soft—and when the arms
Sink softly down, an' th' droopin' eyelids close,
And when the bare
Defenceless head lies snuggling on your heart,
An' when you feel they're yours—your very own—
To feel—— But why should I attempt to tell
What is untellable to you ; " who ne'er
Were plagued nor maul't wi' children," as you say.
But I was proud o' mine—so proud o' mine—
I could have laid my life down, inch by inch ;
They frisked around my knees, an' each in turn
Climbed on my lap, and throwed its rosy arms
About my neck, an' kissed, an' called me mam ;
And big and little come to me wi' all
Their early troubles, secrets, pains, and cares ;
Their boisterous merriment was joy to me,
Their laugh my music, and their joy my life.
Ay ! I was proud o' mine i' those bright days,
The happiest an' brightest of my life !
Folk said how blessed I was—a homely cot—
A lot o' winsome bairns, all fair and sharp—
A honest-hearted, steady working man—
An' blessed indeed, I was ; poor John, poor John !
He was as good a lad, my husband was,
As ever wench was tied to.   Kind to me ?

Ay, an' as fond o' me as if I was
The queen herself—God bless her !—on the throne.
He travelled wi' a "Thrasher" for the squire,
An' tented th' squire—ay, a hearty job.
Sometimes he came home twice a week ; sometimes
But once ; but always spent th' week end wi' us ;
He never missed when Sat' night came round,
And so it was a busy day wi' us :
I scrubbed an' cleaned all up, got th' hearthrug down,
An' th' table set, his arm-chair fix'd i' th' nook,
His trashes warming 'fore a glowing fire ;
An' did for th' morrow all that could be done
(So that we might enjoy the day of rest
Without incumbrance or worldly cares ;)
Then washed an' titivated th' children up,
An' comb'd their locks, and kissed their glowing cheeks,
Then let them run to peep for dad's return,
While I put on clean apron, frock, and cap :
This done, I closed my door an' stood at th' gate
Wi' hooded head an' knitting in my hands,
To watch for him, an' list to th' childer's shouts,
When first his grummy face came bobbin' o'er
The little knoll, an' see the legs an' arms,
Spin on, while hair and clothes streamed back i' th' wind,
And my unwieldly John stoop stiffly down
An' kiss them one by one, then take the youngest
Up in his arms, fix the next upon his back
An' so come on ; while the next clung to his laps
Or danced along before.—Ay, I was blessed !
I always met him wi' a smile and kiss,

Some folk might think it maudishness, but I know
Had I once missed, it would have snapped a link
O' that firm bond that closely knit us all.
We were not like some folk, whose tenderness
Wains wi' the marriage moon—John often said
Our courtin' days had never known decay.
He got him cleaned an' shaved, while I prepared
His favourite dish ; an' then wi' th' younger bairns
Upon our knees, an' th' older sitting round,
We fell to work, ay, I was happy then !
An' after that when th' supper things were cleared,
An' th' lamp was lit, and John had th' weekly news,
An' I my knittin'—everlasting pegs
John christened it—for why ? because it was
The companion of my leisure hours.
He first would grope his pockets o'er for nuts
Or haply sweets, or gingerbread, which he
Wi' th' little ones would barter for a kiss ;
Then proudly draw his hard-won earnings out.
I seem to see, tho' 'tis so long since now ;
His stiff, thick, fumbling fingers sort it o'er,
Then toss it wi' a smile into my lap.
Ay, those were happy days, such happy days !
Folk said I must be happy, and I was,
Why even th' squire an' 's lady riding past
Would stop and watch my little ones at play,
An' beckon 'em toward, an' talk to 'em ; sometimes
The lady would strip off her glove an' wi'
Her lily hand would pat their frizzy heads,
An' now an' then they'd take one for a ride

G

A hundred yards or so ; then set it down
Wi" sixpence in its hand to buy it toys.
They had no children, bless you ! an' I thought
They always looked wi' longin' eyes at mine.

   Ay, happy days indeed ! so bright ! but soon—
Too soon, the darkness came ! my own poor John
Got badly hurt somehow ; I scarce know how.
His leg was crushed wi' th' wheels ; they brought him home
Insensible : ah, me, all through that week
I had had something on my mind—a fear,
A secret dread, a sort of· heart-break, which
I'd never felt before : when nought was near
I felt so grieved, so lone ; the tears would come,
I knew not why. The very night before
I dreamed three times I saw him dead and white ;
And when they brought him suddenly ; stretched out,
Still, cold, and white, besmeared wi' dirt and blood,
I could not scream, nor run, but only stare
Upon the senseless face, as tho' my eyes
Were fascinated—so a moment then
I dropp'd down mute, and senseless as the dead.
'Twas long ere I woke up again, to know
My horrid state ; to feel the agony
Too deep for words : I've often heard it said
That sorrow ne'er comes single-handed, so
I proved its truth, ah, me ! that very night
A little lifeless babe was born to me :
I gazed just once upon the little eyes
That never ope'd—the lips that never breathed.
I weeping, kissed an' pressed it once, and then

They wrapt it up, an' in a small square box
One took it sadly, quietly, i' th' dusk,
And hid it mutely 'mongst the churchyard mould
Deep in a corner, 'neath a dusky larch.
I wept to have it buried like a dog,
Without a single prayer, a sigh, or tear,
Or ever a word o' Christian burial ;
It seemed cut off alike from me and God !
But not shut out from love ; no, no ! alas !
No whit less dear to me, because the soul
Had never spoke within, was that wee form :
It lies a still life scene, strewn round with sighs
And dew'd with tears, amid the many shades
And memories of the dead—nay, living past !

 'Twas weeks and months ere I could rise again,
And sorrow, like a shadow, draped our cot.
My poor lad's groans fell hourly on my ear ;
Sometimes he raved an' rambled 'bout his work ;
Sometimes his pain would drive him mad.
The surgeon said he might, and he might not live ;
'T might mortify and then 'twere certain death.

 It grieved me sore to see the little ones
All hanging round so silent and so sad :
Their bonny cheeks grown pale and dimpleless ;
Their curly love-locks tangled round their brows ;
Their bits of things that formerly I'd ta'en
A mother's pride in keeping whole and clean,
Hung round them, grey wi' dirt, and limp, and rent.
They'd lost their prop, you see, a mother's care.
Friends may be kind and do their best, but ah !

There's nothing that can fill a mother's place ;
No hand, alas ! that's like a mother's hand !
Time dragged away, and things cheered up a bit ;
My health and strength came slowly back to me ;
But John, poor lad ! lay there for months an' months
At th' door o' death, in anguish terrible,
The shadow of his former self.   *I'm* ——
And th' wind blew briskly in my poor old face
As I came o'er the moor.   My eyes are weak,
An' now I'm come to th' fire they smart and run ;
Forgive me ; I'm a foolish, childish frame ;
Leave me a bit, and I shall soon be right—
He bore up bravely, hopefully through all ;
But when our little treasured hoard was gone,
And he was still a-bed, and I but weak,
And th' haggard wolf came peeping in at th' door—
'Twas on a dismal day, I recollect—
He turned his great shrunk eyes on me, an' on
The tiny shadowed things that hovered round,
Wi' such a look of wordless agony—
Or if it spoke one word it was despair !
He tried to raise himself, sank back, and groaned.
I ran and raised him up, and twined my arm
Around his shrunken form, and laid his head
Upon my breast.   I never shall forget
The look he turned on me, the kiss he gave ;
Then gazing sadly on the little ones, he stretched
His thin arms out, and mutely laid the right
On th' oldest's, th' left on th' youngest's head—
" Poor helpless things ! God help you now I'm down.

What will become of you ! Had I but strength
I'd work, ay, day and night if flesh could bear ;
I'd wear my fingers to the bone, and spill my heart
To save you from one breath of harm.
But now what can I do? too weak to rise ;
Bound down and forced to see you pinched and pale,"
He bowed his honest head and groaned again,
Then fell to weeping like a very child.
I could not comfort him, not even speak :
But only sob and cry for company ;
An' th' children, seeing us, burst out as well.
Ah, then we had not learned the mystery—
The one great end and purpose of our life :
We had not learned to look up yonder, where
The sad, sorrow-bowed, and burdened ones
Alone may look for help. We had not sinned
With head—strong turbulence as some have done :
We were not steeped in crime—lived moral lives—
Were honest, peaceable and such ; but then
We had not felt that halcyon peace within,
We had not seen the light, nor felt God's love—
Ah, no, no, no !
        That day when th' gloaming came
I sat beside his bed ; he lay and slept,
And in their tiny cribs our darlings slept :
But I—I could not sleep, nor could I cry.
My heart was like a stone, my head on fire.
Around the cot the March wind soughed and moaned ;
And upward through the window I could see
The monstrous clouds with crazy turbulence

Surge to and fro, and bulge their paunches out
And bloat their leaden cheeks, and fiercely scowl
Wi' brazen eyes at me ; then double up
And swell like some huge monster gorged ; then spread
Their phantom wings and mutely disappear,
While others came in endless line—strange things !
With sheeny upper sheens of steel-like light,
And undershades of sullen, hateful black ;
Sowing beneath a misty veil of gloom.
I looked upon the dreary, frowning world,
And everything around seemed chuckling with
A demon mirth, a mocking, devilish bliss
Seemed hugging to its torture maddened heart
In wild malevolence—huge ecstacy
The horrid joy of seeing one more form—
So happy once—brought low to share their gloom,
Their utter desolation and despair !
    'Twas strange, but just that moment o'er my mind
Came back the shadow of a former dread—
The memory of a sermon I had heard
Six months before :—the same before me rose
In vivid power.   I heard the preacher's voice,
And saw his waving hand.   The text he took
Was this :—" Our God is a consuming fire."
Then came the flashing of his steely eye,
The awful shade that brooded on his brow,
And then the thunder of his eloquence :
He seemed to look into my very soul !
" Our God is a consuming fire," he said,
" And all that sin must die, and day by day

He sees your very act, and weighs each word,
And reads each secret thought; and by-and-bye,
It may be soon—e'en suddenly—He'll come;
The trump will sound; the ghastly dead be raised,
The living changed—and then! what then? ah, then!
The wicked shall be judged, the sentence passed,
'Depart ye cursed! ye who scorned my sway
And crucified the Lord of Life afresh—
In everlasting torment, fire and chains.'"

   Much more he said, and each impression seemed
To burn into my soul: the good Lord God
Seemed brought to human mould with human powers,
And human passions; not a God of love;
Whose spirit yearned towards a fallen world,
Who gave a darling Son to plead and die,
And bear the burden of His creatures' sins.
Not a kind Father, caring for His bairns
And mourning o'er their crimes and miseries—
Remembering that they are but feeble flesh,
And waiting, lovingly, with open arms
To take them to His heart: but a fierce Judge,
With thunder-brooding brow, and scorching breath,
And flashing eyes that watch and never wink:
A grim inquisitor, who takes delight
In torturing the erring, straying ones.
All this came rushing through my maddened brain,
And everywhere—on earth—mid clouds and gloom—
No matter where I cast my eyes—appeared
A dark enormous face, whose vision fierce
(As constant as a statue's changeless eyes)

Glowered down or up on me, and seemed to scowl
A mocking exultation at my fall.
  I know not why, but when I looked on him,
My suffering lad, and my poor inn'cent bairns,
I seemed to feel a sudden, desp'rate strength,
A clenching of the hands, a knitting of
The thews, a setting of the teeth, a stern
Determination in my heart to live,
To work and strive—yes, I could work ! and they,
My helpless ones, should never want, no, no !
I've thought since then 'twas wrong and heinous sin—
Defiance 'gainst the purpose of my God.
But from that day I toiled and strove for them—
For him who once so bravely wrought for me,
I seemed to have new life, new strength and heart ;
I hardly knew myself; felt quite surprised
To find so dauntless and so strong.
One thing alone seemed clear to me—they need,
So I will be their prop and win the bread ;
And so I did, worked day and night almost,
Took linen in to wash, and sewed, and knit,
Went twice a week to th' mill, and washed and ironed ;
And all seemed nothing to me ; for when tired
The sight o' them, the sound of one sweet voice
Would cheer me up again, and make me strong.
But once, I call to mind, 'twas nearly o'er ;
They'd almost lost their last remaining prop—
'Twas in the winter ; I had been to th' mill,
And washed for th' miller's wife, an invalid :
All through the day the snow had sifted down,

And whitened all the frozen hills and plains.
Towards night a breeze had brisken'd up, which sent
The fleecy snow, with sudden, angry puffs
In spray-like jets about. 'Twas late ere I
Who had been rather cast i' th' morn, could start,
And o'er the hills the great black night had come,
And from the north the piercing, piercing wind
Grew every moment stronger ; and the light
Died out completely from the wrath-browed sky,
But on and on I went with quickened breath,
With panting pulse, and wildly fluttering heart.
Ah me ! two weary miles lay 'fore my face.
I never could recall the horrors of that night,
Or how I struggled through. It seemed to me
A maddened dream, a conflict hand to hand
With demon death ; a horrid phantasy ;
A desperate wrestling, wrenching, battling on ;
A plunging, scrambling, 'mid huge drifts of snow :
A grappling up ; a phrenzied struggling forth,
With clogged and slippery feet and frozen skirts,
While round me raged the deaf'ning hurricane,
The shuddering trees, bent double, howled again ;
And from the adjacent fields, like powdered glass,
Caught up and hurled by the furious wind
Upon me poured a thick perpetual storm
Of cutting, blinding, suffocating snow.
    I'd almost conquered—home was nigh—when lo !
I plunged headlong into a mountainous drift.
I strove to rise, but all my strength was gone :
I tried to shriek, but scarce could draw a breath.

My limbs grew numbed, but God was merciful !
A neighbouring youth, returning home from work,
Came stumbling up, and found me lying there,
('Twas poor Joe Plant, the wheelwright's only son,
A quiet lad was Joe—subjects to fits.
They found him one day lying dead i' th' close,
Dropped in a fit—was suffocated—so
Th' Cor'ner and the jury brought it in.
His mother, poor old woman, took on so,
They had to hold her from him at the grave ;
And when the sods fell on she fainted—dropped,
They had to bear her home ; and after that
She fell into a rambling, withered state ;)
He picked me up and bravely helped me home,
But I was speechless, wholly overcome ;
And when the anxious, tearful faces flocked
Around, and th' glowing embers shone on me,
I fainted right away and lay for hours
Insensible.   Again, 'mid tears and pain,
A tiny breathless babe was born to me,
Again the weakness, want, despair, and gloom ;
Again the desperate fight for life and bread ;
And so the years wore on till twelve has passed
Without a change—except that all had changed.
I worked and strove and bore up under all
And kept a shelter o'er our heads, and want
At bay ; and still my strength held out, although
The ruddy bloom of health had faded long :
No change, said I ? ah, I was wrong.   A change
Had come o'er me ; I once was blithe and gay

And fair and buxom as a lass need be :
But now my face was shrunk, and pale, but calm ;
My forehead trenched ; my hair fallen off ; my form
Was thin and bent ; my heart was meeker, sadder ;
But then my arms were strong—thank God for that ;
And John was with me still : he braved the storm
And turned a narrow, very narrow point,
And after months and months of anguished doubt
Was raised again.   But from that fatal shock
He never more recovered ; ne'er again
Looked fairly up ; but from that day became
A pale, enfeebled, bent and lame old man.
But then, you see, we had him still to love,
To look up to, to guide the helm as 'twere.
He filled his arm-chair in the corner still ;
His word was still the law, his joy our joy.
And I was glad of this, for I could work
And win the bread.   Ah, poor old John, in Heaven !
But no, not old and way-worn as thy mate,
For there the tired grow young again—I think
I loved thee dearer, ay if that could be,
In thy dark hour, than in thy prosperous state ;
And if thou couldst be near and see me now,
Or hear my words, or look into my heart,
As disembodied souls, they say, can do,
It surely would be sweet to thee, to know
How dear is the remembrance of that love
To thy old wife's lone heart, brim full of tears ;
How fondly chequered memory conjures up
That tender, suffering, sorrowing look of thine,

Fraught with a something never felt before.
God recompense thee there !
       He got in time
To be of use ; helped me of busy days ;
Did little jobs for th' neighbouring folk, and such,
And bits of fancy gardening for th' squire,
Who ever after that was kind to us ;
And so we scrambled onwards pretty well.

 No change, said I ? ah, all was changed, except
The weary round of toil, the fight with want,
The race with fate, the pains, the shades, the tears,
And sad realities of life.   My bairns
Were nearly all grown up ; all gone from me
But one, my youngest born, a gentle lad.
Two blooming lasses and a stalwart lad
Were out in service, far from home and me—
Gone from the little nest, with untried wings,
With beaming eyes, and eager hopeful hearts
To buffet with the great deceitful world—
Gone forth alone, pure lambs, not dreaming of
The lurking wolves, the pits, and shifting sands—
Full of bright dreams of future ecstasy,
Of fairer realms, and skies of summer hue—
That far-off, golden summer-land of youth !
With kindling passions, faculties, and needs ;
Dim dawnings of the ends and aims of life,
Awakenings of affections light and deep ;
Perceptions of the chaste and beautiful ;
Sunrises of the bright that yield the sad ;
(Sweet visions that, alas ! but fade too soon ;

But youth is youth, and ever will be youth.)
Gone out with truth—stamped brows, but feeble wills ;
With inexperienced, unsuspicious hearts,
Unarmed to brave Temptation's demon siege.
Ah ! many an anxious hour I thought of them,
And hoped and wept ; oh ! had I prayed as well,
The brooding cloud of anguish might have passed.
But ah ! spirit's light was darkness yet,
A fourth, my eldest born and dearest now,
Was in a foreign region, far away.
Two years before, a wondrous tale had swept,
Like some mad storm-wind, o'er the thirsty land ;
Its burden gold—a fortune in a day.
Sublime discoveries— a golden paradise—
A country pregnant with the precious lore,
Begemmed inside and out with richest ore ;
And through the startled land rough heads were bent,
Wide-opened eyes grew bright, and lips agape,
To catch the luscious sound ; and kits were packed,
And many a noble heart went forth, to brave
The tempest and the tropics, to secure
The wealth that only needed picking up.
Alack ! how few came back, and those how spent,
To tell how false, how hollow was the tale !
And John, my eldest, after his father named,
And th' very picture of him at his age—
Among the rest, drank in the sugary tale.
And naught would satisfy but he must go,
Although I begged him not with tearful eyes.
He met my prayers with stronger arguments ;

" Bless you, my mother ; you were always kind !
You would not hinder me from doing well?
And this may be my fairest chance in life ;"
He said, and pictured what good things he'd do
When he returned.—We ne'er again should know
The pangs of want, and I should no more toil,
But live quite like a lady—so he said—
Well, in the spring, he and a neighbour's son,
Staunch mates from boys—both of an age and size—
Swore lasting friendship, to defend and aid
And see each other safely home again,
And hurried off with buoyant hearts, to cross
Tempestuous seas and unknown lands for gold.
    Just twelve months after that, my second-born,
A chaste and tender lass, with auburn hair
And lily features soft and delicate,
Had yielded up her maiden life to one
Ralph Wooliscroft, a brawny collier lad.
They took and bought and milked a cow,
Across the moor some half-a-mile from us ;
And now had proved one year of married life.
Ah me ! a twelve years' lapse works change indeed.
The bairns that then all crowded in one nest
Were widely scattered now, and one a wife,
Would soon be mother too, if all went well.
But I had little time to think and brood ;
My hands were full of work : beside my own,
I had to look to her.   She always was
A very delicate and feeble thing ;
But now she looked so tender and so frail,

No gaze fell on her, but the spirit sighed ;
She was a very sadness to the soul.
It seemed impressed upon her mind for weeks
She should not live it o'er ; and though I coaxed,
But oftener chid her for her childishnes.
She soon forgot herself and rambled on—
"If aught should happen to me, you'll see to all ;
You'll lay me quietly in such a nook,
And so and so I'd like to bear me there.
If aught should happen me you'll take this dress,
And when 'tis trimmed afresh, and bits let in,
'Twill make a nice warm winter's frock for you.
If aught should happen me, you'll love poor Ralph
Dear as your own ? Ah me, he'll be so lone !"
And though I rallied her, pooh-pooh'd and such,
Yet, heavens ! how my yearning spirit ached !
    "If it should live, and should be motherless,
There's such and such I'd like stored up for it :
And this or that will make it something, when
'Tis grown a bit : and in the chest of drawers
My work you will find, the key of which
Is in my pocket here ; if you will look
Deep in one corner, 'neath my Sunday cuffs,
There's three scrawled notes, a valentine, a rose ;
And in one frame, portraits of Ralph and me,
Mementoes of our joyous courting days ;
Please lay them by, till it shall understand
How dear they should be for a mother's sake.
And, mother, I have something on my mind ;
Say, will you promise me, if I should die,

To take my child and bring it up for God ?"
This was too much, 'twas like a serpent's sting,
Or dagger's thrust to me ; to think that I
Who ne'er had taught my children how to pray ;
Who on the hearth of home had never reared
A hallowed shrine, round which the wandering feet
That toiled all day, might meet to pray at night ;
To think that I, a mother, godless yet,
Should, 'neath so searching gaze, be asked by one
Who might have lived to brand me with neglect,
Nay, might in time have cursed me in the pit,
To take her child and bring it up for God !
My heart was bubbling up, my throat was full.
She took my hand in hers with fond caress,
And stroked it restlessly with either hand,
And looked at me with tender, pleading look—
 " It would be better so," she said, as in
Apology for having asked too much,
" Ralph might ! I do not know ;" she looked at me
Half sadly, half enquiringly—" might in
Awhile—a good long while you know ;" she paused,
Then added, "when the first fierce storm was o'er,
And he had grown more lone than sorrowful,
Might find another he could love so well ;
One who would love him not more dear than I,
But one who might be stronger, and might live
And fill his home with lots of winsome bairns,
And all his great good heart with tender joy.
If this should be—I do not say it will—
But if it should ; in the far years to come,

When all the past was dead and I forgot
Except in name, and may be, now and then,
In melancholy hours, and truant thoughts,
My child might——" Here she stopped and bowed
Her head upon her breast and sobbed ; and I—
I sobbed as well ; for oh, my heart was full,
I drew the drooping head upon my breast,
And stroked the glossy hair, and kissed the lips,
And pressed her close, so close, as though she were
A little child again. .   .   .   .   .

       And from that day
A shadow gathered slowly round my heart ;
I never once believed the words she said,
But deemed them drooping thoughts, love phantasies,
Or plaintive babblings of a sick, spoiled child.
And yet, in quiet hours, they haunted me,
Like prophet-whispers from an unseen hand.
 The days went on, and came the dreaded time,
And sick anxiety, strained by suspense
Unto the highest tension, settled calm,
And waited still, with fever-starting eye.
 'Tis strange how calm one is, in hours like these,
When only *half* the weight—the pain we feel,
Would make us rave and weep a sea of tears.
'Twas in the gloaming that I stood and gazed
Out through the windows on the far away—
The misty twilight settled softly down,
And from the drowsy blue, the solemn stars
Stole silently ; and came a flittering breeze
With soothing cadence like a lullaby,

H

And rustled mid the garlands of the hills,
And uttered by the reedy, lisping brooks,
Low whisperings of prayer.   'Twas strange that I
Should think, " How mild it is for April weather,
How sweet a night 'twill be for the tired soul
To start upon its wanderings, should she die."

   At last 'twas o'er, the anguish, doubt and dread,
And racked suspense, and agonizing hope,
Were with anticipation buried in
Uncertainty's dim grave ; and glad surprise
Rose up with kindling eye and quivering lip
And dropped upon their dust a rain of tears—
Relieving tears of thankfulness and joy !
As bright-eyed Spring wakes from the lethargy
Of sorrow's mute prostration, and comes forth
And o'er the tomb of patriarch winter, weeps,
The soothing droppings of her April grief.

   The child was born—a wee, white, darling boy,
And all went well, ay, marvellously well ;
Grim-harnessed death seemed never farther off ;
And sweet security, and new-born joy
Incontinently laughed, with feverish mirth,
At credulous fancy brooding in the shade—
Pronounced, for once, a lying prophet sprite.

   How beautiful that morn my sweet child looked !
How quietly she lay ; how softly smiled
In all the luxury of listlessness !
How tenderly she kissed her fair first-born !
What glad gleams of gratitude she cast above !
What blessings quivered on her voiceless lips !

How full my heart was as I bent o'er them,
To feel their warm breath flutter on my cheek ;
Ere from the cot I stole, and left them there
So angel-like, so peaceful, sleeping, turned,
The mother, fair and spotless as the child !
My heart was light, e'en girlish, as I sped
Across the dim expanse that April morn.
The restless soul of day was slumbering yet
So quietly, that not one breath of air
Swept with awakening kiss the earth's damp cheek.
The curtain of the dawn half drawn aside,
Let in a flush of drowsy, flossy light,
Which changed the myriad, myriad pendant drops
To coral studs, and wreaths of crystal beads ;
As virtue's charms, obscured, unheeded here,
Dim while the dusk of earth enclouds them round,
Burst into splendour 'mid the dawn of heaven.
A great blank, freckled shore of high-up clouds,
Whose ether tide-line stretched above me, marked
An undulating coast from north to south,
Floated its dark uncertain substance far
Upon the dim sea of retreating night.
And all the western world was lost amid
The swooning mists, that lounged their sluggish bulk
Along the rear of night from hill to hill.
The solemn east glowed 'neath a sky of blue—
Intensely dusky blue, unflecked, ungemmed,
Save that the morning star, dull as a knob
Of rusted brass, with red and sleepy eye
Winked drowsily above the heathy ridge.

But, oh! the rapturous chorus of the birds
That fluttered 'mid the many-jewelled trees,
And skipped about, and shook the limpid drops
In one another's wings as if in play ;
As fair-haired children, 'mid the orchard's bloom,
With many an antic, laugh, and shout, shake off
The snowy blossoms on each other's heads ;
The robin with its crimson pulsing breast
Sang hopefully mid the spray—like lime ;
And e'en the frogs amid the misty pools
Croked lustily a morning chant of joy,
And on I went with feelings glad and strange ;
The rapture of the scene was on my soul.
I turned upon the threshold of my home, and gazed
Again upon the fascinating scene :
A crimson glow grew dimly up the east
Till half the blue had blushed to daffodil.
The first stiff yawn of day was flushing o'er
The quivering lashes of the dreamy hills.
A great lank fork of cloud stole up the front
Of the red glory.   Silently I watched ;
It rose and rose until a mermaid form
With long, low, luminous hair, and weird white head
Bent down and eastward turned ; one arm upraised
With long, fair, maiden fingers reaching far ;
The other downward thrown below the rim,
As beckoning up and pointing out the course
Of the great sun, with fate-like potency,
Stretched out its shape upon the sheeny sea
The light and glory of the world and God,

Like a great deluge surged around me there,
And rose and rose, and burst into my soul,
And snatched it from its sordid shrine of clay,
And bore it up and up upon its tide,
And filled it so with worship of the good—
Spontaneous worship of the good, until
It seemed nigh bursting with unspoken praise.
How long I stood there 'tranced, I scarcely knew :
The sun was teeming out a dazzling flood
From every rift and crevice of the cloud,
And all the scene was breaking into life
When I awoke as 'twere, and found my hands
Clasped right before me, 'neath the awful God.
With conscious sin I turned and went my way,
Whilst from each cheek slid off a pendant tear.
'Twas strange that it should move me thus, who ne'er
Looked up to Him in prayer, nor read His word :
It seems a sort of instinct which we have
In common with the soulless things of earth.
How strangely every object, every scene,
Ah ! every thought and action of that day
Is fastened on the page of memory.
'Tis even so when some unlooked-for blow,
Some sudden withering blight falls on the heart—
The common objects of the world and life,
The scenes most trivial, insignficant,
Seem stamped into the soul, or photographed
E'en as a sudden lightning's blaze will limb
The leafy trees upon the stolid pane—
Seared in or buried down, to rise again

With all their natural hues, and shapes and scents
In the sad dreaming of the after calm.
I entered in : John looked into my face,
And his less wistful grew, and opened out,
And broke into a smile, the while he scanned
The happy light of peace that glowed on mine.
"How is she, Mary?" "Very well, thank God."
"What is it?" "A sweet boy," said I, and each
Went forth without another word to do
The duties of the day, with lightened hearts.
There was a singing in my soul that day,
A joyous undertone, that now and then
Swelled up and quivered on my tongue and lips,
In the broken echoes of the songs I knew
And loved in that lost life, my maiden-day.
How tenderly they linger on the soul,
Those sweet refrains —those spirit-stirring strains !
They cling amid the fibres of our hearts,
Through all the tangled warp and weft of life.
How sweetly comes their soft aroma back !
And yet how sad—how sad the spirit grows
Beneath their influence.   There seems to be
A wailing in the soul when they come back,
A welling upward of a font of tears ;
A grieving, which we have when Autumn's hand
Lies mutely on the tresses of the world,
When low winds mourn, and flowers fade silently ;
An undefined something, which we feel
When leaves are falling—falling noiselessly ;
A sort of bending o'er a fading form ;

A brooding watching of the sun go down
Upon the glory of a day of joy
Looked forward to, through long and darker days,
Now dawned and vanished all too suddenly;
When in our hearts we feel a consciousness
That few such glories dawn upon a life;
A musing o'er a sleeping infant form,
A gazing o'er a solemn stretch of graves;
Ah! all things sadder grow; and none, alas!
Are what we deemed them when we sang those songs.
And yet we love them; would not part with them—
Ah, God! no, no! we could not part with them—
They seem a portion of that hidden life,
An undercurrent of that spirit-world
We share not with our kind, nor ever may.
I often think that those we know the best
Are mysteries to us still, and will be aye;
Ah! strange! the soul hath depths unfathomed e'en
By its own plummet; only now and then
Some haunting voice or presence surges up
A train of echoes, undefined and deep,
Which sound it not, but only hint its depths,
Like pebbles tossed down chasms vast and deep;
Such echoes are these dim-remembered songs!
 The thought came once, "they'll call me granny now,"
And thereupon a shadow, wan and lorn,
Peeped through the curtain of the future's dusk;
A tottering shade of sour decrepitude,.
Of withered cheeks and thin and snowy hair,
And head bent downward towards the dust again,

A chilling whisper from the frosts of age,
A sort of creeping back into the dark.
    The tide of day was ebbing silently
O'er the brown mountains of the saffron west,
When, all my duty done, I clomb into
My upper room, and dived into a row
Of ancient drawers, from whose capacious maws
I musingly disgorged a heap of things
That long had lain in darkness undisturbed;
Half worn-out garments, ruffled caps and cuffs
Too little grown for those that wore them long;
Brown faded, mildewed, memory-haunted things,
I'd cherished long for love of those that grew
And cast them, as the callow young its shell,
And passed into the world away from me—
And hunted from the midst a pair of socks,
A tiny baby-cap, and crumpled dress,
That, long ago, I'd stowed away in grief,
Half thinking that the time would come when they
Would be of use, and wondering if it would;
And while I called and mused the time had skipped
In noiseless haste away : and in the dim,
Obscure recesses of the room, the dusk
Had gathered, with its sallow, silent brood.
I gathered up my waifs and rose to go,
When palpable and plain before my eyes,
A tiny milk-white form, with infant face,
Stole noiselessly from out a sombre nook
And glided, glided, with a glow of eyes
Turned full upon me, so mysteriously,

Across the narrow space and faded out.
I was not scared at first, for reason, thought,
And every faculty seemed merged in sight,
I only watched and watched in a dazzled calm
Until the apparition faded out, and till
Stunned, startled consciousness awoke, and sent
A rush of frenzied blood along my veins,
Was I quite sure I saw it ? Yes ! although
The folk of now-a-day, grown more acute,
And wiser than their fathers—so they think—
Would call it superstition or the like ;
Say I'd been dreaming, thinking over-much,
Until my senses had deceived themselves,
And conjured up a waif of air, to give
To give a shape to all their dark engenderings.
The bold would ridicule me openly ;
Those more considerate would listen to
My childish babblings, with an inward yawn,
And smile incredulous as you now smile,
But then such things were seen, and, ay, believed—
I stood a while in idiotic trance,
Then fled with awful swiftness down the stairs,
And on the hearth came face to face with John
He stared into my white scared face a bit,
And neither of us spoke ; I scarce could breathe.
He gasped ; " Good heavens ! what ails you, Mary ?"
Oh, John ! I've seen a token." There we stood,
Till sudden we both burst out, "Our Girl."
I felt like fainting for a little while,
And dropped my head face downwards on the squab.

Just now a hesitating step was heard without ;
A trembling hand came fumbling at the latch.
The shadowed features of a neighbour's lad
Looked in upon us mutely—furtively.
" Ralph wants you, mother, now," the urchin said,
And paused and coughed, then clenched, "the child is dead,"
And hastily withdrew himself.   I looked
In John's face, grown intensely white, and he
With painful soul-intensive eyes in mine,
But neither of us spoke a single word ;
Insentiently I rose and donned my shawl
And hood, and hurried out, and closed the door,
And sped across the moor.   I reached the cot,
I scarce knew how ; my senses all seemed dazed ;
My feet scarce seemed to touch the ground they trod.
Ralph sat besides the fire with head bent down
Upon his hands ; and though I went to him
And laid my hand in silence on his head
He neither looked nor spoke.   I sought the couch
Where, in the dawn, I'd left my child asleep,
She lay there quietly, as if asleep,
With Ralph's old mother bending o'er her head.
I went and touched her cheek ; the eyes unclosed
With such a weary sadness in their depths.
Her cheeks had paled ; her lips grown white and dry.
I did not speak, but felt an agony
To weep myself, and make her weep away
The stony agony that filled her soul,
I kissed the lips, which quivered quietly,
As if an utterance struggled in the throat,

But nothing came ; no word, not e'en a tear.
She feebly raised her arm, and pointed, mute.
I turned, and found the tiny-curtained crib.
I drew the snowy sheet down silently,
And the figure lay, all cold and stiff.

. . . .

Just then Ralph's mother came and stood by me.
I said, " How did it happen ?" and she said,
" Convulsions took it, and it died in one."
I kissed it reverently, and cloaked it up ;
Then doffed my shawl, and calmly set to work
To tidy up the room, and drive away
The tearless gloom which hung around the house ;
And hoping to divert the sorrow-stunned,
Gasped down the bitterness within my heart ;
Yet even stealthily I watched my girl.
Sometimes her eyes were opened languidly,
And watched my motions, oh ! so listlessly ;
Sometimes she raised them to me wistfully,
But never spoke, or sighed, or wept at all.
I cannot speak the agonizing pain
That draped the cot, and would not if I could.
At last the day arrived ; we nestled it,
Ah ! snug within its tiny downy box,
And sat in silence in the darkened room.
We two old women looked on it and wept,
Wept heartily at last, and seemed refreshed.
She raised her hand and laid it on its face,
And then we raised her up to look at it.
She gazed upon it long and earnestly,

And kissed it once, and backward dropped again ;
And only when they screwed the coffin lid,
And hid the darkened face for evermore,
Her features quivered —quivered brokenly—
And solemnly a great, bright, swollen tear
Slid off and made a spot upon the sheet.
And when they bore it off, she followed it
With great, wide, dry, and hungry eyes, until
'Twas lost to her, and then she turned them up,
Far up to God.   I left her then, for, oh !
I felt accursed in the breath of prayer.
We buried it, and went our ways again.
The days went on, sadder and slower, perhaps,
But ever on, and sunny June arrived,
And she had risen from her couch of pain,
And had assumed the duties of her home.
We never heard her murmur, never once ;
She bowed her will, and bore it patiently
As far as outward seeming went ; no word
Or sad rebellious tear gave potent sign !
But, ah ! we knew how deep a bitterness,
How keen a want was hungering in her heart.
Far less we judged from what she said and showed
Than what she said but half, or left unsaid.
Sometimes when self-restraint was off its guard,
And the strong will had ceased its vigilance,
The prisoned soul would wander mournfully
Amid its dead and buried loves and dreams,
And suddenly betray its sorrowings
With some great sign, or far-off dreaming gaze :

A sudden pause amid her work, as if
She wanted something which she had forgot,
Or sought to bring to mind some cherished thought
That had escaped her puzzled memory,
And now and then would say what might have been,
"If it had *only* lived." Thus picturing,
By contrast sad, how deep the loss must be.
But though she bore it all so patiently,
And though she strove to work again and live,
Yet something sad had fallen upon her life,
Or something bright, a charm, a vital power
Had gone from her and fled for evermore.
We watched her day by day with anxious eyes
And felt she was not, could not be the same,
And yet we knew not why; but only hope
With sighing hearts that all might turn out well;
But evermore the shadow deeper fell.
'Twas but the twilight of the night of death!
A little, thirsty, intermissive cough,
A frothy, restive, indecisive cough,
So silent and so subtle that it passed
For weeks and weeks almost unnoticed, came
And fretted sedulously at her life.
Her form grew frail and thin, her garments hung
In flaggy, windy folds about her limbs,
And even seemed about to drop from her;
Her long white lady-hands disclosed to view
The shape of bones and joints, the muscles' play;
Her features sharper, more intensive grew,
And ever whiter, save that evermore

On either cheek a small unnatural spot,
A vivid star of crimson came and went ;
Her brow grew smoother and more prominent.
And yet she murmured not, nor took alarm,
And never pined, nor spoke her thought, although
I think she knew her fate, ay, from the first ;
And so she faded, faded as the world
Fades in the mournful Autumn, constantly ;
And by-and-bye we came to realise
The truth, which in our hearts so long had lain
In mute impressions, never shaped in words.
One night I went to her, as was my wont
When I could snatch an hour from my own toil,
To help her out a bit, and found her worse.
Her strength had given out ; she lay at rest
In listless attitude upon her couch.
I bent o'er her, and, as she did not speak,
But seemed too tired and weary e'en for that,
I felt a breaking, bursting in my heart,
And fell a weeping, baby that I was,
(I could not help it for the life of me),
And sobbed, and gushed out my storm of grief,
So long fermenting, but compressed within,
And, child-like, cried until I could not cry.
She got my hand in hers and bade me sit,
And looked on me with fixed and languid eyes,
And spoke anon, " There, you'll be better now.
I saw you coming o'er the paddock stile,
And thought to tell you all that now you know.
Or why these tears ?   Well, it is better thus.

It pains me much to see you sorrow so
Because the truth has proved itself at last.
It would have pained me deeper to have been
The truth's interpreter to my mother's ears.
And now we'll talk of what you know, and I,
I know, have known and felt so long ago,
That I am going, going noiselessly,
But feel that I am going, like the brook
That runs adown the dingle variously
Amid the broken rocks, all joyously
It skips and trips awhile, and sings a song—
A glad, unshadowed song—and ripples back
The trickling laughter of the sun.   Anon
It comes into an almost level course ;
The banks grow narrower, closer to the brink
Of a great chasm.   There the waters move
So silent and so deep within themselves,
Without a smile, a ripple, or a song,
Till suddenly they drop themselves amid
The yawning gulph that opens underneath."

THE DOOM OF BABYLON.

REVELATION XVIII.

THE blaze had faded from the fecund sky ;
The awful wonder of the scarlet beast
Upon whose seven-fold forehead's brazen front
In glaring characters of sulphureous light,

Great blustering names of blasphemy were writ.
I bowed myself unto the earth and moaned ;
The heaviness of death was on my soul ;
The burden of the future's unborn woe,
In all the harrowing blaze of prophesy,
Like scorching embers, glowed on Memory's shrine.
. . . . I lifted up my eyes and peered around.
The desolated island placid lay ;
The sky was silent, dark, and slumberous,
Serene and signless.   Ghost-like, here and there,
Long dusky trees were limned against its night.
Great flexuous shapes of strange uncertain bulk,
But by their hideous blackness visible,
Inertly crowded in the midnight south.
The shapeless masses of the fissured hills
Rose breathlessly around me everywhere.
All things were frightful in their death-like rest,
Portentous, hideous, undefined, and foul !
And darkness ! oh, a darkness horrible !
So horrible ! lay like the hand of death
Upon the shuddering forehead of the earth,
So clammy cold !   No sound disturbed its rest
But the tumultuous sobbings of the breeze,
And far away amid the night, somewhere,
The guttural mutterings of a cataract,
Like the dull murmur of approaching storms,
Or distant clamour of awaking winds.
I bent my palsied limbs—a weariness !
And felt amid the dark, and closed my book,
And turned my fevered eyes far heavenward,

And clasped my hands before my breast and prayed,
And sobbed and prayed, " Dear God, be merciful !
Be merciful, and leave me here in peace !
The awful presence of Thy might, Thy wrath,
Thy majesty—the horror of despair—
The awe of judgment, torment, wailing, woe—
The midnight of the future, like a pall—
'Tis on my soul, with all the agony
And utter desolation of the lost.
Thy burden is too heavy for me, Lord,
Oh ! I am crushed and weary unto death ;
Oh ! let me see Thy face no more, dear God,
Until my fainting soul, unearthed, has gained
A God-like power, a more than mortal strength.
Oh ! take Thy hand from off me, lest I die !
Oh ! I am broken, broken, broken, crushed !"
My head sank earthward, and I wept again—
Wept in my weakness, as a child might weep.
  . . . I raised myself ; the scene was all unchanged ;
The damp, morbose sudations of the earth
Commingled with the dank miasma of the marsh,
Clung with a mucid chillness round my frame,
And drizzled from my moulting hair and beard
In drops of humid, fetid dew, upon
The saturated robe which clogged my frame ;
A mortal dampness chilled me to the soul.
I shivered, shivered with an inward gasp,
And shrank into a heap from the cold damp,
That like a cloud of fog enwrapt me round. . . .

I

A restless aching, yearning for repose
Stole o'er me, and I groped and groped around,
If peradventure I might find a stone,
A tuft of weed, a little mound of earth,
Or block of wood, however small, whereon
My throbbing head might drop, and rest, and sleep
In dull forgetfulness, until the dawn,
The far-off dawn of day ; or till the light
Broke round my spirit from the morn of heaven.

Oh, never to be forgotten
    Is the rapture and glow of that night ;
The stars seemed half dropped from the skies
    In a torrent of mystical light.
The soul of the passionate night,
    The heavens, the earth, and the air,
The ocean that stirred in its sleep
    Was one palpitation of prayer,
    Of wonder, worship, and prayer.
The crests of the desolate hills
    Glowed still in a glamour of white
Like foreheads of prophets upraised
    To the God of the glory of night.
The long lustred tops of the trees
    Seemed grappled and twined in mid-air,
Like hands that are nervously clasped
    In the agonized cravings of prayer.
Yet not one articulate sound,
    No sighing or sobbing was there,
No breath of the passion suppressed
    Gave voice to that trouble of prayer,

    Ah ! felt, deeply felt, but not heard
    Was that midnight emotion of prayer.

I watched them in a wondering, gloried trance,
Those solemn shapes communing with their God ;
I felt no terror, but a passive awe.
I knew that God was round me, and that soon
Those teeming skies would be withdrawn, e'en as
The curtain from the tented Holiest,
To unfold the infinite wonders of the night.
I felt that " He that liveth and was dead "
Had ministered unto and strengthened me ;
For now the shuddering sense of nakedness,
Of cold and hunger, weariness and pain,
And all the shrinking weakness, and the dread
Had left me in a glow of happiness,
Serene, expectant, gloriéd, and calm.
I watched the pulsing stars a little space,
And thought they seemed to fade and tremble, dim
And mutely, imperceptibly withdraw
And lose themselves amid the monstrous space.
 . . . . .   All suddenly they vanished in the depth
And on the scene a pale-like glamour fell—
An awful blackness dropped on every thing,
But nothing stirred except amid the air.
And there a quivering, quivering seemed to be—
A something not defined, as if a shoal
Of denser, blacker night had formed itself
Into a mighty sea, where voiceless winds
Contended in a deadly tournament,

And lashed its breasts into a rage of waves—
Of quivering, billowy waves tempestuous,
But half discerned against the lesser dark.
. . .   Just now an ominous change, not seen, but felt;
A sudden pause, fell on the darkling scene—
No pause of voice, for not a sound was there;
No pause of motion, for no object stirred
Except the tremulous motion of the air,
And that had vanished ere this speechlessness,
This breathless dumbness came, and yet a pause
Of griping hand was left upon the scene—
A ghostly, ghostly pause. . . . .   All passively
Long misty shoots of stilly, paly light
Streamed with a lingering 'fulgence 'cross the sky,
And with an awing calmness lustred there,
And stood out palpable, but mingling so
With the still blue, that outline there was none,
Like dim moon-dawnings over crouchant waves,
They lay there silent, visible, but deep
And dusked with amethyst   'Twas strange, so strange.
I clasped my hands across my darkened face,
And bowed my head upon my knees, and thought,
Or strove with vain essay to think ; for sense
And faculty alike seemed numbed and tranced.
Anon, a fluttering rush of wings swept round.
Instinctively I raised my head, and felt
A pinion soft.—Ah ! naught of earth, not e'en
The silkest flush of dawn that e'er lay 'neath
An owlet's wing, could match its suppleness—
Swept cross my face, and brushed the daze away.

Yet not one shape appeared, no point of light,
And yet the dark was held in check ; a glow,
A stilly pallor haunted earth and air,
And where'along the heavens the niveous light
Glowed spectrally, the sky was vastly deep
Withdrawn almost beyond all human ken ;
But in the midst, half seen, and blackly grey,
A huge chaotic mass of umbrose shapes,
Globe-like, immense, upheaved, revolved, and surged
Like gourmand billows on a monster sea.
On earth the lustre lay intensely still.
It was not bright or glinting, but a dim
White crepuscle, in which the eye discerned
The shapes of things, without their minutiæ.
. . . . Anon, a rumbling roll fell on the ear,
A little murmur very distant, silent, faint
As the last wave of sound that crimps the air
From dying echo of a thunder-clap,
Or soughing croning of a wheezing wind
Amid a larch tuft on a distant hill,
And all grew silent—listening. . . . By degrees
It dawned upon my senses that a stream
Of stronger light fell on a mountain's brow
That lay afar to south of me ; and yet
Intensely as I gazed, when piercing straight
Upon it still, 'twas undiscernible ;
But when I cast my restless, puzzled eyes
A little to the east or west of it,
A soft irradiance seemed to muster there,
Which formed a reflex in my passion orbs.

. . . I turned my eyes above, and there appeared,
Half down the southern sky, a wondrous thing,
A shapeless boss, a frosty nebula
Surrounded by a tiny atmosphere of haze,
A rayless nucleus of snowy light
With effervescent sparkles oozing forth,
The soulless eye of a dead universe!
A circumambient coronal of light ;
A misty halo, dim and half-defined,
With intermediate space of blacker sky,
Went circling, circling round the mass of light,
Like to the diadem which crowns the moon
When 'neath the awnings of an Autumn's sky,
The hardy shepherd to his mate remarks,
"The morning will be stormy, for I see
A circle hovers round the moon to-night."
And 'mid the vacant concave, where the stars
Should be, but were not, ever and anon,
In odd uncertain places, far and near,
Dull globules of pale vitrescent light
Bulged out—a moment stayed, and sank again ;
And through the air a whispering, whispering went,
A voiceless breathing of an unknown fear,
A wordless talking of tremendous things,
A nameless horror paralysed the scene.
. . . . The wonder larger grew and brighter, while
I looked. . . . The lurid stars crept ghastly out,
Stood still, and gazed with awful eyes apace,
And hid themselves again. . . . On earth the light
Lay brighter, denser ; and the stream that erst

Fell on the mountain's brow, had travelled thence
A little to the right and nearer me.
   But oh ! the terror that was on the earth !
A creeping, creeping ran along the hills
With rising motion, as a sudden horror
Raises the prickling hair, and knits the skin
In wiry knots.   The bulrush and the flag
Upon the marsh fell backward, as the corn
Before the fury of Euroclydon.
And yet no breath of wind was loose that night ;
The bosky leaves with motion odd and strange,
Turned up their undersides, that glimmered white,
E'en as a seagull's wing gleams white against
The black-browed background of a thunder-cloud,
Or hoar-frost spray upon an inky sea.
The veteran trees seemed blanching suddenly,
And great gnarled branches heaved with motion strange
As men upheave their arms to shield their eyes
From the fierce glory of a sudden glare.
The waves of ocean checked their course and turned,
As women turn from some tartarian sight,
And rolled their monstrous chariots back again.
.   .   .   The wonder grew and grew ; the circlet glowed,
And wider spread and deepened ; and the light
Flushed every moment brighter.   Still I gazed.
.   .   .   .   Adown the southern sky, below the light,
The flank was reft asunder, suddenly.
The sky rolled up and formed a circle round
With ragged, undulating selvages,
And through the orifice a lurid flash

Poured out—a moment played—then cleared away,
And far along the vista lay a moontide stretch of sea,
With a war of glistering white waves rolling up tumultuously,
Where, serenely rising, falling, dashing wide the yeasty
    cream,
Forward a far-seen-gormand harbour, floated many a rich
    trireme
With a thousand slaves and captives, bending to the galling
    oars,
With the gods of many nations, and the signs of many shores;
With the voices, shapes, and costumes of an hundred sea-
    strewn strands ;
Freighted with the offerings of an hundred tributary lands ;
Gaily onward rode the galleys o'er the flushed and jewelled
    tide,
Proudly as their gods and heroes, all defiant in their pride.
  A moment only danced the marvellous scene
  Before my startled vision, ere a fume
  Of sooty vapour, sifting from above,
  Dropped like a curtain, fold by fold before,
  And all the detail faded—then the shape,
  Till nought remained beyond the red, red glare.
  'Twas awful, that great, bald, blear blotch of eye
  Staring so blankly, senselessly, from out
  That ragged fringe of black and brooding sky !
  . . . . A little space, and then 'twas raised again,
And arose a vasty region, flushing 'neath a summer sheen,
With a tower-embattled city in the haze-wrapt distance seen;
And along an ocean's margin lay an emerald sweep of
    plain,

Where a thousand white pavilions stood like bubbles on the
    main ;
And a richly-mounted army, glittering in a frost of gold,
Bore aloft the flashing ensign ; tossed the banner wide the
    fold ;
All unnumbered as the leaflets, as the matron trees unfurled,
Ere the form of Autumn withers all the beauty of the world ;
Or, with many a warlike movement, swept they at a chief-
    tain's nod
Proudly as Assyrian legions ere their overthrow of God.
    Again the red dusk quivered down ; again
    The vision visibly dissolved away ;
    Again insensate horror, staring, white,
    Threw out its mouldy sceptre o'er the night world ;
    Again the curtain quivered much, and rolled
    In gorgon folds its volume up the front.
And a hugely bulwarked city, vast and mighty rose to view ;
Came a din of boisterous music, from a river glancing
    through ;
And a thousand gorgeous temples, domes, and turrets raked
    the air ;
And a maze of streets, like serpents, struggled, twining
    everywhere ;
Where, mid flashing wreaths of jewels, in a thousand gay
    costumes,
Strode the youth and swept the maiden, flushed with gross
    unhallowed blooms ;
And the minstrel, chief, and minion, demi-god, and devotee,
And the bondmen passed among them, cursing in his heart
    the free ;

Nebo, Bell, and fiery Moloch, on their shrines, mid heaps of
　　　spoil,

Stood exacting rites as senseless as their priests, but not
　　　more vile,

Where amid unholy incense, dropping down and grovelling
　　　flat,

Surged a host of fawning votaries,—not sincere in even that.

Came a change : a rush of twilight swept across their
　　　sapphire sky,

And the flashing lamps of Dian paled the stars that trembled
　　　nigh.

Came a change upon the city, when the misty spirit of night,

Spanned huge shadows 'neath the arches ; .kindled high the
　　　glaring light ;

There the slave of prurient passion, gormand, vaunter,
　　　debauchee,

Sought their like amid the gatherings, in the haunts of
　　　revelry ;

And the ghastly-visaged spoiler, lurking thief, and ravisher,

And the wizard, and the slayer, and the gross adulterer,

And the bestial fool, and strumpet, were revealed, unscreened
　　　to me,

Mid their haunts and assignations, where they dreamt no eye
　　　could see ;

All the crime-bespotted city wallowed in its demon-laven,

And the stink of its corruption, like a curse, went up to
　　　heaven.

Once more changed ! above the city swept a huge and
　　　wrathful cloud,

And the dread avenger, Ayrael, from its bulging entrails
　　　bowed,

And upon the midnight revellers fell the creeping of a fear:
And the deathly waiting shadow of a horror crouching near—
Came a tumult, and a flashing, mingled with a wail of woe,
And the vision faded, vanished in one whelming overthrow.

      *   *   *   *   *   *

    Dark grew the fire-wreathed brow, and from the lips
Thus : " Babylon the great is fallen ! is fallen !"
Oh, mighty city ! thou hast grown unto
The acme of thy splendour.   Thou shalt be
A waste of desolation.   Thou art as
A summer's day grown to its glowing noon.
In calm unshaded splendour, which the mad,
Dark, terrible cyclone shall suddenly
Insepulchre in devastating night.
Thou art a river on a level stretch,
Unruffled in thy calm, complacent roll,
And gorged and flattered by the tribute tides
From all surrounding lands ; but thou shalt meet
A fearful cataract : the earth shall ope
A wide, dark, brazen mouth, and swallow thee,
Even as a fierce volcano, issuing
From out the trailing bowels of the earth,
Heaps out its unlaved sides and builds on high
A dark ambitious summit, terrible fire
With its own vomit, blackening the pure
And virgin heavens with putrid blasts and fumes,
Standing in proud assumption vauntingly,
Till some convulsion dire with spasms huge
Rip up the iron rocks, and heaving its base
And hurl it back into the hungry gulf

Itself had made—entomb in its own ashes.
So hast thou risen from the o'er-gorged earth,
And swelled on high a mouth of blasphemy
Big with the fiery lava of thy own
Corruption-gendering heart; so shalt thou fall;
So shalt thou lie—thy name thy execration!
  Great Babylon! exalted as the heart
Of Lucifer the proud, is fallen, is fallen—
Sunk in the abyss of utter filthiness—
Stained with the scorching brand of every crime—
Glutted with all the excess of every lust—
Blotched with an utter taint of leprosy—
The subtilest essences of every base
And vile, unnatural, execrable thing;
And every devil, every spirit of ill
That walks the fiery pit, or haunts the earth,
Hath found a home in thee.   E'en as the heart,
The centre of the human system, pours,
In myriad streams, the vital fluid through
The wondrous frame instinct with life; e'en so,
O, wonder of the world! hast thou poured out
Through myriad fiery veins, the deadly spume
Of thy corruption.   Every land has grown
Intoxicated with the heated draught.
The glutted denizen of every realm,
Is sated with her vapid luxuries.
The nations from afar, enamoured with
The vision of her pomp, have bowed themselves
To basest servitude; and kings have sunk
In utter prostitution at her feet.

But thou art fallen, art fallen !
  How hast thou padded round thy ghastly frame,
With all the huge proportions of thy pride,
The grandeur of thy dawnings and thy deeds,
The triumph of thy genius, science, art—
Thy ships on sea ; thy harnessed hosts on land ;
Conquest, achievement ; wealth and luxury ;
Pompous display and glorious ancestry ;
Thy long illustrious line of mighty kings ;
A great, grand past, strung o'er with proud exploits,
Thy host of heroes—names of wide renown,
Where mind o'er matter triumphed and achieved
Wide victories, that might raise the wondering blush
To future people who had deemed themselves
More wise as earth was older—in the van,
In the van of all the people—deeming intellect
Progressive as the stately march of time.
These are but feeders of her huge conceit—
But ministers unto her consequence—
But idols which she worships in her heart.
How hast thou decked thee in the gorgeous robes
Of commerce, learning, nationality,
The pride of power, of pomp, and ancient fame,
And liftest up thy face to heaven, and wreathed
Thy sensual brow with stars, and proud hast said,
" I sit a queen ; all the nations bow before
The glory of my presence, and all lands
Yield up their choicest unto me ; I rule
A goddess o'er the petty realms of earth :
I stand a rock, firm as the ages strong,

To overawe the petty frets of time;
To hurl defiance at the ghouls that lurk
With rage malignant round the tattered skirts
Of old departing eras—Change—Decay,
Fate! Desolation! and Oblivion last!!"

SIMPLE POEMS.

RUDYARD.

SUNSET MUSINGS.

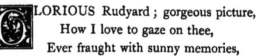LORIOUS Rudyard ; gorgeous picture,
  How I love to gaze on thee,
  Ever fraught with sunny memories,
  Ever beautiful to me !

Whether blushing Spring enwrap thee
  In its robe of virgin pride,
Whether golden Summer steep thee
  In its mellow gushing tide ;

Whether drooping Autumn flood thee
  With its dreamy chastened light,
Whether chilly Winter drape thee
  In its vest of spotless white ;

Whether storms sweep grandly o'er thee,
 Light or gloom their charms impart,
Ever grand, sublime, majestic,
 Ever beautiful thou art.

And I love to roam in twilight,
 From the busy haunts of toil,
From Oppression's galling fetters,
 From Deception's soulless smile,

Here to sit and gaze upon thee,
 As I gaze upon thee now,
With the balmy zephyr playing
 On my hot and aching brow.

How sublimely grand the picture
 Stretching out before my gaze ;
Deluged with the glowing splendour
 Of the sun's declining rays,

Lies the lake in tranquil beauty,
 Like a model mimic sea,
Like a brightly polished mirror,
 In a frame of ebony ;

Like a flood of molten silver,
 Froth of gold and sapphire dipped,
Flashing back the efflorescence
 Of the summer's blazing light.

And away, far up the valley,
   Rising from the sunlit tide,
Towering hills in stately grandeur,
   Bound the view on either side.

Turning, twisting, undulating,
   Sinking low or peaking high,
Throwing up a jaggy outline,
   Quaintly cut against the sky.

Bulging mounds and blocks of granite
   Rise in beauty all around,
Lichen grown, and moss enamelled,
   Ivy wreathed, and bilberry crowned.

Rugged cliffs of mouldering sandstone
   Break abruptly here and there,
Like a patch of coarsest fustian
   On a robe of beauty rare ;

In whose fossil-bedded strata,
   Like an ancient crypt unsealed,
Lies the bloom of bygone ages,
   To the curious eye revealed,

Seeming placed to point this moral
   To the thoughtless and the gay,
All that's fair must fade and perish,
   All that's beautiful, decay.

K

And above and all around me
  Stalwart trees bedeck the scene,
Tendril-twined and ivy-mantled,
  All enrobed in richest sheen.

Like à mighty host of giants,
  Armed and ready for the fight,
With the lightning's gleaming falchion,
  And the tempest's awful might ;

And the sun in haze of beauty,
  Sinks in solemn peace to rest,
'Neath the bright and mystic curtain
  Of the crimson-glowing west.

Fleecy mists of gorgeous splendour,
  Clouds of shapes and forms untold,
Sail like argosies of tinsel,
  O'er a sea of burnished gold ;

Softly breaking up and parting,
  Gently gliding to and fro,
Mirrored in the glassy bosom
  Of the peaceful lake below.

And the mason's busy hammer,
  And the mower's tinkling scythe,
And the whistle of the teamster,
  And the song of milk-maid blithe—

All are hushed, and peaceful Silence
　O'er the scene its mantle throws ;
Not one sight or sound discordant
　Breaks the swell of sweet repose.

And the stilly, dreamy motion,
　Of the vapours gliding o'er,
And the plashing of the wavelets
　As they break upon the shore,

And the calm and saintly murmur
　Of the tall and stately trees,
As they chant their thrilling vespers
　To the music of the breeze—

All combine to soothe my spirit,
　Panting, yearning, sad, and sore ;
Waft my thoughts from present sorrows,
　To the happy days of yore :

When I met my noble Mary
　Oft amid this shady bower,
When the flush of day was fading
In the mystic twilight hour ;

When together oft we wandered
　Through the flower-enamelled glade,
Sat in silent contemplation
　In the cool and leafy shade ;

Watched the unsuspecting rabbit
  Frisking through the bushy grove,
Heard the rooks in noisy confab
  In the giant trees above ;

Went in search of curious flowerets,
  Climbed the rocks for fern and heath,
And together, for her forehead,
  Twined a rainbow-coloured wreath ;

Watched the mighty locomotive
  Rushing grandly on its way,
And the snow-white wreath of vapour
  Softly break and die away ;

Sought for shells amid the shingle
  On the lakelet's rugged side,
Watched the ever busy swallow
  O'er its shining surface glide ;

Launched our skiff upon its bosom,
  When the wind was calm and still,
Gazed enraptured on the picture,
  And of beauty quaffed our fill.

Then when passion or ambition
  Filled my soul with wild unrest,
Or, when sorrow or affliction
  Quelled the demon in my breast,

Standing grandly there before me,
  With her cool hand on my brow,
Gazing fondly, sadly on me—
  Ah ! I seem to see her now—

She would breathe the balm of kindness
  O'er my sufferings and my wrongs,
Read me thoughts of grand old authors,
  Sing me sweetly soothing songs ;

Speak in strangely thrilling accents,
  Of that land beyond the sky,
Where " the weary, heavy laden"
  Find eternal rest and joy—

Till my brooding soul, enraptured,
  Soared on Fancy's glowing wings
Far beyond this realm of turmoil,
  Up to brighter, nobler things.

But those days of halcyon glory
  Like a vision passed away,
Like a fitful gleam of sunshine
  On a dreary winter's day ;

Leaving nought behind to cheer me
  Through this world of storm and blight,
But the sweetly soothing memory
  Of their evanescent light ;

For the summer waned and deepened,
  Softer grew the twilight's hush,
Meeker grew the morning's dawning,
  More subdued the noontide flush ;

And disease, like deadly night-shade,
  O'er my Mary cast its blight,
Paler grew her cheeks of beauty,
  Grew her eyes more large and bright.

Whiter grew her brow of marble,
  Softer grew her hand of snow,
Fainter came her voice's music,
  Feeble fell her steps and slow.

Then we wandered here but seldom,
  For it only seemed to cast
O'er our lives a deeper shadow—
  We were dreaming of the past—

And the tender, chastened aspect
  Of its beauty, seemed to say,
" All that's fair, alas ! must wither,
  All that's beautiful decay."

But we never spoke of parting,
  Though we knew that we must part,
Either strove to hide that knowledge,
  From the other's bleeding heart.

But the Summer passed, and Autumn,
  Meek-eyed Autumn, came again,
With its wreath of faded flowerets,
  · And its wealth of golden grain.

'Twas the solemn hour of midnight,
  And the moon shone clear and bright,
Silvering o'er the silent landscape,
  With its weird mysterious light,

When I stood among her kindred,
  Gazing on her features fair,
Stroking back the silken tresses
  Of her wavy ebon hair.

And she looked so like an angel,
  In her mute and dreamless sleep—
All the past came flooding o'er me,
  And I turned away to weep.

Came her voice, serene and saint-like,
  " Do not leave me yet awhile ;"
Then I looked, her eyes were brilliant,
  And her features wore a smile

As she gazed around upon us,
  Pointing with her snow-white hand,
Through the vista of the future,
  To that brighter, better land.

Softly whispering, " Loved ones meet me,
   On that far celestial shore,
Where the noble faithful-hearted
   Meet again to part no more."

Then her hand dropped down beside her,
   O'er her features passed a change,
Pallid grew her lips and rigid,
   Glassy grew her eyes and strange.

And I knew, though almost frantic,
   As the dear white hand I pressed,
That the worn and weary spirit,
   Had at last gone home to rest.

Time passed on, and sunny Summer,
   Came again to deck our bowers,
With its robe of gold and emerald,
   And its wreath of ferns and flowers.

All around was love and beauty,
   All seemed happy as of yore,
But the bliss of vanished moments,
   Came to cheer my heart no more.

And a weary, weeping wanderer,
   O'er this wilderness I roam,
Till the summons come—" 'Tis finished !
   Leave thy toil and hasten home."

THE PAUPER CHILD.

HERE they lay upon their pallets,
   In that crowded Workhouse room—
Not a sound disturbed the silence,
   Not one ray relieved the gloom :

All that band of little vagrants,
   Branded with the awful ban,
Justice visits on the children,
   For the crimes of fallen man.

*   *   *   *   *   *   *

They had ate their scanty pittance
   Long before the day had fled,
And were marshalled by the matron,
   Like a mimic troop, to bed.

Long ago was hushed each whisper,
   E'en the grieved had ceased to weep ;
All oblivious of their sorrows,
   Side by side lay fast asleep.

All but one poor little sufferer,
   And alone she panting lay,
None to speak a word of kindness,
   None to wipe her tears away ;

No fond hand to mix the cordial,
   None to soothe her bosom's pain,
None to smooth her ruffled pillow,
   None to cool her aching brain.

Wildly throbbed her little pulses,
  With a strange, inconstant beat,
And her throat was parched and thirsty
  With the burning fever-heat.

Slowly rolled the perspiration
  From her brow in muddy streaks ;
Now and then a tear-drop trickled
  Down her flushed and wasted cheeks.

Strangely fixed was every feature,
  And the brilliant, restless eyes
Seemed to gaze beyond the ceiling
  Up into the dusky skies ;

And the little hands were folded
  O'er her bosom thin and bare,
And the lips, so parched and swollen,
  Slowly moved as if in prayer.

There she lay, nor sigh, nor murmur,
  Till the clock within the tower,
Waking up a thousand echoes,
  Boomed the solemn midnight hour.

And the sounds so weird and ghost-like,
  As they pierced her throbbing brain,
Broke the spell that bound her senses,
  Brought her back to earth again ;

And she longed to reach the window,
  Longed to sit and dream once more,
With the grated casement open,
  As she oft had sat before,

Looking o'er the silent city,
  To the mountains hoar and bare,
Listening to the night's low whisperings,
  Drinking in the balmy air ;

Gazing out into the distance,
  Where the wondrous orbs of light
Roll in calm mysterious grandeur
  Through the misty realms of night ;

Gazing, till a sad, sweet feeling,
  O'er her listening senses stole,
Veneration, love, and wonder,
  Thrilled with solemn joy her soul.

For she seemed to see a vista,
  Opening through the dark blue sky,
See a snow-white throng of minstrels,
  Hear a rapturous strain of joy ;

See a host of happy children,
  Free from harsh rebuke and toil,
Dancing round a crystal fountain,
  'Neath a loving father's smile ;

And she thought they seemed to beckon,
   And to murmur softly, " Come !
Leave that world of pain and darkness,
   Come and share our radiant home."

Yes, she longed to reach the window,
   Longed to scan the midnight sky,
But her limbs were far too feeble,
   And no other help was nigh.

Turned she slowly on her pillow,
   With a weary, weary moan :
Oh ! it seemed so hard to suffer,
   Loveless, hopeless, all alone.

Faster came the scalding tear-drops,
   Fiercer still the fever burned,
And the patient little spirit,
   With a strange persistence yearned

For a sweetly sympathising,
   Loving face to gaze upon,
For a word of fond endearment,
   Just one kiss, if only one :—

Ah ! poor, patient, plaintless sufferer,
   Thou hast never known the bliss
Which entrances all the being,
   Neath the pressure of a kiss ;

Thou hast never proved the value
Of a tender mother's care,
Ne'er received a brother's blessing,
Never heard a father's prayer ;

Never romped with happy schoolmates
Through the sunny summer hours ;
Never roamed among the meadows,
Culling dew-besprinkled flowers.

All thy life has been o'er-shadowed
With a cloud of darkest woes,
Un-illumined by the halo
Pure affection round it throws.

And in place of loving-kindness,
Gentle words and tender looks,
Vile abuse, contempt, subjection,
Harsh commands and stern rebukes.

Ah ! weep on, for thou art wretched,
And 'twill ease thy grieving breast ;
After sorrow comes rejoicing
After labour cometh rest.

Time moved on, though slowly, surely ;
And the clock within the tower
Sang a solemn, dirge-like requiem
Over each departing hour.

Agonised she lay and listened,
　Till it changed the hour of four ;
Then a change came stealing o'er her,
And she mourned and wept no more.

Sorrow, sighing, grief and anguish,
　Gloom and darkness passed away ;
Round her burst a flood of glory,
　Brighter than the noon of day ;

And she stood upon the borders
　Of that calm untroubled shore,
Where in blissful dreams and visions,
　She had often stood before.

All the traces of affliction,
　All the rags and dirt were gone,
And the disembodied spirit,
　With a dazzling lustre shone.

Came a host of shining children,
　Floating through the lambent blaze,
With a loving shout of welcome,
　And a joyous song of praise,

Came and kissed the little stranger,
　Led her softly by the hand,
Through the groves of sweet promegranate,
　O'er the silvery shining sand.

Through the rich and fertile valleys,
　Where the tree of knowledge grows,
Where the crystal fountains sparkle,
　And where milk and honey flows.

O'er the gem-bespangled mountains,
　Through the palm and olive bowers,
Through the verdure-mantled pastures,
　Decked with never-fading flowers,

By the margin of a river,
　Which in smiling grandeur rolled
Through the landscape and the city,
　Like a thread of molten gold ;

Led her through the gorgeous portals,
　Of " that city bright and clear,"
Singing sweetly, as they journeyed :—
　" But the pure have entrance here."

Through the shining ranks of angels,
　Onward to the centre seat,
With a shout of " Hallelujah,"
　Laid her at her Saviour's feet.

With a smile He stooped and raised her,
　Placed her kindly on His knee,
Whispered softly as He kissed her,
　" Suffer them to come to Me."

Rest in peace, enraptured spirit,
  Free at last from all thy pain,
From unkindness, hard and cruel,
  From Oppression's muffled chain."

They will hide thy little body
  'Mongst the many nameless graves,
Where the heather scents the breezes,
  And the mournful cypress waves ;

They will read a pauper's portion
  Of the solemn funeral prayer,
They will heap the mould in silence
  On the coffin rough and spare.

They will leave it light and tearless,
  And it soon will be forgot,
But an eye will watch above it,
  Though they comprehend it not.

Sweetly rest, pure little spirit,
  Ever happy, ever blest,
" Where the wicked cease from troubling,
  And the weary are at rest."

"HALLOWED BE THY NAME."

A SABBATH EVENING SONG.

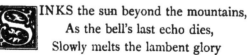INKS the sun beyond the mountains,
    As the bell's last echo dies,
  Slowly melts the lambent glory
    From the hazy western skies.

Upward from the east in silence,
   Comes the great calm empress, Night,
With her dusky tresses trailing,
   From her forehead gem-bedight ;

Softly creeping through the valleys,
   Closing up the drooping flowers,
Flooding all the nooks with shadows,
   Blotting out the distant towers ;

Healing parched and languid nature,
   With her wealth of balmy dews,
As a word of gentle kindness
   Failing strength and hope renews :

Steeping in the balm of Lethe
   Mortal senses, sorrows, woes,
Lulling, as a gentle mother
   Lulls her darling, to repose.

From the silent meads and valleys
   Misty exhalations rise,
Like the incense of an offering,
   Up into the milky skies ;

Nature cheered and and renovated,
   Vocal woods and streams exclaim,
In a thousand whispering voices—
   " Maker, ' hallowed be Thy name !'"

L

All those orbs of wondrous beauty,
   Spangling o'er the firmament,
Constellations slowly rising
   From the shadowy orient ;

Mystic signs for ever moving,
   O'er one vast unmeasured track,
Gems that stud the wonder-girdle
   Of the circling zodiac.

Moons and satellites empyrean,
   Wheeling round each central blaze,
In the hazy ebon concave,
   Far beyond our finite gaze ;

Teeming worlds on worlds of chaos,
   Sweeping on with silent grace,
Round the myriad suns and systems,
   Through the vasty realms of space ;

All are chanting in their motions,
   In their bright, unflickering flame,
In their wondrous revolutions,
   " Blessed and ' hallowed be Thy name.'"

Weary frames, worn out with battling
   In the restless, feverish strife,
Pressing o'er the toiling, moiling,
   Panting, wrestling, race of life.

Hearts bowed down and almost broken,
    Shrinking 'neath their fleshly load,
Tempted, tried, afflicted travellers,
    Almost fainting on the road,

Taste again the sweets of comfort,
    Bask in Love's all-healing looks,
Read again each precious promise
    In the well-worn Book of books.

Lay their failings on the altar,
    And for grace and pardon sue,
Feel the hallowed influence stealing
    Softly o'er them, like the dew ;

Till each soul, renewed and strengthened,
    Quits in thought this mortal frame,
Murmuring, as it soars unfettered,
    " Father, ' hallowed be Thy name !'"

Oh ! thou great all-glorious Being,
    Omnipresent everywhere,
Thou who read'st each secret motive
    Hear'st the softest whispered prayer ;

Thou, whose mighty hand has written
    Nature's grand stupendous tome,
Thou, who scatterest worlds like sand-grains,
    O'er yon blue ethereal dome ;

Thou, who mad'st and fashioned all things,
    Gave them motion, light, and breath,
Fixed'st laws, by which creation
    Works her own strange birth and death;

Thou, before whose face adoring,
    Angels veil themselves and fall,
Thou, whom seraphs chant for ever,
    Holy! Holy! Lord of all;

Thou, whose power exalts the humble,
    Teachest babes to lisp Thy fame,
Oh! Thou great all-ruling Spirit,
    Blessed and "hallowed be Thy Name!"

SPRING.

EAUTIFUL Spring! Beautiful Spring!
    Coming again on the wandering wing,
    Sunshine and beauty and pleasure to bring,
Gladly we welcome thee, beautiful Spring!

Virgin of purity, rapture is thine,
Bright is thy brow, as the lore of the mine,
Fair is thy cheek, as the flush of the rose,
Sweet is thy smile, as an infant's repose.

Robed with a mantle of gorgeous array,
Girded with tendrils of amaranths gay,
Jewelled with flowerets of every hue,
Frescoed with sunbeams and spangled with dew;

Hollow-cheeked sorrow and sadness and gloom
Vanish away to their wintry tomb ;
Grief bows her fennel-crowned head to thy sway,
Time like a phantom glides swiftly away.

Genial laughter and frolicsome mirth !
Herald thy coming again upon earth,
Welcome thee back to thy throne in our bowers,
Queen of the empire of beauty and flowers.

Everything lofty and noble, or grand,
Wakes into life at the wave of thy wand ;
Earth dons her mantle of radiant sheen,
Azure and purple and scarlet and green.

Hedgerows and forests burst out into bloom,
Flowers load the air with delicious perfume ;
Winds hail thy coming with boisterous cheers,
Clouds in their gladness gush out into tears.

Birds sing thy praises with jubilant voice,
Trees clap their broad waving hands and rejoice,
Lambkins and fledglings the chorus prolong,
Streamlets gush out into rapturous song.

Mortals enamoured bow down at thy shrine,
Painters pourtray thee a goddess divine,
Poets, the landmarks of every clime,
Praise and extol thee in epic sublime.

Everything radiant, rapturous, bright,
Hails thy approach with a shout of delight,
Welcomes thee back with a jubilant ring,
Radiant, sunny-eyed, beautiful Spring !

HEART STRAINS.

THE DISCARDED.

A REVERIE.

NEW Year's Eve ! and I am sitting
    By the glowing ingle-side,
      Watching, listlessly, the smoke-wreaths
        Dancing up the chimney wide ;
And the quaint, fantastic shadows,
  Which the flickering fire-light flings
On the floor and walls and ceiling,
  Flapping, phantom-like, their wings.
And the storm's mysterious spirit,
  Raging in the outer air,
Shrieking round the eaves and gables,
  Hissing through the poplars bare ;
And the drowsy hum of voices,
  And the cricket's carol clear,
And the clock's monotonous ticking,
  Are the only sounds I hear.

Though the crackling yule-log blazes
  On the hearths of joyous homes ;
Though the heartfelt laughter echoes
  'Neath a thousand frosted domes ;
And the New Year's trees are twinkling
  With their myriad starry lights,
Loaded down with toys and trinkets,
  Circled round with romping sprites.
And the ivy-green and holly,
  Hang in festoons from the walls,
Decorate the lamps and vases,
  And the statues in the halls.
And a myriad hearts are swelling,
  Pulsing, panting with delight ;
Sunny eyes are gushing, glowing,
  With affection's tender light ;
Youthful hands are clasped in others,
  Which for long have been astray,
All their toils and cares forgotten,
  All their sorrows cast away ;
Some are coining jests and riddles,
  Some are whispering sweet and low,
Some are stealing, snatching kisses
  'Neath the mystic mistletoe. ,
Swells the dreamy gush of music,
  And the young, the fair, the brave
Dance in undulating circles
  Round the Old Year's yawning grave.

Though, in days gone by I gambolled
  With the laughter-gushing throng

Of the peerless and the fearless,
  Of the joyous and the young ;
Though I trod the dance's mazes,
  With the gayest of the gay ;
Shod Old Time with silver slippers,
  Banished gloom and care away ;
Though I wooed the goddess Beauty,
  Knelt at Pleasure's gaudy shrine,
Looked in eyes whose timid lustre,
  Thrilled their rapture back to mine ;
Though I clasped fair hands, whose pressure
  Gave the impulse to my own :
All have vanished ! and I'm sitting,
  Sadly dreaming, " all alone."

Ah ! 'twas in the days of sunshine,
  When my heart was wild and free,
When the air was full of music,
  And the world was fair to me ;
Ere my soul had learned to sorrow,
  Long before my heart had dreamed
That the forms revolving round me
  Could be aught but what they seemed ;
Ere affliction cast a shadow
  O'er the glory of my youth ;
Ere deceit and wrong and falsehood
  Banished trusting love and truth ;
Ere I proved that lips might flatter
  While the heart was full of guile,
And the blackest thoughts lie hidden

'Neath a sunny face and smile ;
Ere I'd found that grand proposals
    Might be only gilded lies,
And the fiends of lust and passion
    Slumber 'neath a fair disguise.
Ere the gaudy shams had withered ;
    Ere the paint had worn away ;
Ere my gold had turned to tinsel,
    And my idols, soulless clay.
Ah ! 'twas then the sparkling current
    Of my being danced along,
'Neath a sky of cloudless radiance,
    To a constant gush of song.
Now, alas ! those days have vanished,
    And the friends of youth have flown,
And I'm sitting by the ingle,
    Sadly dreaming, " all alone !"

Oh ! what forms and faces haunt me
    As I watch the dancing blaze !
Visions, fraught with painful meanings,
    From the scenes of other days ;
All the memories of my anguish,
    Of my deep and bitter wrongs ;
All the venomed shafts of slander,
    All the spleen from double tongues.

Comes SHE, now, and, stands before me,
    (Like a phantom from the tomb),
As when first my eyes beheld her,

In the glory of her bloom ;
Stately as the fabled Juno,
   As the young Aurora fair,
Dimpled cheeks of summer roses,
   Shining cataracts of hair ;
With her words of lofty meaning,
   And her noble-souled pretence,
With her looks of sham affection,
   And her gloss of innocence ;
Acting up the rôle of virtue,
   And the pure and lofty mind :
Only now the mask's transparent,
   And I see the fiend behind.
Then, my heart was pure and simple,
   Full of hope, and joy and truth,
Hovering 'twixt the pride of manhood,
   And the innocence of youth ;
Unsuspicious, fond, impulsive,
   Dreaming of no meaner state ;
With a passion-love of Beauty,
   Of the noble, good, and great.

Then, my soul was softly waking,
   To a new and joyous sense,
Softly quivering 'neath the breathings
   Of a rapturous influence ;
That which casts a dreamy lustre,
   In the far-off, vacant eyes ;
Sets the " Fairy Fancy " wandering
   After fonder, holier ties.

That which thrills the human bosom
　With an unimagined bliss ;
Gives to youth a feeble foretaste,
　Of " the Better World in this ;"
Sets the giddy brain a-musing,
　When the sun sinks in the west,
And the raptured thoughts a-dreaming,
　When the body sleeps at rest.
In the bosom softly stealing,
　Unacknowledged, undefined ;
Indistinct, as mellow·whisper
　Floating on the vesper wind.
As the flush precedes the coming
　Of the glorious " God of Day ;"
As the streamlet slowly gushes
　Ere the torrent bursts its way ;
As the flower first springs, then opens,
　To the radiance from above ;
So my soul was gently thrilling
　'Neath the power of dawning love.

Then ! my thoughts were mildly grieving,
　O'er my childhood's broken toys,
O'er its sunshine calmly fading,
　O'er its vanished hopes and joys.
I was stepping o'er the threshold
　Of a new and sterner life,
Gently floating on the margin
　Of the whirlpool of its strife ;
Only tasting of the hardships,

Which the future had in store,
Looking out into the shadows,
    Which its sorrows cast before ;
Feeling strangely, sadly conscious
    Of the transientness of things,
That the hopes most fondly cherished
    Ever have the fleetest wings.
'Tis, alas ! the spirit waking
    From that blissful childhood's dreams,
When our life's a barque of pleasure
    Floating down a golden stream :
'Tis the first cold breath of sorrow
    On the pulses fresh and warm ;
'Tis the shade that damps the sunlight
    At the coming of a storm.

Then ! Ambition smiling whispered
    Of a grand and lofty name ;
Pointed out into the distance,
    To the mountain-heights of Fame,
Hung a wreath of verdant laurels
    On the highest of its towers ;
Hid the pitfalls in the pathway
    'Neath a screen of moss and flowers.
O'er me came at times a longing
    For a loving, kindred soul,
Which, with sympathy, could urge me
    Onward, upward to the goal ;
For a gentle smile to cheer me,
    For a pure and noble breast,

Where my thoughts might find an echo,
  And my weary head might rest.

Then "She" came and thrilled my being
  With her preference and her praise;
Twined herself so closely round me,
  With her lofty winning ways;
Till she seemed to me an essence
  Floating o'er me everywhere,
Every bitter cup to sweeten,
  Every hope and aim to share.
Thus I fell a blinded prisoner,
  In the meshes of her toils;
Fascinated by her beauty,
  And the glamour of her smiles.
Need I tell the "old, old story?"
  How I listened and believed;
Told my tale of youthful passion,
  Trusted, loved, and was deceived.

Oh! 'tis hard to have the heart-strings
  Snapped asunder at a stroke:
Twining round a darling object,
  As the ivy round the oak;
Hard to feel the spirit clinging,
  Hoping, praying—all in vain!
Have the love, so blindly lavished,
  Tossed unvalued back again;
Hard to don a gay appearance,
  Wrapt around by wounded pride,

Whilst the heart is bleeding, breaking,
  Evermore an empty void.
Harder still to have suspicion
  Planted where affection throve ;
Lose all faith in human nature,
  Human virtue, truth, and love.
Have the flowery palm of honour
  Turned to ashes in my grasp,
And the worm my bosom cherished
  Rise and sting me like an asp.

Ah ! but think not, haughty maiden,
  That I envy thee thy power,
Or the grand and lofty beauty
  Which was all thy virgin dower ;
Think not, either, that I would be
  Unconcerned and gay and free ;
Doff a love, and don another,
  In a twilight, like to thee.
No ! I sooner far would suffer
  All the agony of heart—
Ay, an age of desolation—
  Than be fickle as thou art.
For it proves to me, my spirit
  Has not lost the stamp divine ;
That my nature is not shallow,
  Is not mean and base as thine.
Neither think thou that my being
  Yearns towards thee even yet ;
That a smile of thine would banish

All I never may forget ;
That a look of thine would make me,
  All I dreamed I once might be ;
That one gleam of love would chain me
  Once again a slave to thee.
Oft returns the tidal volume
  Cloaking wile with amorous speech ;
Bar'st his breast with kiss and welcome,
  Evermore the grey old beach.
All in vain ! the fickle Nereid,
  Laughing, slips the fond embrace,
Mocks the moans, the tears that trickle
  Down the sad, pain-wrinkled face.
Ah ! I know thy fickle nature,
  Thou art like that wily wave !
And should Hebe, doling, give thee
  All that Tyche ever gave,
Should the richest of the carver,
  And the fairest of the loom,
And the choice of art and nature
  Lustre round thy beauties' bloom ;
Ah ! should all the gifts and graces
  Gather round thee, and conspire
In thy form to fix their essence,
  Flush thy face with spirit-fire ;
Nay ! should'st thou in tears, forgetting
  Beauty-love is calm and proud,
Should'st thou humble thee, and bow thee
  Where I once so meekly bowed :
Having once deceived me, never,

Never more, whate'er thy mien,
   Could'st thou be to me the being
      That thou mightest once have been.
No, alas! thy tears might give me
      Less of pride, and less of scorn,
Deeper pity, deeper shadow,
      Make me sadder, more forlorn.

Oh! my proud and peerless Jenny,
      Loved so madly long ago!
Why, oh! wherefore didst thou win me
      Only to deceive me so?
Wherefore did'st thou trifle with me
      For the sport it gave to thee?
Caring not that such diversion
      Might be agony to me.
Had it been thy lot to suffer
      With the bright and youthful band,
'Neath the scourge that slays the fairest,
      And the noblest of the land;
Though 'twere sad to see thee wasting,
      Slowly fading, day by day,
As the stars fade at the dawning,
      As the shadows shrink away;
Sad to see grim death presumptuous
      Seal the lips that spoke the vow,
Lay his finger on thy pulses,
      Cast his shadow o'er thy brow;

M

Sad to see that form so queenly
    Rifled of its summer bloom,
Laid by weeping friends to moulder,
    In the dark, the lonely tomb.
Had I known thy spirit landed,
    Far beyond this wintry blast ;
Had I known thee pure and noble,
    True and faithful to the last ;
Oh ! I could have borne the parting,—
    Could have borne to let thee go ;
Though my hopes were buried with thee,
    Though I idolized thee so !
Then I might have toiled and suffered,
    Suffered patiently my woes,
In the hope to meet thee, darling !
    Where the weary find repose.

But to make me scorn the being
    In my blindness throned so high ;
See her proudly, gaily careless,
    Dancing on, a living lie ;
See the lips on others smiling,
    On whose breath my spirit hung,
In whose vows my hopes were centred,
    To whose truth my being clung—
Oh ! 'tis terrible to struggle,
    With that old and bitter pain
Ever rankling in my bosom,
    Ever throbbing in my brain.

But I will not curse thee, Jenny,
    No ! but bid thee flutter on,
Till thy Summer day be ended,
    And thy beauty faded, gone ;
Till the Flatterer's tongue is silenced,
    And thy hopes are buried low ;
Till reflection comes to taunt thee
    With the deeds of long-ago.
Then, perchance, thou'lt weep in sorrow
    O'er those broken vows of thine ;
Then, perchance, thou'lt learn the value
    Of a heart as true as mine.

Fare-ye-well : begone, ye phantoms !
    Who have marred my summer prime ;
Cast a blight o'er all my being,
    Made me old before my time.
I will look among the lowly,
    Till I find a bosom true,
Then I'll plant my modest lily
    Where the poisonous Upas grew.

* * * * * *

How the time has flown ! 'tis midnight !
    And another year has fled ;
Hark ! the bells ring out a requiem
    O'er the faithless, lost, and dead.

WAITING FOR DEATH.

This Poem refers to the illness and death of the Poet's beloved sister,
Hannah, who returned home to die ; and now rests
in Endon churchyard.

WAS in the waning of a glorious day :
     The sun had sunk beyond the mist-swathed hills,
     Crowned with an halo of celestial light.
The gaudy clouds, in various attitudes
Of light and shade, and changing constantly,
And moving slow, fringed with a golden blush,
Like festooned curtains draped the rosy west.
'Twas in the dawn of Autumn, and the scene
Was beautiful, but o'er it hung a hush,
That pensive, sad, half-sweet, half-mournful calm,
That quietude which quells Ambition's stride,
And sets the heart a-weeping vanished loves :—
That lull, when Nature in her glowing robe,
With all her charms matured, would seem to pause
Upon the brink of darkness and decay,
And sadly, tearfully in retrospect
Review the radiant but withered past.
'Twas thus when in a quiet room we sat,
A mournful band ! for one, a birdling loved,
That long had fled the parent nest, had come
Again ; a poor, wan, wasted thing, to die !
We sat beside her couch, and watched, and wept.
Awhile she lay, nor looked, nor moved, and then
The eyes blazed up, she smiled and thus she spoke—
" Oh, come and sit beside me once again,

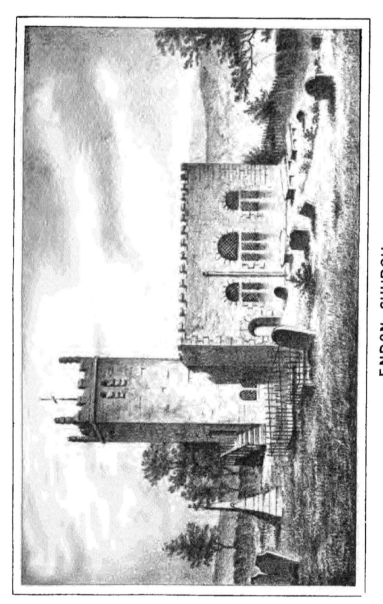

ENDON CHURCH

And lay one cool hand on my burning brow,
And with the other closely, fondly clasp
This wasted, shrivelled hand of mine ; no ! yours !
All yours, my husband ! even more than when
I stood beside you at the sacred shrine,
And vowed to love and honour and obey ;
For now the bickering storms and cares of years,
The sunshine and the shadows we have shared ;
And more than all, that strongest, tenderest tie,
Sole offspring of our union, beauteous flower !
Our fondest, brightest hope ! our angel boy !
By kind and pitying Heaven a moment lent,
To shed a ray of brightness o'er our path,
To teach our hearts that strange deep tenderness,
To unlock that hidden fount—a parent's love ;
Then taken, as the shepherd takes the lamb,
To draw the wandering sheep back to the fold.
All these have knit our souls intensely close,
In bonds of kindred suffering, hope, and love !
   Come closer, closer, dear one ! to my side,
And let me gaze with these fast-dimming orbs
Once more into the fountain of your own,
And watch the liquid tenderness gush out !
And let me hear again that low, deep voice,
Whose tones grown tremulous in days of yore,
Erst woke my virgin soul to ecstasy ;
Call me once more your darling one, your own !
The mother of your seraph-boy, your wife !
Soothe me with gentle words, and let me lean
Upon you, downward to the river's brink.

How dark it grows, I scarce can see your face !
Is it the daylight fading, or my sight ?
Perchance 'tis both !
                    How fast my poor heart beats
At times, then almost stops ! this burning heat,
This rattling cough, and fever of disease ;
This acrid thirst, and constant gasp for breath !
This weary stretch of patience, hope, and faith !
This useless clinging unto earthly love ;
The world so beautiful, and worldly dreams
Will soon be o'er ; the reign of flesh and sin,
The fightings, struggles, griefs, will soon be o'er,
And I shall be beyond them all ; at rest !
Unbroken rest ! Oh hasten, happy hour !
    *   *   *   *   *

" Have I been sleeping ? could it be a dream ?
So beautiful it was, so real seemed,
A light broke softly round me, and a strain
Of thrilling music crept upon my sense :
A seraph form appeared, enrobed in white,
So radiant ! I scarce could look ; when, lo—!
The veil was lifted from its face, it smiled
And murmured ' Mother !' 'twas our angel Boy.
I strove to rise and follow him beyond,
When, all at once, in shining robe I stood
Upon an eminence, whose glittering brow
O'erlooked the universe ; and far below
Vast worlds, and numberless, and bright, revolved
Through realms of space too vast for human thought ;
I saw, but comprehended not, the power

That whirled them on ; and heard their low, weird song.
I stood entranced, when came HIS thrilling voice ;
' O mother, come !' I turned, and lo ! a fount
Of crystal whiteness, and a mansion grand
Rose up beside me.

               Trees and flowers and fruits,
Of rarest loveliness, and shady bowers,
And tinkling waterfalls, and shrub-fringed hills,
And landscapes fair rose up before and round ;
And through the trees, vibrating softly, sounds
Of far-off music floated to my ear.
He led me on, our Boy ! low whispering : ' Come !
' Oh, come and share this Paradise with me !'
I strove, but could not clasp him to my heart.
I bent to kiss the gorgeous flowers ; they fled !
All fled, and night was round me, but a voice
Came from the distance : 'twas his voice, it said ;
' Oh, come ! and bid my father, too, to come.'

    *   *   *   *   *

" Draw nearer, nearer, husband, kindred—all,
I am so cold ; my heart ! O mother ! read
That beauteous Psalm you read me yester-e'en.

    *   *   *   *   *

" How sweet ! it falls like balm upon my soul !
' Thou art my shepherd, Lord ; I shall not want,
Yea, though I walk the valley dark, and though
The shade of death encompass me about ;
No evil will I fear, for Thou art there,
Thy rod and staff sustain and comfort me.'
Oh, Saviour, come ! dear Lord, I wait for Thee !

My flesh and spirit fail, my heart doth faint;
Be Thou my strength, my joy, and endless hope!
'Tis long to wait! I'm weary, weary, sick!
I languish, panting, on the river's brink,
And wait for Thee, and yearn for Thee; oh, come!
Come now, Lord Jesus, quickly, quickly come!

        *   *   *   *   *   *

"Oh, moisten just once more my burning lips,
And raise my head, and wipe my fevered brow;
Then sing to me, with voices soft and low,
That song I love so much: 'The Better Land!'

        *   *   *   *   *   *

"How beautiful! how strangely beautiful!
Your voices, oh, how sweet! and yet methought
I heard deep strains from far, commingling with,
And heightening much, the rapture of your own.
Hush! list! again they come, and rise and swell,
And wrap me up, and melt my soul away:
Soft, tremulous, intensely grand, they rise,
Then fall and die away; see, see, they come!
A vista opens; Angel hosts appear;
Light! Light! a blaze of light! our darling boy!
And far beyond my Saviour beckons me!
I go—farewell—meet me—at home—in Heav—!"
A moment more the white lips faintly moved,
But all was still; the voice had gone for aye;
A moment more the brilliant eyeballs rolled,
But saw not; for the soul had fled to rest!
The muscles strung, relaxed; the pulse grew still;
The eyelids drooped, the death-sweat came and stood

In beads upon that calm and sainted brow.
The pain, the grief, the anguish, all were o'er !
We knelt and wept in silence there awhile ;
But half in grief, and half in hope and joy :
Then rose and pressed the weary eyelids down,
And stretched the worn, thin limbs, and kissed the brow ;
And wrapt her in her pure and snowy robe,
And on a dark, cold day, we bore that form
To where the loved of many kindred sleep !
· We laid it there, and o'er it dropped a tear ;
" Dust unto kindred dust," and all was o'er !

THE PEASANT POET'S DESPAIR.

E still, O my desolate heart ;
  Crush back the wild sobs that would rise ;
 Reseal the hot fountain of tears,
  That gushes in streams to my eyes !

Forget that thou ever hast dreamed
 Of wrapping with glory thy name,
Of climbing the mountain sublime,
 Where stands the bright temple of Fame ;

Of winning a deathless renown,
 Of standing among the vast throng,
Whose brows are with amaranths wreathed,
 The glorified children of song !

What art thou, that thou should'st aspire
   To mix with the noble and pure ?
To rise from the scum and the mire,
   Where wallow the nameless obscure.

What art thou ?—a portionless clown,
   A fungus exhumed from the soil,
A graft of that plebeian throng,
   Whose portion is sorrow and toil.

Be still, O my heart, and forget
   The shrine of thy passionate love ;
Forget that sweet being whose thoughts
   Are pure as the spirits above !

Forget that calm, beautiful face,
   Lit up with such glorious eyes,
Forget that thou ever hast hoped
   To win, and to wear such a prize.

A scion of honour and wealth,
   Beyond thee in virtue and worth,
As far from thy reach as the stars,
   That smile on the slumbering earth !

Such lofty ambitions and hopes
   Are but for the favoured of Fate,
The wealthy, the learnèd, the wise,
   The beautiful, noble, and great.

Forget, O forget, if thou canst,
   Those wild aspirations and schemes,

That radiant being whose charms
Exalted thy loftiest dreams.

Go back to thy menial toil,
Crush out thy ambition and pride,
Float down with the passionate host
And sink in obscurity's tide !

Already insidious disease
Has tainted and baffled thy breath ;
Be resolute, silent, and calm,
Awaiting the coming of death !

TO MY MOTHER.

 HOW calm, how bright the dawning
Of my blissful childhood seems !
Where the first faint rays of memory
Penetrate the land of dreams.

Dim and shadowy scenes and faces
Pass like spectres o'er my mind,
Seize their misty robes and vanish,
Leaving scarce a trace behind ;

But, e'en as the venturous wanderer
In the pyramidal tomb,
Sees the light that marks the entrance
While around him all is gloom ;

So, amid the glooms and shadows
  Of my dawning life I trace
One serene and sunny presence;
  One unchanging form and face.

And through all those hours of weakness,
  Through my boyhood's hopes and fears,
Through the tempests, sorrows, trials,
  And the cares of later years;

Firm, alike, mid storm and sunshine,
  Through Affliction's feverish night,
Runs that presence o'er my pathway,
  An unbroken stream of light.

O! my fond and tender Mother,
  'Tis thine image, purest, best!
Utmost on my range of vision,
  First on memory's scroll impressed;

Constant sharer of my burden!
  Guardian of my transient day!
Like an angel ever pointing
  To the Life, the Truth, the Way!

Ah! I have not yet forgotten,
  All thy counsels and thy tears,
All thy warnings kindly spoken,
  All the bliss of vanished years.

And till round me falls the death-mist,
    Till the sun of life has set,
Never shall I cease to love thee,
    Never, never once forget.

———

GOOD NIGHT.

ROM the calm, burnished west,
    O'er the radiant world
    Growing silent and dim ;
O'er the dew-besprinkled flowers,
O'er the grass-mantled hills,.
And the valleys and meads,
Comes a murmurous breath ;
Mid the trees breathing slowly,
        " Good night !"

Through the mist burdened air
Come the forms of lost friends !
In the by-gone how dear !
Forms, so graceful and straight,
Forms, so shattered and bent ;
Faces laughing and bright,
Faces tender and sad,
As I saw them the last !
Now they grasp my thin hand—
Wave a smiling, or sighing—
        " Good night !"

Far away, far away ·
Is the maiden I love,
Lying wrapt in repose,
On a pillow of down
Rests the beautiful head ;
Loving angels watch o'er !
Now she smiles in her sleep,
And in dreams coyly whispers—
                    " Good night !"

O World, dim and sleeping !
O waifs from the bygone !
O loved one reposing !
Ye fade from my vision ;
A drowsiness steeps me ;
Dull Somnus enwraps me ;
I rest and 'tis peaceful—
My conscience is easy,
And my hope is beyond
In the skies ! fleeting shadows—
                    " Good night !"

THE POET'S GRAVE.

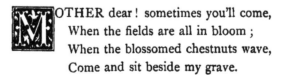OTHER dear ! sometimes you'll come,
When the fields are all in bloom ;
When the blossomed chestnuts wave,
Come and sit beside my grave.

THE POET'S GRAVE

For, alas ! I soon must lie,
Where the willows wave and sigh ;
Slumber 'neath the mouldy stone,
All unheeded, all unknown.

Come and strew my grave with flowers,
Culled from Nature's wildest bowers ;
Those I love, the modest ones,
Hiding 'mongst the moss and stones.

For, alas ! etc.

Come when waves of sorrow roll,
Fiercely o'er your shrinking soul ;
And, if sainted spirits may,
I will soothe you while you pray.

For, alas ! etc.

Come when age has flecked your hair,
Seamed your brow with lines of care ;
Sit and muse upon the time,
When we'll meet in yonder clime.

For, alas ! etc.

You will not forget, I know,
Where my " mortal " sleeps below ;
Though the proud may pause and sneer,
You will hold it sacred, dear !

For, alas ! etc.

MINNIE, EDITH, AND LIZZIE.

UNNY-haired and bright-eyed maidens,
          Brimming o'er with fun and frolic,
          Gushing out with joyous laughter,
Singing, dancing 'mongst the flowers,
Ever radiant, ever happy.
All unconscious of the darkness,
Looming in the distant future,—
Ye are like a streamlet gushing
From the summit of a mountain,
Skipping over rocks and pebbles,
Dancing round in mazy eddies,
Laughing out in merry cascades,
Toying with the moss and flow'rets,
Frisking, sparkling in the sunshine,
Ever dancing, ever singing,
Ever gushing out with gladness,
Filling all around with music ;
All unconscious of the valley,
Where its waters, darker, deeper,
Roll with low and mournful cadence
Through the sedges and the shadows,
Onward to the boundless Ocean.

SONNET.

AY, can it be, that those bright phantasies :—
          The forms of beings, loved in days gone by,
          (Our noble ones long passed into the sky ;)

Those radiant visions, fair-eyed Fancy sees
When thought steals back in dreamy reveries,
  Who, when the soul would linger and despond,
  Breathe evermore that glorious thought, " beyond !"
Who, soft as moonlight falls on troubled seas,
Steal o'er the burden of our nightly dreams.
  And soothe and nerve us when we need it most,
And point from earthly cares to Calvary's streams,
  Say are they spirits of our loved and lost,
Lent for a time our angel-guards to be ?
For oh ! to deem them such is sweet to me.

SUNRISE.

SLOW creeps the light athwart the concave still,
  Steals a low whisper on the breathless calm,
    Bringing the scent of opening flowers, a balm ;
Breaks o'er the earth a grand, a rapturous thrill,
The chant of waters, and the song-bird's trill ;
  The clouds fold up their curtains, snowy white ;
  The sleeping stars fade noiselessly from sight.
Bright Phœbus mounts above the crimson hill ;
The sheeted mists like baffled hosts retire,
  Wan Zephyr comes to wanton with the flowers,
The stream meanders on, a string of fire,
  And light and music fill earth's sylvan bowers !
Bright dewdrops shine and tremble everywhere :
O Sceptic, look and blush, for God is there !

MAN O' MOW.

REMINISCENCES.   INSCRIBED TO G. H.

ET me ship my oars a little—
 Drifting idly down the stream,
From the twilight towards the sunlight—
 While I live again that dream.

On the cragged sun-tinted summit,
 Of a mountain pile I stand,
Hugely grand and wildly lovely,
 Visions rise on every hand.
Calms of sky are blue about me,
 Windy currents on me beat ;
Broken fissures dark with thicket,
 Cliffs and gaps are at my feet—
To the Northward sweeps the mountain,
 Turret-spurred and larch-embrowed—
Heaving, swelling, crouching, curving,
 To the awful headland " cloud"
Which o'erlooks a widening plain-land,
 Flanked with rugged outs and ins,
Whence the damps arise that, floating,
 Mist the foreheads of the Mins.

To the South a dusky turret
 From the highest apex climbs,
Like a fragment of some giant
 Bulwark of the feudal times ;
 Thence the mountain breaks and straggles

THE SUMMER HOUSE, MOW COP

"TO THE SOUTH A DUSKY TURRET,
FROM THE HIGHEST APEX CLIMBS." —*Page. 182*

Roughly to the vale afar,
In a score of ragged plateaus,
  Girt with gleaming shale and spar.
And among the knolls and hollows,
  Villas, blocks, and chimneys rise ;
All astir with toiling livers,
  All a-pant with enterprise.

Eastward, where adoring Eos
  Wakens Gœa's Memnon lyre,
Rise the many-shaped and broken
  Torrent-hills of Staffordshire ;
Crowding upward like the billows
  On a tempest tortured sea :
'Mongst whose scalloped crests and curvings
  Throbs a monster Industry.

To the West a vast campagna,
  Where a bay might once have been
Suns its wide, recumbent substance,
  Liveried o'er with gold and green ;
Forest-braided, with a prolix
  Growth of huge umbrageous trees,
Shrinking 'neath a tickling wind-sprite,
  Like the laughter of the seas.
Sudden gleams of rural mansions,
  Sloping roofs, and glinting walls,
Many-gabled, many-windowed,
  Pinnacled, patrician halls,
Where the beeches crowd the thickest

On the sward ; and here and there
   Taper spire, and browning belfry
     Climbing, clasp the upper air ;
Far-seen stacks of grimy chimneys,
     Rolls of smoke, and jets of steam
Crowd upon my sweeping vision,
     Stud the current of my dream.
And afar, where, mid the ether,
     Grows a white translucid mist,
Where the scene is distance-softened,
     Summer-shot, and silver-kissed,
Glamour-wrapt, as wraiths of wonder
     Hover round old fairy tales,
In a wild serrated sky-line,
     Rise the frontier rocks of Wales ;
And around them vaguely blended,
     Vapoury hues are grouped and piled ;
And above them, cloud-wreath curtains,
     Protean-gleamed, are looped and coiled.
Radiant is the vasty vision,
     Sun-lit, or dawn, or noon ;
Thrilling ! 'neath the sleepless vigil
     Of a white September moon.

Other forms and other features
     Rise before me, pause, retire ;
Stately forms endued with manhood,
     Noble son and generous sire ;
Budding children, blooming matrons,
     Mother-faces calm with care ;

Forms with coils of woman-glory
  Circling foreheads, passing fair !
And the thrill of music haunts me
  Like the thoughts of master-minds,
And a tender voice a-singing
  Sweet and low as autumn winds.
Ah ! But not the gorgeous landscape
  'Neath the still cerulean sky ;
Not the shapes of grace and beauty,
  Though a sweetness and a joy ;
Not the music, not the singing,
  Revelations though they be,
Strike the deepest chords within me,
  On the harp of memory :
But the strings that throb the sweetest,
  And the bonds that closest twine,
Are the hands that came to clasp me,
  Are the eyes that glowed in mine ;
Are the lips that bade me welcome ;
  Feet that came at sorrow's call ;
Are the hearts that rose to love me,
  Though a stranger to them all !

Oh ! 'tis sweet to feel the twinings
  Of a fond solicitude,
Stand amid the charmed circle
  Of a noble brotherhood !
And I tell you, ye who loved me,
  Tell you now and once for all—

Though the winds of sorrow wither,
　Fortune deal her bitterest gall,
Though deserted, scorned, forgotten,
　Evermore the memory
Of your kindness—never fading—
　Will come back to gladden me.

Heaven bless you ! God, I thank thee
　That, although of much bereft,
Much—so much—of beauty, blessing,
　Joy, and tenderness is left !

ICARUS; OR, THE SINGER'S TALE.

"TO-DAY, our obituary readers will find
    A name—Thomas String—not unknown to his
        kind,
And 'twill be remembered, we doubt not, by those
Who've read us through twenty long summers and snows,
    That some of his rude, plaintive snatches of rhyme
Appeared, years ago, in our " nook for the muse,"
    And excited no little surprise at the time.
As far as we know he was born in the west,
    Of poor, toiling folk, in a tenement mean,
Whose shelter he left in a mood of unrest,
    Whilst still very young, for the world he'd not seen.
He wandered afar in most pitiful plight,
    And earned a scant living in various ways ;
Won food for the raw, hungry stomach by light,
Sought food for the soul from his books in the night,
    Gained knowledge of life in its stubbornest phase.
He published, it may be a decade ago,
    A volume of scraps with indifferent success,

Which brought him the semblance of fame—but a show—
Which faded, and left him more bitter and low,
   Proportioned to the height of his sudden access.
Not much of his subsequent path can we trace ;
   But few in the districts he haunted have known him ;
He passed like a cloud-shadow o'er the earth's face ;
   He had not a friend, at least none that would own him.
A character changeful, erratic as wind,
And strangely anomalous e'en for his kind,
   Wild, sensitive, bitter, exulting and grieving.
We think that no person of taste is so blind,
   As to read his rough scraps without talent perceiving.
A lover of Nature, akin to her moods ;
A power-spirit chained to a spirit that broods ;
A wide scope of vision, a child-like simplicity,
E'en such was the man that among us has passed,
   So thoroughly human, unnoticed for years ;
Gone home to his grave ; and the proud world that cast
   But hardly a crust to him, reapeth no tears.
Much genius he had, which we deem might have shone—
   Chaste powers, which we feel might have raised him to
      fame—
Had fate been propitious ; had fortune but thrown
   One ray of her star in the scale of his claim."

(From the " LYNX, *" a month afterwards.)*

" We are glad to inform our subscribers to-day
That Sir Hodge Poyson, Baronet, writes us to say

That seeing our notice, a short time ago,
Of the life of poor String, and his troubles and knell,
Deeply pained and amazed, he determined to go,
To the scene of the conflict, to earth out and know
The deep yearnings and sorrows, and all that befell
The true 'Bard of the Sad,' and his merits as well,
The gentleman laudably strives to pourtray
The strange scenes that he witnessed, and goes on to say,
'In the hole where he crept with his pain and his pride,
Mournful song-scraps were littered on every side ;
I read the damp slips till my eyes were tear-blind.
'Neath the couch where he wrestled with hunger, and died,
In a dirty, damp litter, of mouldering straw,
Stood a rude alder box, which, when opened, supplied
Such proofs of a vastly superior mind,
As filled me with anguish, and wonder and awe.
And sitting up there, in the fast fading glow,
I thought that there was but one act we might do
For the man who has lived for us, toiled for us, wept for us,
Bourne our contumely, caught for us, kept for us,
Fondly embalming their voices and themes,
Star-dawnings of beauty, emotions, and dreams ;
Frost-waifs, that i' th' living eluded and slipped ;
Entwinings, that Time in his transit had stripped from us.
For the man whose heart broke in the effort of giving—
Yet, spurned like a dog from the land of the living,
Too late for our pity—one justice alone
On the long-trampled list still remained ; and that one
Is to lustre his sky in the set of his sun,
Is to rescue his works from the terrible jaw

Of impatient Decay, and Oblivion's maw.
Therefore, seeing my rôle, I determined to bring
   Out the works (in two vols.), with a portrait complete ;
With an essay prefixed, and a life of poor " String,"
   And can promise my readers a marvellous treat.'

We doubt not subscriptions will speedily flow
   (See advertisement elsewhere) from those who admire
The conflicts of genius, have pity for woe,
   Or tremble and throb with the beat of the lyre.
When ready the vols. will be duly announced,
And a suitable critique, in passing, pronounced.
We scarcely need say that no pains will be spared
To render them ample, success to secure.
The surplus, if any, will go to procure
A suitable mark for the grave of the bard."

(THE SINGER'S TALE.)

Bless thee, my harp, thou wert true to me ever :
   Soft while I weep o'er thee, kiss thee, and waken
All the sad, sweet things that murmur and quiver !
   True to me still, though of all else forsaken !
No more I strike for the far generations,
   Lost to the hope of fame, glory, or pelf;
And the wild songs that I sang for the nations
   Now in my sadness I wail to myself.
Still are ye dear, O my only-begotten,
   Born in the travail and pulse of my heart,
   Sown in my soul, of my being a part.
Ah ! but 'tis sad, to be quite, *quite* forgotten,

Sad unto one who has wrestled and striven,
  Lived in the life of the world as I have ;
Sad unto one who has gotten and given
  To the cold world the new voices I gave.
Ah ! I am tired of the ebbing and flowing,
     The coming and going,
     The seeking and seeing,
The trouble of effort, the fever of being.
And what is the wonder ? I'm utterly beat.
     Soon 'twill be over—
     Oblivion will cover—
Rest cometh after the toil and the heat.

(Women Loquentur.)

Soft—let us raise him, nor yield to the shrinking;
  Ah ! it is sad to have never a dear one ;
Sad to depart in the night to my thinking,
  Up in a garret, with nobody near one !
Have we no feelings as women and mothers ?
Arn't we, from Adam, all sisters and brothers ?
Have we not, all of us, weans of our own ?
  True, they have each a true friend and a home, too ;
We know they ARE cared for—have been in the gone—
  But know not, alas ! as yet, what they may come to ;
Let us be kind, then ; they are where he's gone to—
Do as we'd wish our own weans to be done to !
Stay, what is this 'neath his hand on his breast ?
How stiff the long fingers ! 'Tis rumpled and creased !

Long lines all awry, blotted, jumbled, and stark !
Poor fellow ! ay, true, it was done in the dark.
" Ah, me, for a mother's fond hand for a little—
        That tender retriever !
Oh, love for the soothing of woman to quiet
        This burning and fever.
Ah, dying is bitter in darkness and hunger,
        When lonely I wish ;
I dreamed not in days that have summered and fallen
        Of coming to this !
But patience, take courage, my spirit, trust calmly,
        Be firm in assurance :
Learn bravely this last and most difficult lesson
        Of lofty endurance.
The sin shadows shift and the mist films are breaking,
        The vision grows clearer ;
New gleams of the beautiful come, and for ever
        The wonder draws nearer !
I hate not the world, have no wound nor one memory
        Of wrong that I cherish ;
I censure no longer ; grown wiser, the race that
        Have left me to perish
I pity them even, and grieve for the shackles
        That earthward have bound them,
While all the wide ocean of Truth throbs in beauty
        Undreamed of around them.
I grudge not the labour, the sweat, and excitement,
        Since all that I knew
And felt in my heart of the truthful, and trembled,
        I find to be true ;

Since all the fierce throes of my being, the yearning,
    The passion that fed me,
The impulse of beauty, the instincts I followed
    Have never misled me,
Since all the misgivings that clogged me, the doubts of
    The truth of my mission,
The tauntings and lashings, the ghoul eye of darkness,
    Have fled like a vision !
And all the great hem'sphere I dreamed of and fought for
    With restless commotion,
From which came but glimpses, as weeds to Columbus,
    Along the drear ocean ;
And all the grand system of wisdom, the workings,
    Inweaving agreeing,
The goal of my yearnings I groped for in blindness
    Grow clear to my seeing.
The soul cannot rise from the base to the noble
    By pausing and thinking,
Nor grow to the triumph, and clasp the great mystery
    By suddenly drinking
One draught of the pure.   It must grow from a point, and
    With constant endeavour,
Rise upwards in circles expanding and growing
    To Godward for ever.
Ah, well ! for my soul, if't has strung every chord of
    The harp that was given ;
Ah, well ! if each string will respond to my touch mid
    The quiring of heaven.
Still shift the dim shadows, and the mist films are breaking,
    The vision grows clearer ;

New gleams of the beautiful come, and for ever
    The wonder draws nearer."
 Others there are that are passing my reading,
   Blotted, disfigured, and tangled among ;
 Something there seems of a sadness—a pleading—
   Something of triumph, of rapture, of song.
 Hum ! It is strange that he should sing at such time
   Something we feel to be tender and grand ;
   Something we read but may not understand:
 Ay ; and how well it comes in with the rhyme !
" Daft" though they called him, who stooped to despite,
   Still he had something we none of us thought of ;
   Something beyond us, unreached and undreamed of,
 Though he was wanting in thews for the toil.
   Yet he was not of the vagabond race,
   Not of the lazy who sink in disgrace.
   Something that held him aloft from the base
Shone in the depths of his far-looking eyes.
Yes, and he ever had kind words to speak,
   Ever for children a pat and a smile ;
Ever for woman, the suffering, the weak,
   Something of tenderness, nothing of guile.
Some of his sayings sound wondrous wise,
Some of his singings brought tears to my eyes ;
So let us wipe the white ooze from his lips,
Stretch his long arms by the side of his hips ;
Press down the lids o'er the sorrowful eyes,
Staring so vacantly up at the skies,
Through the grim lustre the grey twilight leads him,
Find him a man who will strip him and clean him,

Lay him out decently here where he lies ;
No one will lose by 't, who, pitying, befriends him,
  Make him, and swaddle him up in a shroud,
Get him a suit, if our pittance affords,—
Nothing more costly—a box of deal boards.
  That'll be all we can do for him now,
Save that we find him a long home somewhere,
Should there be e'er a wee corner to spare,
  Bring him and hide him away from the crowd,
Drop him a tear while the rude heap is piled,
Mourn him a little—he's somebody's child !

YEARNINGS.

Excellent Father! benignant Sire !
Calm on Thy throne, high, solemn, and eterne,
What myriads of Thy marvellous works around Thee burn.
My soul, uplifted with a great desire,
Would rise to Thee, be filled, and then expire.
O, the rapt worships trembling on my tongue !
O, the vast yearnings quivering into song !
When shall I lose this sense of prisoned feet ?
When shall I rise to Thee and grow complete ?

O Font of Wisdom ! centre, source, and spring,
Of Being vast ! Thou Good of everything !
Thy hand hath strung with luminous films the night.
Our day—the night of Thee, who art the Light of light,
Hath ordered all things, great and small to be
A gradual ladder leading up to Thee.

The god-like soul—as water, prisoned deep
From sources high, doth heave and pant to leap
To its own level—wrestles with its chain,
Its cell, ribbed clay, until the light it gain—
The level of its own divinity attain.

My life drags o'er me in a great distress ;
Earth's brutal current-tides around me press ;
The rage of pride—the froth of littleness—
Hate swells and deepens—hope grows less and less—
Vice spreads her gay enchantments to my view—
Hot passion piles my veins with fiery dew—
Fate conjures dawnings deep that threat to gulph—
Hardships grow monstrous—doth press me hard ;
My soul cries out in pain, but none regard.

But ever and anon my thought escapes,
Spurns the cold shackles that would prison it,
Leaps to the light, moves o'er the wondrous shapes
Wherein the marvel of Thy name is writ,
And ever as their music dawns on me,
My spirit trembling gropeth after thee.
And if I from this yearning feel of wings,
Deem Thou hast given the eagle's majesty,
And so essay to rise and soar and sing—as sing
The morning larks : O not presumptuously,
I am, though frail, thy own begotten : steady me.

Sustain me through the first malignant rush
Of shrivelled natures, scornful, mad to crush ;
While from me fades the din of earthly strife,
And the new meanings gather o'er my life ;
While o'er the widening circles calm I move,
With brow adoring lifted to Thy love.
Bear me till all created things—earth, air, and seas,
Their workings, powers, and properties
Configured, pass before me ; till all images,
The parts revealing, links all agencies,
Together fitting, make one awful whole—
A royal garment, godhead for my soul.

Hold thou my right hand, while around me break
The illuminating radiance all objects take
That unto thee approach ; while clouds that scowled
Above me erst, pass 'neath me golden-cowled—
Give me to touch with trembling finger-tips
The minor chords of thy stupendous lyre ;
Flow in my soul their harmony and fire,
So all things pass to music on my lips ;
Hold me, till the warm skirting hazes, fold
The charméd in their glow of roseate gold ;
Till clothed in robes of Truth and Chastity,
My being wholly moves to melody ;
Till from my soul the earth-shade softly goes.
The damp weight drops, sweet dawns the mystery ;
The golden portals of the stars unclose,
And my whole being grows absorbed in thee.

ENAMOURED.

When lost in dreams of twilight's power,
   The windings of a vale I trace ;
I caught her in a hazy bower,
   With birch and willow interlaced.
Around her feet the primrose shone ;
   The languorous boughs hung low with dews,
She saw me not, but plaited on
   A wilding wreath of many hues.

Her robes were looped with garlands fair;
   Her shaded eyes were full of dreams ;
Around her fell a glow of hair
   That stirred like weeds in beds of streams.
Her hand was rosy, fresh, and pure ;
   Her heart lay on her lips in smiles ;
Yet fire and yearning trembled sure
   Beneath the bosom heaving whiles.

And bluebells, violets, snowdrops white,
   And wild rose, vetch, and lily chaste,
And golden thyme, and daisies bright,
   With laurel twined, her forehead graced ;
Her sandals green of woven moss,
   With strings of berries red were tied ;
O, what a strange bright thing she was—
   Too wildly fair for mortal bride.

Amazed, I paused ; then, smitten, dared
   One hasty step : she fled in fright !

I followed; 'passioned, and despaired
    Beneath the day, beneath the night.
A grand new radiance took the skies;
    A fairer glory wrapt the earth;
I saw all things with other eyes,
    And wakened to a wider birth.

I loved the hills she touched with light;
    The glowing flowers that thronged her wake;
The stream she strung to wild delight,
    I loved all Nature for her sake!
She dropped me here and there a flower,
    But would not list my constant prayer;
She coyly fled o'er field and moor;
    I followed—followed everywhere.

A SONG SCRAP.—A FRAGMENT.

My soul, like the soul of a desolate woman
    In barrenness pining,
Burned aye with the fever and passion of grasping,
    Conceiving, divining.
Full of hope I pursued the dream-visions so fair,
    Till the moment of grasping;
Then to find them but clay of the common world, sank back
    Despairing and gasping.
I felt all the fever, the heat, and the stir of
    The moulding and sowing,
But came seeking fruit from my toil ere
    My bud had done blowing.

I hope to lift high, like a beacon, a light
    O'er humanity's sea ;
To remain while the tide-waves of being rose, sank, and
        subsided,
    And 'twas not to be.
I dreamed that my voice down the chords of the ages
    Should sweep some high theme ;
I dreamed I would shine like a star fixed in heaven,
    And 'twas but a dream.
And what if I grasped not the prize; if my soul grew
        enlarged,
    My vision more wide,
And my being more noble than theirs who disowned me,
    And stung me with pride?

(WINTER.)

    Fierce blows the boreal wind, and the breath
Of crazy old Winter comes, harsh and keen.
Fled are wool-laden clouds o'er the distant horizon
Which sleeps in its vapoury caul, like a lazy old Friar.
Old Phœbus has drawn on his night-cap, and gone to his
    pillow,
And over our heads in the leaden-hued watery welkin,
The laughter-eyed stars are hiding and coyly out—peeping,
And all things are hushed, and the world in its quiet
Turns round to the slumberous night with its myriad toilers.
   'Tis a beautiful scene for the eye of a winter sick prisoner.
The fierce winds have folded their wings and are sleeping ;
The thrush and the starling are piping away in the bushes,

And aye and anon the red robin joins softly the chorus.
The fowls are departing to roost, and the children
Are joyously lending their laugh to the chant of the songsters.
Away on the patriarch mountains the sunset is burning,
And huge floating cloudlets, begloried with crimson,
Move silently o'er with a sleepy and peace-breathing motion.
It is March, and the battle-god rides in his chariot of
    tempest.
Keen Euros comes over the hills with his white banner
    waving,
And over the landscape the sleet and the snow flakes are
    scattered,
And under the hedges, and out of the sight of meek Phœbus,
The snow lies in long broken patches of glittering whiteness,
And Winter, stretched out on his death-bed, revives for a
    moment,
And wrestles with virgin-eyed Spring in a deathly encounter,
While newly-roused Nature looks on with a sleepy vication.
How can I describe thee, thou demon-eyed terrible Winter—
A terrible wind, coming furiously down from the mountains.
A frost-knit and snow-whitened earth, sad and shivering ;
An ice-bound and icicle clogged murmur of brooklets and
    rivers,
A host of sad songsters, half starved, mid the brakes and
    the hedges ;
An army of sparrows and tits 'neath the eaves and the gables.
No sound but the turbulent roar of the wind meet the
    tree-tops.
    Ah me ! I am sickly and lonely, a weary-souled prisoner.

———

Give me, dear Hannah, a sister's love only ;
Lavish on others thy maiden regard ;
Pass to the death on thy virgin path lonely,
Sooner than love the wild soul of the Bard.
Bard !" said I ! "rather the essence of moods,
Trembling, wrestling, loving, and dreaming,
Proving the real while hoping the seeming,
Passionate, pitiful, weeping, and burning,
Grasping and throbbing, and longing and yearning,
Suffering the bitter world's terrible learning,
Climbing huge mountains in hope of reward,
Finding, instead, the dread hate that broods.
Pardon me, girl, for forgetting one moment
All it has taken so long years to learn me,
If I but dreamed of the poet's endowment,
Crowned with a love and a life such as thine.
Let it pass ; love me not, hate not nor spurn me;
Brief was the dreaming, and quickly the waking
Brought back the terrible phantom of aching.
Ah ! 'twere a crime, could I win thee, to linger !
Sad is the lot of the seer and singer !
Sad, for the poet, if true to his mission,
Over rough pathways, thro' oceans of brine,
     Draggeth no tender feet,
     Goadeth no bosom's beat,
     Wringeth no woman's shrine
     In the transition.
Calm ! with the great and noble upsoaring
All the grand impulse and triumph revealing,
Shadow-hung depths of the fallen exploring,

All the temptations, and tryings unsealing,
All that needs human-eyed pity unveiling,
Aiding the weak when oppressed by the strong,
Backing the right when beleaguered with wrong,
Lifting a champion voice for the low,
Scaling the dim heights of passion and madness,
Groping the dark depths of suffering and sadness,
Running the hard race of panting endeavour,
Echoing each heart throb and pulses sob quiver,
Pointing at tyranny's stern prophet finger,
Teaching the pure, the heroic, forgiving ;
All the wild pathos of striving and living ;
Waking each chord on the vast scale of feeling,
Telling each tone that the people may know
All the world's beauty and piteousness,
All that they feel but can never express.
Such is the lot of the poet—the singer.
Yet would I covet to be to thee, dearest,
Fondest and first, as a friend and a brother,
Twine round thy being the closest and nearest,
Live in the pulse of thy life till that other
Wakes up that highest chord seraph inspired,
Then I would pray in tears, banish me never,
Let me be all that I have been to thee ever ;
And when aweary and beaten, and tired,
On to the verge of insanity driven,
Wounded and broken, embittered and riven,
Sick of the winter world's weakness and vanity,
Fainting I came for a kind word and smile—
Came for the joy of thy healing awhile—

If I but came, as a brother should, purely,
Asking but tenderness—HE would not surely
Drive me away from thy sheltering haven.
Surely not ; else 'twere not common humanity.

     *   *   *   *   *   *

Why did they come in their trappings unto me,
Crowding the wake of my fancied success,
Vaunting the many grand turns they would do me,
Stooping to flatter, and pat and caress ;
Just for one moment betrayed to surprise,
Waked from the torpor of cold apathy,
From the complaisance of self-satisfaction,
Round to the semblance of living and acting.
     Wild curiosity,
Greedily spurring them onward to see
All the surroundings, and bearings, and size
Of the great mushroom-spring,
     Latest monstrosity.
Why did they dam the rude surge of my life,
Gather the volume and deepen the force,
Only to loose it, to laugh at its strife,
List to its murmurings troubled and hoarse :
Why did they ? but for their pleasure and mirth.
Lift me on high but to dash me to earth !
Why did they shine on my twilight estate,
Wrapping me round with a Midsummer fold,
Only to teach me how bitter the cold ?
Better have left me alone to my fate.

     *   *   *   *   *

Impulse is dying; the mirage is parting,
Energy flaggeth, and life glimmers low;
Sick of the struggle, aweary and smarting,
Spurned of the world, and deserted, I go.

———

Awkward-shaped, country-shod, sensitive, shy,
Open-faced, lustrous-eyed, heavily-browed,
Almost unnoticed, a many-haired boy,
Wanders the country o'er, thoughtful and bowed,
Slipping away from the clamour and noise,
Spurning the countryman's toils and his joys,
Haunting the hollows, where alders and ashes
Bend over rivulets sparkled with eyes,
Softened with drooping, long pale willow lashes,
Where a wind passeth 'mid shadows and sighs,
Haunting, to watch the light change o'er the skies;
Wandering in lonely unforbidden ways,
Down dim lanes, o'er moorlands, thro' dimbles and dells,
Peering at all things with questioning gaze,
Lost in the mist of melodious lays
Of ouzle and linnet, and robin and thrush,
The quiverings of treetops; the tingling swell
Of Argent brook warblings; the musical droppings
O'er the water-kissed lippings,
Round lichen-trimmed basins of many a cascade,
The Summer morn's throb, and the twilight's grand hush,
The chantings that ran
In wind, wanton wan-lights, 'neath the thick shade

Of forests huge-pillared ; the still murmur made
By knitted-winged insects that dance in the sun,
Bending so reverently over the flowers,
Even to cull one—so tenderly ! sighing,
Treading so lightly for fear of destroying ;
Watching, a-dream, peckled windows for hours ;
By pebble-marged windings of silver frill dimplings,
Up gorges where waters dash storming and stuttering,
Where winds from the mountains rock mourning and
          muttering,
Prone 'mid the grass while in marvel and might,
Through the cloud temple dome, dusky the night,
Sweepeth on misty wing dripping with dew,
Sparkled with star-streams glimmering through,
While the far westward is shorn of its gold,
And up the east cometh in lustrous fold
Silver-cupped Cynthia, saintly and solemn,
And wait-shadows cluster round buttress and column,
And riseth the weirdness on earth's sleeping face,
And the flames seek the nymphs and the wood satyrs chase;
Standing entranced on the brow of a hill,
Steeped in the sunset and panting, but still
Tears on the lashes, and all things forgot,
Hands clasped before him, and knowing it not.
Climbing through fog curtains, cold summits, where
Eos first shakes the gold-flakes from her hair ;
Pausing till webbed in the tissue of braid
Helios weaves over mountain and glade.
Always some treasure, new found, in his hand—
May be a flower, shell, or crystal of sand,

Things that the world spurned as refuse, were worth
Far more to him than jewels of earth.

———

Acquaint with all beauty, or lofty or low,
Thirsting for freedom and panting to know,
Marvelling at all that is under the sun,
Tired with the deeds that the mighty have done,
Or shadowed in books :—Now, the hero who fears
Neither foeman nor friend ; now the patriot pure ;
Now the noble who rights ; now the wronged who endure ;
Now the lover, the poet, the maiden in tears ;
By all impulses swayed ; all impressions their light,
Or their shade on him fixed, to all customs his mind
Stirred responsive and various as harp to the wind.
Now stirred with a sudden convulsive delight,
Now languidly lying, now revelling wild ;
Now sad as a man ; now gay as a child ;
Most tender to all things, and feeling, but shy,
Deep-pained o'er the mangling of even a fly.
Most gentle and docile where love holds the reins,
But stubborn and fierce 'gainst the pride that o'er weens ;
Touching by accident tremulous keys
That vibrate i'th' distance, and die by degrees,
Waking strange dawnings of music, that cause
Sudden dream vacancies, tremour and pause.
Finding stray clues into mazes of thought,
That gleam on the spirit and vanish uncaught,
Now dropped in despair, and now taken again,

While the heart goads the blood to the worrying train ;
Pressing hot, passionate lips to the dews ;
Sending bright eyes after mingling of hues,
Like a bird in the wind, full of awe in the storm,
When the thunder-tongues bellow round lightnings warm.
The song of the lark up the misty March air,
A shimmering of leaves in a sunshiny shower ;
A quiver of stars in a water-world deep ;
A red streak of cloud line ; a flash from the bare
Solemn wails of the night, or a wind sob, had power,
To arouse in him yearnings that prompted to weep
Thoughts vague, dim, and awful as night wheeling birds ;
Troubled gulfs far too deep for the plummet of words ;
  Feeling a strange intuition of tears,
The fire damps that heralded the gathering of years,
A consciousness deep of the conquering despair,
E'en fancy the prospect drew never so fair.

FRAGMENTS.

Probably intended for Icarus.

Rolls of light in wide gradations,
  Melting upwards rim the sky,
Streams of glory up them sweeping,
  Reach the apex, melt and die.
Golden hands about the sunset
  Lightly touch a thousand strings ;
Sweeps their music through their twilight,

Like the mellow fall of wings ;
Splendour upon splendour falling
  On the mist emerald woods,
Splendour upon splendour sinking
  In the deeps of beauty floods ;
Dewy whisperings, westward stealing,
  From the flossy wraith of mist ;
Crystal shoals of brilliant dawnings
  From the purple amethyst.
Dion shakes a sea of tresses
  O'er Endymion mountain sweeps ;
Hesperus a wrapt Narcissus,
  Woos his image in the deeps.
Splendour flooding copious over
  Heaving clumps of foliage ;
Swimming high the crystal chalice
  Of the dreamy saxifrage ;
Wrapping fulgent uplands girdled,
  With a crystal water plinth ;
Winding hedgerows, blossomed, bending—
  Flossy banked with hyacinth.
O'er mazy masts of blossoms
  Where the myriad toilers hum ;
Honied pyramids of chestnuts,
  Nectar snows of thorn and plum.

* * * * * *

Twilight spreads her wide pavilion ;
  Wraps us in her syren realm ;
Pipes the blackbird in the thicket,

Trills the throstle in the elm.
Softly slide along the portal
　　To the caverned calm of night,
Hung with blue and silken auros
　　Lit with radiant chrysolite.

*　　*　　*　　*　　*　　*

Fades the western solemn glorid.
　　'Neath the red'ning casque of Mars ;
Falls the night all palpitating
　　With the wonder of its stars.
All the great warm under-breathings
　　Of the drowsy earth upsoars
To the cooler drifts, and scattering,
　　Drops again in diamond showers.
And the great pulse of existence
　　Beateth ever on the scene ;
Though the heavens in panting splendours,
　　Reeling out stars and shreds of flame ;
Though the air in currents eddying,
　　And in clouds that brush the hill;
Though the human harp is silent
　　And the earth lies sleeping still.

*　　*　　*　　*　　*　　*

Shreds of wild witch clouds upbreaking
　　Steep amid the rosy wine ;
Elfin locks and draperies sailing
　　Through the orient hyaline.

Earth in drowsy radiation
  On the void her cadence pours,
Move the frequent airs about her,
  Soft distilling diamond showers.

———

" FRAGMENTS."

(From Geo. Heath's Diary, January and February, 1869.
  Probably intended for Icarus.)

And the nereid willow, coyly
  Dips her tresses in the stream,
While the silken sensuous waters
  Trembles downward in a dream.
Did I dream that Summer twilight
  Was a crisis to my fate,
That the currents thence diverging
  Led to issues strange and great,
There are moments when we tremble
  When we pause amid the strife ;
When we feel our acts will influence
  All the tenour of our life.
There are sudden branching currents
  In our being's headlong force,
Which, if entered, bear us softly
  To a milder, calmer course ;
To the realms where life is fullest,
  Where our hope with fruitage teems ;

Where our life sweeps grandly onward
   'Neath the Summer of our dreams—
Which, if missed, are lost for ever,
   Chancing never more, alack !
Never agony—entreaty,
   Prayer, or tear, can bring them back.
Hearts may break that know too late ;
   One false step may be as fatal
As the deadly hand of fate,
   And the " might have been," add poison
To the sting for ever lost !
   O ye reft of love—of manhood,
O ye blinded, vexed and tossed.

     *   *   *   *   *

Mid the air, the twittering swallows
   Touch each other as they pass,
And a million things are kissing
   As they sing amid the grass.
And the graceful poplar, bending,
   Strokes the birches lady hair ;
Lean the glowing flowers together ;
   There is moving everywhere.

     *   *   *   *   *

Somewhere in the dusky eastern,
   Solemn, silent light'nings fly ;
And the misty corruscations
   Tremulous leap from sky to sky.

Earth is still and watchful, listening
   For the space lost thunder-tongue ;
And the star-spots dim and brighten
   As the quivers flush along.
" While the silken sensuous waters
   Trinkles downward in a dream,"
Winding into tingle tangles,
   Gliding lithely in and out ;
Over shoals of polished boulders,
   Under roots among the trouts ;
Shivering into silver-listenings,
   Washing groups of islets green ;
Filping flowers that flank its margins,
   Making lordly sedges seen.
Simpering over gravel hurries,
   Skimming into golden braids ;
Springing over whirls and rapids,
   Spurring hills and making raids ;
While the flossy bed-weed, streaming,
   Closes now, and now expands,
Like the tresses of a Neriad,
   Hidden just a'neath the sand,
Hangs the sun's last ray upon it,
   And the varying shadow shifts,
While the eternal music rises
   And the passion water drifts.

       *   *   *   *   *

Human life's a harp majestic,
   And the chords diversely strong,

P

Various tensioned chords—we bicker
   Loosely as we.drift along.
Some—the sinew-proud—rush headlong ;
   Harshly twang each chord in course,
Pausing not to 'list the discord,
   Meeting nought of tone or force.
Some—the frailer, finer natures,
   Thrill them with a trembling hand ;
Fathom all their depths of meaning—
   All 'tis pain to understand.
Should we miss one string by clinging
   Unto one we're drifting from,
Or by straining to the future
   For a chord we dream will come ?
Then we lose a charm, a colour ;
   Then we feel a want unknown,
And our lives grow compass narrow,
   Circumscribed in range and tone.
Happy he who, vision widened,
   Bravely strikes each chord in turn,
Gathers all the music essence,
   If it make him joy or mourn ;
Borrowing neither sheen nor shading
   From a future or a past,
Living each in turn completely,
   Knowing none in turn will last.
For no single gush of fortune,
   And no sudden stroke of ill,
Never circumstance, or sequence,
   Never sudden stand of will—

But the life built whole in littles,
　But the mighty aggregate,
Forms the basis of our being,
　Makes the grand result of fate.
Yet one string there is, whose music
　Wildest thrills the human breast,
Hath a fuller lingering cadence,
　Harmonises all the rest.
From its height a nobler meaning
　Down the vanished strings is cast ;
Moves the future, grandly radiant,
　In the memory when 'tis past.
Woe for him, who, vaunting prudence,
　Calculates—the coward pluck !—
Shifts the grand horizon further,
　Leaves the perfect chord unstruck.
Never shall his sordid nature
　All the ennobling raptures own ;
He shall find, to vex his future,
　But a feeble aftertone.

*　　*　　*　　*　　*

No ! there came no shade of all things
　That the waiting test years taught ;
Nothing of the sturdy knowledge
　That the after pleading brought.
Say my gems of truth and wisdom,
　Hidden deep in unwrought mines,
Unconceived how vast the struggles
　That accomplish young designs.

All untried the field of fury,
 Where, 'neath tempest gloom, or sun,
All the spoils of sage experience
 Are in deadly combat won.

  * * * * *

Bold I stood in perfect manhood,
 With a brow made grand by hope ;
All existence round me stretching
 Wider than my vision scope,—
Lay encalmed in all the splendour
 Of my spirit's light intense.
So the sun his orbit charges
 With his own pre-eminence.
Mingled with anticipations,
 Conquest glows in planned extremes,
With the fervour of excitement,
 And the after hues of dreams.

MISCELLANEOUS POEMS.

A BUNCH OF SNOWDROPS.

ENDER snowdrops, wee and white,
   Go to her whose beauty lies
On my being, like the light
   Of the stars on brows of skies.

When the moon hath not a streak,
   And the night all gloom would be,
But for those still gems that break
   Through the mirk on land and sea.

Go to her I love, and say
   " Fearful love is ever true ;
Say I cherish her to-day
   With a thought as pure as you."

And, as ye are hands of hope,
   · Stretching out to broken things,
Toiling up the winter slope,
   And the year's first blossoming ;

So is she the Iris-light
　　Stretching to me through the years ;
First for her, my soul in might
　　Woke and gave me love and tears.

And as ye, frail things, are soon
　　Riven of your modest bloom ;
Morn of Spring, and Summer's noon
　　Lustre o'er your living tomb.

So, if she should spurn my love,
　　Scorch my hope with cruel breath,
On and on the years will move,
　　Blooming o'er the living death.

YOUNG AMBITION.

'D scorn to swell the toady rout,
　　Or bow before the gilded elf ;
　　I laugh at Fate, and sing and shout,
　　　　" The man's the man he makes himself."
I strike my breast—its ring is sound ;
　I feel my wrists—they're shackle-free ;
I look above, before, around,
　And scoff the prate of Destiny.
I think my life—my nucleus lay,
　And toil around it patiently ;
The circle widens day by day ;
　The man's the man he wills to be !

No golden key, no magic door,
　No royal road for any man ;
All naked born, the rich, the poor,
　The autocrat, the plebeian.
I have no patience for the sect
　Who dream of crowns, and covet thrones,
Yet sit and murmur, and expect
　The world to lay them stepping-stones.
I love the man who bears his thews,
　Trusts his own strength, his path pursues,
And makes him what he wills to be.

Am I not strong and hardy-faced ?
　Hath he not given a harp to me,
A soul to love and feel ; and placed
　Within me my eternity ?
Have I not feet to climb the stair ?
　A mind to think, a brain to plan ?
Have I not hands to do and dare ?
　Shall I not stand distinct a man ?
O yes ! I'll live ; not drift, not dream ;
　Fate, circumstance, my steeds shall be :
I'll mould each moment to my schemes,
　Becoming that I fancy me.

I'll grasp the skirts of light, and link
　A mortal to a heavenly goal ;
Anoint my lips with truth, and drink
　The universe into my soul ;
I'll sow a stream of radiance there,

A moon-track on the wrestling seas ;
My songs shall bow the hearts of men,
    As tempest winds bow forest trees ;
I'll lift my voice and send it far
    Along thy shores, Eternity !
I'll bear my forehead—shine a star—
    The man's the man he wills to be.

SONG.—OCTOBER.

HEN the herds were picking the dead ash leaves,
            Under the trees,
    When winds were bringing a trouble of death
            On many seas,
                        She died, alas !

She in whose life I had lived and moved
        So long, so long !
Who had made all my days like the ravishing change
        Of a passionate song ;
                        She died, alas !

She, who was ever a delicate bud,
        Wee, weak, and frail ;
For whom I so anxiously watched and met
        Chill, damp, and gale ;
                        She died, alas !

She, who was blythe as a bird one day,
    The next without strength ;
Whom I dreamed, could she tide o'er a few more years,
    Might grow strong at length ;
            She died, alas !

She died, and the light of my life and hope,
    Went out, went out !
And my heart sobs now, as the shuddering leaves
    Drift dead about ;
            She died, alas !

———

NEW YEAR'S RESOLVES.

 WILL be useful and happy yet,
    Though my path hath been shaded long ;
Though, frail and dependent, misfortune hath
    damped
    The dawn of my life and song.
I will be patient, and strong, and brave,
    And true to my purpose set ;
My being shall gloriously rise over self—
    I will be earnest yet !

The rare woman-form that is all too dear,
    And the love that may never be mine,
And the fair home-ties I have dreamed of so,
    My soul shall be brave to resign.
The calmness will come in God's good time,

And the yearnings will cease to fret :
I'll sow all my tenderness wide in the world—
   I will be conqueror yet !

And those who have scorned me shall blush to scorn,
   The haughty shall cease to sneer ;
And those who have deemed me ambitious and proud
   Shall learn to esteem and revere.
The wounded shall seek me for sympathy,
   The erring, the hard-beset :
I'll live in all hearts 'mongst their treasured things—
   I will be cherished yet !

I'll gather life's sunbeams into my heart,
   And focus them round me free ;
And many a sad heart and weary eye
   Shall brighten to light on me.
Kind words shall cheer. loving deeds rejoice,
   And pity shall soften regret :
The friendless shall want for a friend no more—
   I will be useful yet !

I'll forge me links to enmesh my world
   In a boundless charity ;
I'll clothe all objects in robes of song
   And a wide-souled piety.
My life shall be empty and barren no more,
   Its ills shall be bravely met ;
The interests of all whom I love shall be mine—
   I will be noble yet !

I'll sow a flower when I may, and dull
  When I can the galling flints;
And future fathers, when counselling youth,
  Shall reverently point at my prints.
And women shall ease them with weeping and say,
  As they point at the greening sod,
"The man that lies there was as true a man
  As ever went up to God."

OVER A FEW WITHERED SNOWDROPS.

WHERE is the beautiful face
    Flushed with the wide, dark eyes?
  Where is the yearning face?
    Only the gloom-wind sighs;
And out of the door in the yard
  The sycamores moan and stir,
And the clouds mope onward, but none regard
  The wail in my heart for her.

Oh! where is the beautiful face
  Framed in its mass of hair?
Where is the haunting face?
  Hark! on the tremulous air
Comes the boom of a funeral bell
  Heavy as my despair—
'Tis well, I am answered, well, right well!
  Would I were sleeping there!

Where art thou, mine elect ?
  Oh ! but to hear thy voice,
To see thee once more, mine elect !
  Afar in thy paradise,
In the peace of the realms of calm,
  Dost dream of our troubled shore?
Oh, love ! my spirit hath lack of balm
  In thy absence, evermore.

I follow the shafts from the crest
  Of the hill, when the east grows warm ;
And now I am turned to the west,
  Where the day sinketh down into storm ;
And alike when the night is pearled
  I pour my complaint, oh, love !
My heart goeth out over all the world,
  To return like the weary dove.

Oh, when will it all be done?
  And when will the mourning cease?
Slow are thy wheels, O Sun,
  Fickle thy wing, O Peace !
Ah, woe ! that our dreams will fly
  Like feathers, when winds are rude,
That we shroud up our dead from the world's cold eye,
  And rot in our solitude !

LIGHT IN THE DARKNESS.

HEN the soul is o'ershadowed with gloom,
    With sorrow, and sadness, and care ;
When the future seems dark as the tomb,
    And the present a gulf of despair ;

When life seems a desolate blight,
    A burden we loathe every day ;
When hope swiftly wingeth its flight,
    And pleasure doth vanish away ;

When the soul broods in sorrow alone,
    And chides its unchangeable fate !
When the heart seems congealing to stone,
    'Neath misfortune's unbearable weight—

Perchance a sweet, innocent child
    Has pressed on your pale cheek a kiss,
And said, " How I love you !" and smiled
    With a look of ineffable bliss.

Or perchance an affectionate wife
    Has bid you hope on to the end ;
Or your hand has been grasped 'mid the strife,
    In the warm-hearted clasp of a friend.

When beautiful, eloquent eyes
    Look tenderly down on your own ;
When hearts with your own sympathise,
    And show you, you are not alone ;

What a beam of ineffable light,
    What a soul-thrilling, heart-cheering ray
Disperses the gloom of the night,
    And turns all your darkness to day.

How it gives you new courage and hope,
    And lightens your burden of care ;
Gives you strength with affliction to cope,
    And bids you no longer despair.

———

TO IDA (A SWISS LADY).

IDA, the sunny, the happy, the bright !
    Ida, the youthful, the happy, the free !
      Blythe as the sun birds that sport in the light,
        Follow the dance, joyous Summer, of thee !
Waif from the land of the gushing romance ;
  Sprite from the realm of the ardent blue skies,
Where the wild streams o'er the white boulders dance,
  Where the rude mountains to heaven arise.
Land of the picturesque lakelet and rill,
  Where the huge cliffs and ice-crystals gleam,
Where the weird glaciers stand snow-wreathed and still—
  Beautiful realm of the poet's first dream !
Child of a people whose banner still waves,
  Liberty's ensign by heroes unfurled—
Heroes too noble of soul to be slaves—
  Heroes whose deeds are the theme of the world !
Maiden, the beautiful, noble, and wise,

Beats the pure heart with a passionate glow ;
Deep are thy eyes as thy own native skies ;
  Pure is thy brow as thy own native snow,
Stately of bearing and lofty of brain ;
  Joy gushing out with each pulse-beat and breath ;
Health dancing on through each vessel and vein —
  Radiant life on the dim plains of death !
Fair as the earth when the sun was first given ;
  Grand as the night when the stars first arose ;
Richest of earth and the purest of heaven ;   ⸱
  Softest that darkles and brightest that glows.
Being as pure as the virgin-eyed Truth,
  Maiden whose days like a Summer breeze flows,
Dost thou e'er think, mid the rapture of youth,
  " Ah ! there are some that are weeping and low
Some on whom beauty smiled never at all ;
  Some to whom health is, alas ! but a name ;
Some to whom life is bitter as gall,
  Fickle in hopes, and uncertain in aim ;
Some who must mourn o'er youth's premature blight ;
  Some who must languish in sorrow and pain,
Yearning for daylight and panting for night,
  Seeking for rest and relief, but in vain ;
Some on whose lips never joy wrought a smile,
  Strangers to star-eyed laughter and mirth ;
Some who are fainting from anguish and toil,
  Gazing eye heavenward, weary of earth !"
Fairest of earthborn, how calm is thy day,
  ⸱ Glowing and cloudless thy sun-glory shines,
Flowers spring about thee and brighten thy way,

Hope evergreen round thy virgin heart twines.
Friends press around thee with greetings and smiles ;
 Hands clasp thy arm and full eyes on thee shine ;
Love at thy feet pours the wealth of his spoils ;
 Souls that are noble thine image enshrine.
Hearts, faithful hearts, beating over the foam,
 Panting and love-lit await thy return ;
Ever toward thee, abroad or at home,
 Dreaming eyes languish and fond bosoms yearn.
Maid, for whom genius sparkles with song,
 Music bursts out with its loftiest thrill,
Dost thou e'er think, 'mid the mirth of the throng,
 " Ah ! there are some that are friendless and still ;
Some who have bosoms as earnest and free ;
 Some who have feelings as keen as thine own,
Yearning for friendship and fond sympathy,
 Asking for bread and receiving a stone.
Some who of confidence know not the bliss,
 Know not how trusting the spirit expands,
Know not, alas ! what a bosom friend is ;
 Feel not the thrill of the clasping of hands.
Some on whose toiling no voice's sweet tone
 Suddenly falls, or the beam of an eye ;
Some whom the proud, cruel world will not own,
 Passing in silence insultingly by !"
Maiden ! the dreaming when hushed is the sound,
 Vanished the pomp and the gay pageantry,
When on thy finger thou circlest round
 Love's shining token, *he* gave unto thee ;
When in the trust of the moon-lustred night

Wakes in thy bosom the rapture and glow,
Wells from those soul-eyes a chastened love-light,
Looking on days of bright summers ago !
Days when he knelt for thy love and was silent ;
Sunsets beglowed with hand-clasp and vow ;
Times when a heart beat against thy pure breast,
Lips dropped Affection's chaste seal on thy brow !
When those long missives come over the wave,
Tender, impassioned, persuasive to thee—
Oft hast thou pictured him, noble and brave,
Dream'st of the hopes in the future that be—
Dost thou e'er think, 'mid the dream of thy joy,
"Ah ! there are some who are loveless and lone ;
Some who ne'er basked in the light of an eye,
Ne'er heard those fond words, 'I love thee, my own ;'
Some who would give all the world for the bliss—
Give all its wealth for the love of a heart ;
Fèel for one moment the thrill of a kiss,
Know the emotions Love's breathings impart !
Some with hearts weeping and eyes slumberless,
Yearning in vain its endearments to prove ;
Some who could die did they only possess
One little heart in the wide world to love."
Ah ! as I sit here 'mid longings and tears,
Brooding o'er dreams that are faded and gone,
Rise up before me the mouldering years
When thou wast with us, ethereal one !
Angel-like moving about 'mongst us here,
. Kindly and pure as the empress of night,
When e'en my dreary and desolate sphere

Q

Caught from thy presence a glimmer of light.
Ah, thou wert dear to us ! dear as our hearts ;
  Dear as our honour—our lives in those days,
Ah ! but as transient as joyous thy stay,
  Fleeting like all things of earth that are bright,
Uprose the white sails and bore thee away
  Far from the reach of our mist-burdened sight.
Grieved hearts and wan eyes wept sadly behind,
  Prayer-freighted breezes soon wafted thee o'er,
Love-sighs to meet thee came borne on the wind,
  Kindred forms welcomed thee back to their shore.
Time hurried on in its frigid unrest,
  Passed without leaving a trace on thy brow ;
Months sped away—joyous months ! thou wert blessed,
  Happy and blithe as the Peri wert thou—
Months that to me brought sorrow and blight,
  Breathed but affliction's soul-writhing breath—
Years ! so they seemed, when I groped mid the night,
  Passed through the vale of the shadows of death—
Ages ! when up from my heart, thy own eyes
  Looking so tender, so hopeful, so glad,
Pointing me up to the rest of the skies,
  Was the one lone consolation I had. ,
Once more the white sails uprose and you came ;
  Once more I saw you, unchanged by the lapse ;
Gay as of yore, all your beauty the same,
  Ripened and deepened a little perhaps.
Once more your fingers swept over the keys,
  Gushed forth a quivering volume of sound,
Sailed my charmed soul on its billowy seas—

Sailed, and was lost in the listening profound.
And as I gazed on thy rapt dreamy face,
  Wildly drank in each voluptuous strain,
I could have thought that the past dreamy space
  Was but a feverish wraith of the brain—
Dreamed that that season of pain and alloy
  Was but a phantom and never had been ;
Fancied I sat, as on Sabbaths gone by,
  Listening entranced with no shadow between.
Ah ! but the song and music was hushed,
  Vanished the singer in sunlight away ;
Over my being the black torrent rushed,
  All the more dark for the brief glimpse of day.
Ah ! there are some without compass or chart,
  Tossing and toiling—the sport of the wave ;
Some to meet friends but to sorrow and part,
  Some who could welcome the rest of the grave.
Some to whom Hope is the wrecker's false gleam—
  Joy but the city-world's far-distant hum—
Love but a beautiful, sorrowful dream—
  Life but a desert : alas ! there are some.

REST IN THE EVENTIDE.

 SAT beside the window, sad and still,
  The gauzy curtains round about me fell,
I looked away o'er misty vale and hill,
  O'er silent field and forest, rock and dell ;

Night's mystic spirit held my soul in thrall,
  A shadowy presence filled the azure void,
A solemn quietude pervaded all,
  And there was—rest—
                    Rest in the eventide.

I wiped my tear-stained eyes, and gazed and gazed ;
  A torrent-gush of moonlight burst around ;
Night's solemn brow grew bright ; the river blazed,
  And floods of glory filled the vast profound ;
The village roofs, the church, the tombs, the spire,
  The landscape stretching out on every side,
The charmèd hills lay steeped in milky fire,
  And there was rest—
                    Rest in the eventide.

And not one pinion clove the dreaming air,
  And not one footfall from the street uprose !
The amorous radiance trembled everywhere,
  And never a sound disturbed the mute repose.
The sad earth turned her wan face to the night
  To woo the rest which garish day denied ;
The pitying sister bathed her brow with light,
  And bade her rest—
                    Rest in the eventide.

The rapt effulgence, sleeping white and calm,
  The slumb'rous presence clasping earth and skies,
Fell on my troubles like a healing balm,
  Or the soul-shadowings of pitying eyes.

The billowy surge of sorrow ceased to roll ;
　Upon my cheeks the scalding grief-drops dried ;
A holy thrill of peace enwrapt my soul,
　And there was rest—
　　　　　　　Rest at the eventide.

I turned my eyes away, and rose and crept
　Up to the curtained couch with bated breath,
Where two wan beings knelt and sadly wept
　O'er one who slept the still pale sleep of death.
One hour agone the weary wheels had ceased ;
　Hope, fear, uncertainty were laid aside ;
The panting, toiling spirit was released,
　And there was rest—
　　　　　　　Rest in the eventide.

I drew the white sheet slowly, slowly down ;
　A rigid object met my yearning sight ;
A round, fair head, with tresses golden brown
　Streaming profusely o'er a pillow white ;
A still, white face with lips all mutely closed ;
　Thin hands stretched meekly down on either side ;
A waxen breast that motionless reposed—
　In marble rest—
　　　　　　　Rest at the eventide.

And can this be, I thought, the hand I grasped,
　The form that learned to love me long ago ;
Is this the being which my glad arms clasped ?
　These—these the lips that, smiling, thrilled me so ?

Are these the eyes that wept whene'er I wept?
This the chaste breast that with me grieved and joyed ?
This the sole head that on my bosom slept ?
The fairest, best !

My love—one year my bride !

Back o'er my soul the old mad yearning rushed ;
I strained the limp form fiercely to my breast ;
Adown my cheeks, on hers, a torrent gushed,
And on the cold, cold lips my own I pressed ;
I called on her with each endearing name,
But still no answering touch, no voice replied ;
Unbroken was the charm, and still the same
That icy rest—

Rest of the eventide.

And yet, how lifelike seemed that quiet face !
The golden glory slumb'ring 'mongst the hair,
Each feature chiselled with divinest grace,
Each outline, graven on my heart, was there :
And yet, 'twas only fairest moulded clay,
The trammel which the soul had cast aside ;
The glory and the light had passed away,
And there was rest—

Rest at the eventide.

And can this marble-like, this placid form,
This mass of earth, I mused, of fairest mould,
Have once withstood the brunt of Sorrow's storm ?
Basked in the sunshine, shivered in the cold ?

Have once been torture-wrung and passion-swayed,
  Crossed, tempted, buffeted, afflicted, tried?
This mute, frail form in cerements white arrayed,
  Proving the rest—
              Rest of the eventide?

Ah, yes! the tempest-rack had o'er it passed,
  And passion fierce had held a brief, dark sway;
Affliction too had racked, but only cast
  A chaster glory round the drooping clay,
But wrought a tinge of sadness on that brow,
  But made her tenderer and more human-eyed,
But scourged that marble breast, so peaceful now
  In painless rest—
              Rest of the eventide.

For when the ocean boiled, the tempest raged,
  And clouds of horror did her bark o'erwhelm,
She cried for help, and One the storm assuaged,
  Came o'er the plaint-wave and took the helm,
And steered it safely o'er the treach'rous deep,
  And moored it firmly on that stormless side—
("For thus he giveth his beloved sleep")—
  And there was rest—
              Rest in the eventide.

I knelt and moaned, "Oh! what is life to me
  Without the partner of my manhood's choice?
A lonely wanderer on the great rough sea,
  With no consoling hand, no cheering voice:

Oh, take me, too, dear Lord! and, free from care,
   Lay me to slumber sweetly by her side;
In death, as life, unparted let me share
   With her the rest—
                        Rest of the eventide."

In one wild quenchless agony of prayer
   The tempest sorrow of my life surged out,
It's idol-dream, its anguish and despair,
   Its passion flame, its madness, sin, and doubt.
Then came a gentle whisper, "Peace, be still."
   A wondrous gladness filled my bosom's void;
A mystic calm, a hallowed strength of will,
   A gleam of rest—
                        Rest of the eventide.

Even so, oh Father! Marvellous, Infinite!
   Thy will be done; Thou judgest truest what is best.
The idol from my heart Thou tookest, that I might
   Grope the darkness through for Thee, my rest:
So lead me on the shadow-land, till I
   Roam where the deathless evermore abide;
And there with her, the lost, the found! enjoy
   That holiest rest—
                        Rest of the eventide.

STANZAS TO—

O thy way, thou fortunate,
    Hie thee from thy mother-lands,
  Get thee wealth, be wise and great,
    Grave thy mark on richer strands;
Seek beyond the great, wide sea—
Calmly, closely, steadfastly—
  But thou'lt never, never find,
'Mid the ravished beauty there,
One wee face so lily fair,
One pure heart that aye will be
Fondly, truly, tenderly,
Ever more as true to thee
  As the one thou leav'st behind.

Darker eyes may on thee shine,
  Gaudier forms around thee start,
Fiercer loves may seek to twine
  Earthy tendrils round thy heart;
In that flushed and ardent zone
Hotter hands may clasp thy own,
  But thou'lt never, never find,
One small hand so soft and white,
One brown eye so full of light,
    One fond bosom that will be
    Bravely, purely, tenderly,
    Evermore as true to thee,
As the one thou leav'st behind.

Get thee drunk with rich perfume,
   And the spell of beauty blent;
Bask amid the hectic bloom
   Of the lucent orient ;
Search among the galaxy
Of the gorgeous and the free,
   But thou'lt never, never find
One low promise half so sure,
One affection half so pure,
One fair being that will be
Fondly, wholly, constantly,
Aye so faithful unto thee,
   As the one thou leav'st behind.

Many a sun must rise and set,
Many a buoyant heart forget,
   Many a season bloom and fall,
Ere again ye twain have met,
   If again ye meet at all !
But I trust that fate at last
May reverse thy flying mast ;
   That, returning, thou may'st find
Breathing still that bosom chaste,
Though the snow be interlaced
With the auburn in her hair,
And her brow be seamed with care ;
   And that thou with passion kind
Cherish her who aye will be,
Fondly, truly, tenderly—

Whereso'er thy steps may be,
Near or far, on land or sea—
Ever faithful unto thee—
    Weeping lonely now behind !

———

AUTUMNAL.

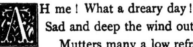H me ! What a dreary day !
    Sad and deep the wind outside
      Mutters many a low refrain,
        Drifts the dead leaves far and wide,
Hurls the thick clouds 'cross the sky,
Scattering torrents in their train ;
Drenching flowers that lowly lie ;
And where'er my sad, sad eye
Pierces, all is gloomy, damp, and drear,
And no sound falls on my dreaming ear,
    But the drip, drip of the rain,
    And that weirdly low refrain,
And, anon, an angry gust
    Splashing 'gainst the window pane.

    Dismantled, unleaved,
    Begloomed, and bereaved,
Wan Nature bends low o'er her dead, lorn and grieved,
    Mournfully drooping, weeping, lone ;
    Uttering many a dreesome moan ;
    Aimlessly rocking to and fro,
While the pelting drops of rain
    On her palsied lips intone.

Choking gutter, belching drain,
   Muddy pool and rindle swell
With the torrent-tears of rain,
Which the clouds, in grief and pain,
    Weep o'er Nature in her dotage fell—
    Shed in sympathy, and cannot quell !
And the landscape, bald and grey,
Sits and broods the livelong day ;
   Mopes beneath the eerie spell,
      Which the sober,
      Sere October
In the dripping air has hung,
Round the droning hills has flung.
Vanished is the gay sunshine,
Fled the song birds o'er the brine ;
      Insect hum
      Is silent, dumb !
Hushed the murmur and the song :
Summer glories every one,
   All are buried, withered, gone !
Faces are shadowed, erst sunny and glad,
Moody, pre-occupied, peevish, or sad ;
The comfortless beggar limps shivering by ;
The flocks creep close to the sheltering side ;
The fowls, one-legged, in the warm nooks hide,
     And each, with its head awry,
     Watches, with bead-like eye,
The huge clouds scud o'er the ink-black sky.
And still the refrain of the wind, well-a-day !
Moans low through the key-hole, and seemeth to say—

"Thus all that is sunny is dashed with shade ;
And all that is earth-born is doomed to fade !"
Ah ! me ! Alack ! What a dreary day !

———

SONG.—SEPTEMBER.

INSCRIBED TO H.

WHEN the prickly balls are bursting,
    On the bending chestnut trees,
  When the sycamore is heavy
      And the ash with clustering keys ;
When the fruit gleams ripe and luscious
  From the nesting leaflets brown,
I will meet thee when the moon-rays
  Fire the mountain's heathery crown.

When the tall bents in the pastures
  Bend o'er mushrooms rinsed with dew,
When the faint winds carol slowly,
  And the skies are softly blue ;
When the partridge 'mongst the grain shocks
  Shrills her wildly piteous tone,
Meet me 'neath the wind-strung alders
  When the fields are silver-sown.

Fear no ill ; I could not wrong thee
  Were my passions ere so base ;
Innocence for shield thou wearest,
  Guardian Trusting's in thy face,

'Deed, I would not taint thy pure life
For a kingly robe and crown !
  Meet me, then, when haws, red-ripening,
Weigh the spiny branches down.

Canst thou say I've ever wiled thee,
  Ever called the hot blood o'er
Cheek or brow, by word or gesture,
  In our wooings heretofore?
Nay ; I see the trust-love misting
  From those glowing eyes of brown :
Meet me, then, when waters whisper,
  And the acorns crackle down.

How my miser heart hath doted
  O'er those memories all and each ;
How I've blest the starting coney
  And the owlet's awful screech,
That they made thee shrink the closer
  To my breast, my choice, my own !
When the night was strange with voices,
  And the earth had shapes unknown.

Hail, September ! mild September !
  Choicest month of all the ring ;
Dearer to my hope than Summer,
  Fairer to my thought than Spring.
When I drop the year-long struggle,
  Quit the black and noisy town
For the wooing 'neath the alders,
  When the stars are lustring down.

Come, then, love ; and harebells, nodding,
   Drones and moths shall 'list our vows,
And the sleepy sparrow roosting
   'Mong the holly's berried boughs ;
Wine of love shall brim life's goblet,
   Mingling thine and mine, my own !
We will quaff it deep i'th' dew-light,
   When the world is slumber-prone.

"NOW THOU ART GONE."

(A LAMENTATION.)

THE twilight shadows, deep'ning into gloom,
   Close thickly round me in my cheerless room ;
      My heart is weeping, weeping sad and sore,
         Now thou art gone !

The book you read lies closed beneath my hands,
The chair you occupied beside me stands ;
   Mementos of the sunny days no more—
      A summer flown.

Anon, the vanished hours before me rise,
And looking at me with those tender eyes,
   Thou, smiling sweetly, sit'st beside me here,
      My darling one !

'Tis but a moment, then 'tis gone again,
But deepening in my heart its aching pain,
 And leaving on my cheek a weary tear,
  Within, a groan.

The leaden days drag on so drearily,
I sit and count the moments wearily,
 I have no pastime and no purpose now,
  And pleasure none.

The sun comes shining o'er the rimy tiles,
All Nature wakens into tears and smiles,
 The moon pours down its lustre on my brow
  Like times agone.

But from them faded sadly is the light,
The grand of earth and sky, the fair, the bright,
 Have lost their charm to me for evermore,
  Now thou art gone !

I strive to lose myself in fiction's maze,
Or fix on learning's page my mind and gaze,
 And pant and struggle, as in days of yore
  I battled on.

Down from the cypress bough my lyre I take,
And sweep its murm'rous strings, and strive to wake
 My soul to noble things, and break the chains
  That bind me down.

But soon my eyes grow tear-bedewed and dim,
And visions of the past before me swim,
    My lyre gives forth but grieved and jarring strains—
        Its music flown.

And no one comes to smile a fond relief,
And no one mourns my weakness, soothes my grief,
    Or speaks a kindly word of sympathy;
        I am alone!

And no one points me upward towards the blaze,
And no one smiles upon my feeble lays,
    And no one thinks of me nor cares for me,
        Now thou art gone!

I might, perhaps, have hoped and wrestled on,
And strained and grappled till the wreath I'd won,
    Till fortune, frowning erst, had stooped to smile,
        All, all for thee!

Nay, this I would have done, (" The will's the way,"
And stern determination wins the day),
    Had but thyself, the guerdon of my toil,
        Remained to me.

But what to me are now the smiles of fame?
Poor shipwrecked thing, without a hope or aim;
    What matters, if I linger, rise, or fall,
        Now thou art gone?

R

What have I here to strive and battle for,
What interest in the game, the race, the war?
  I loved thee—oh, my heart! thou wert my all!
    But thou art gone!

In gloaming time I wander down the lane,
And pause beside the rustic gate again,
  And scan the pathway over which you came
    In days agone!

Your dwelling of those days stands 'neath the hill,
The brooklet ripples on and shimmers still,
  The yew tree nods its dark plumes just the same,
    But thou art gone!

I shrink away, my eyes with tears are wet,
And from my heart swells up a mad regret,
  A silent gush of hopeless lamentation,
    For thou art gone!

Oh! when will cease this constant, quenchless burning,
This rankling grief, this restless spirit-yearning,
  This weary sense of helpless desolation,
    Now thou art gone?

I lift my aching eyes from day to day
Towards where thou dwellest now, so far away!
  The pale horizon bounds my view, 'tis vain!
    My absent one!

I turn into myself, and strive to force
My soul to drink at pleasure's gaudy source ;
    But in my heart still throbs the old deep pain,
        For thou art gone !

I often wonder, dost thou ever think
Of that seared, silent heart thou left'st to drink
    The bitter cup of life, to fight and weep
        Alone, behind ?

Or if those mystic eyes with icy gleams
Shine coldly, if thou think'st of me, as in dreams
    That come to torture this poor brain in sleep,
        Or if more kind ?

You could not see the pain that wrung my heart
When we had met, the last, last time, to part !
    You told me I should see your face again
        No more, no more !

'Twas cruel, cruel ! for if 'tis denied
Our souls the bliss to meet on this dark side,
    Sure we may meet on yonder shore, where pain
        And grief are o'er.

Oh ! grant to me this one fond hope at least,
To meet and love thee when from earth released ;
    Where dear ones never part, no tear drops flow,
        And griefs are none.

But blessings on thee through the coming years,
Whate'er remains to me of hopes or fears ;
Oh, foolish heart ! oh, vain and idle tears !
  Heaven help me ! I am broken-hearted so,
    Now thou art gone !

A CHANT OF PRAISE.

 LIGHT of the Eternal ! round my brow,
For ever circling, moves the fluid air ;
And through the measureless expanse of calm
Glows the empurpled ether, like a sea
Of crystal amethyst ; and far beyond,
In such a hush of peace, the infinite
Unwavering orbs their solemn measure tread ;
And come ten million voices from the earth,
The air, the ocean—rustling steps of airs
That walk the woods in moody glooms and calms ;
The guttural roll of watercoils ; the boom
Of forest-rumbling winds ; the thunderous bass
Of the deep-bellowing tempest-wheels ; the low
Grand undertone of Peace on harp of Eve.
And on my rapt and trembling vision break
In quick succeeding glimpses, power on power
Of all the might and marvel Thou hast made :—
The silken tread of morning on the hills ;
Soft meltings of the sheen into the dark ;
Wide openings of the light in rosy wings ;

Still breakings of the clouds in argent braids
O'er slanting cataracts of moony waves;
The tremulous swell of foliage; the sheen
Of wonder-dreaming waters 'neath the sun;
The mystical magnificence of night,
The light-thronged, rare magnificence of day.
O visions of the mystic! round thee throb
Thy boundless works—a wildering galaxy!
None fixed, but circling all the tireless dance
With measured action, pace, and balanced power;
Conjunct, centrifugal, centripetal,
Immense, harmonious, widening out from thee,
Each in its orbit, none diverging thence.
My gaze sweeps marvelling up the mighty chain,
And grows my soul into a god in thought!
Thou Spirit of the marvellous! I see
In zones, immeasurable, all Thy works
Concentring, circling, Summering to Thee!
Thou the attraction, Thou the moving thought!
O Light of the Eternal! all the stir
And grandeur of the wonder Thou hast made,
Lie on my being like a seraph touch,
And grow through all the grooves of all my life,
And fill me with an infinite, intense,
Untiring gush of wonder, music, prayer.
Maker! had'st thou but given the little day
In which this mortal blossoms, blooms, and dies;
Were this terrestrial span the minute sum
Of our existence—nothing more beyond—
O, I could bless Thee for so faint a glimpse

Of all Thy grandeur-power ; that I might dip
E'en that frail bubble's depth into the sea
Of Thy great magnitude ; that I might drink
So poor a draught of all the harmony,
The wisdom, the beneficence, the light,
The excellence of Thy creative mind
And effluent existence—yea, in sooth,
Were like a dream, a waking from a sleep
To sink into an endless sleep again ;
And how much more when in this mortal glows
A spark of Thine own essence, which must sweep
The myriad circles of a vast, immense,
Untold, unthought Eternity, to which
E'en Godhead hath affixed no boundary-line !
For ever deepening nearer Thy heart ;
For ever learning more and seeking more
Of Thy exhaustless mind and majesty ;
For ever growing more into Thyself.
O Thou unvarying sun, with thy last beams
Flash grieved remembrance in upon my soul—
O watchful stars, with your all-piercing eyes
Deep in my conscience wake conviction's throes—
O stern-browed clouds and mountains, frown on me,
Until within me rise a black remorse
To goad and menace, if for one brief day—
But one brief day—I fail, forget to seek
A deeper knowledge of His wondrous works,
A wider comprehension of Himself;
O soul and harp awake ! O voice awake !
     ⸱ all your strings to the great harmony !

Tumultuous throbbings, break from every hour
And latitude of life—

              Praise ye the Lord !
  Ye mighty Nations ; all ye realm of tongues ;
O men of every clime, of every state,
Or great, or small, or mighty, or renowned,—
Old age and children, youths and maidens, join.
Ye are the grand connecting link betwixt
The mortal and immortal—bare your brows
Beneath the arc of God's great firmament ;
Swell every note of your wide varied minds :—

              Praise ye the Lord !
  O potent Elements, engendered from
The burning heats and calm, awake, arise ;
Assemble from the far four-winds of heaven
As unto strife ; come forth, in all your pomp
And pageantry of sound ; astound the earth ;
Convulse the ocean ; roar amid the woods ;
Gloom all your blackness ; blaze your lightnings forth
Shake your hoarse thunderings loose along the clouds,
And rise and wrestle 'mid the astonished air—

              Praise ye the Lord !
  O fair imperial Day, that walk'st in light ;
O Dawn, with maiden-lip, dew kissed and warm ;
O golden-folded Eve, that sinkest in mist ;
O Night, with the immense, mysterious brow—
Each, as ye tread the pathways of the earth,—

              Praise ye the Lord !
  O splendid portal of the marvel-light ;
O radiant frontlet on the brow of Eve ;

O white, immobile, unimpassioned stars,
I never gaze upon you but my soul
Grows still within me, speechless, dumb with awe,
And rises on my mind of minds the vast—
The sole idea of Eternity !
Still hang your burdens on Creation's harp—
　　　　　　　　　　　　Praise ye the Lord !
　Thou Ocean, roar, and clasp thy ponderous hands,
And kiss thy rage defiant in the teeth
Of the imperious whirlwinds ; shake thyself ;
Spit thy grey froth against the tempest's front ;
Hold thou thy sides, and chuckle 'neath the black,
Stern, cyclopean glooms ; roll thy huge tongue
About thy wooded isles and shoals and shores ;
Or ruffle glimmering scales beneath the calm,
Returning fond, the sunset's kiss of peace—
　　　　　　　　　　　　Praise ye the Lord !
　O solid land, in each successive clime,
'Neath every sky, ream o'er the sumptuous cup
Of all thy opulence ; surge out thy wide
Supreme magnificence in every zone ;
Wreath thy broad brow with all of rare and fair ;
Deck thee luxuriantly ; upswell on high
Thy myriad song—thy God is bountiful—
　　　　　　　　　　　　Praise ye the Lord !
　O mighty reservoirs slung on air,
Ye clouds that drape and film the earth about ;
That float blythe dreams amid the morning gold,
And brood and lie among the mountains, where
The night rolls like the tide from sea to sea ;

Ye mists that hang in ragged fringes round
The edge of darkness—ye white fogs
That swathed the sleeping valleys through the night—
      Praise ye the Lord !
 O all ye soothing dews and showers of rain ;
Ye storms of sleet and snow ; ye winds and hail ;
O frost and ice ; O, varying cold and heat :—
      Praise ye the Lord !
 O all ye waters that replenish earth ;
Ye swollen rivers roaring to the main ;
Ye little lakes ; ye streamlets with your pipes
That run about the woodlands and the wilds ;
Ye effluent springs that spark the mountain side—
      Praise ye the Lord !
 O solemn, solemn mountains ; O ye hills,
Ye calm-browed hills ; ye dusky plains and vales ;
O grey-cragged summits ; O ye chasms wide ;
Ye awful wastes of ever-shifting sands—
Excite with wonder while ye deepen awe—
      Praise ye the Lord !
 Shake out your banners, nod your plumes, ye trees,
That bask the mountains, fringe the glooms and dens ;
Wave, O ye reeds and grass, and picture forth
The wide-wing waftings of the under winds ;
Bend low, O stately corn ; ye thickets thrill ;
O radiant flowers, upstretch your honey-cups—
      Praise ye the Lord !
 O all ye myriad-life that gather up
The fulgent glory of the sun-warmed airs ;
Ye rare-winged birds that vocalise the world,

And skim across the summer wave and wold ;
Ye cattle grazing on a thousand hills ;
Ye beasts that lurk in many dens and caves ;
Ye scaly things that deep in waters glide—
Swell out your being's grand exuberance—
(For earnest life is ever truest praise)—
                                        Praise ye the Lord !
   Slide on, O seasons, in your changeful dance,
Charm the wide earth with mingling lights and shades,
And crown the reeling goblet of the year :
Ye Sabbaths raise your full magnificat—
                                        Praise ye the Lord !
   O thou our orb, amidst thy glittering race,
Made eloquent with beauty by His hand,
How fair thou art ; yea, very fair and good !
O, teem thy myriad pulses forth in praise ;
Pour out thy soul unto the listening hours ;
O take it up, thou ether, take it up ;
Catch the rapt strain thou awful, awful void ;
Ye sister orbits waft the glory on,
And on, and on, until the universe
Is full of harmony, as full of Him—
                                        Praise thou the Lord !
   O all things that have motion, voice, or breath,
Whether ye circle round the Holiest
On wings celestial, or roll amid
Th' unmeasured ecstasies of marvellous space
In light and shadowing ; whether with form
Erect ye walk the world i'th' image of God,
Or creep, or run, or soar, or swim, or glide :

Oh ! all created things—

                  Praise ye the Lord !

  Stupendous Being ! Majesty Eterne !

Triessenced Deity—essential One !

Creator Uncreate ! who veil'st Thy face

In vapoury void ; who in the vast occult

Pavilions of the skies dost hide Thyself ;

Thou Unapproached, Unsearched, Unreached, Unknown,

Whose hidden name no earthly syllables

Could shape for human utterance—to us—

Dim-shadowed in the mystic " GOD."—

O Thou, before Whose face the mad, blind storms

Divide tumultuously the placid air ;

At whose approach the black, confederate clouds

Asunder start with loud convulsive shout,

And drop their half-forged lightnings sudden down ;

Before Whose breath the stars slip from their poles,

The earth hath under-shudderings, the hills

Do shake and melt, the valleys heave and smoke,

The cedars and the oaks abase themselves

And bow ; the forest-realms and ocean-gatherings

Affrighted, roar, afflict, and lash themselves ;

O Thou, Whose might is faintly figured forth

In all the varying pageantry from year to year

Of this the narrow limit of our dim

And feeble ken ; thou Sacred, Sacred Power !

Even as the rain, from earth and ocean drawn

In mists and fogs, thither returns again

In copious showers, so may all essences

All springs of life, all impulses, all interests,

All powers, and motions, erst derived from **Thee,**
To Thee return, in tenfold sympathies
Of praise ecstatic, endless, infinite !

Amen ! Amen !

A PRAYER.

HEN the tempests rage and roar,
    When the torrents beat and pour,
    When the dearest dreams are crossed,
    When my soul is plagued and tossed,
        Son of God, remember me.

When my day is full of light,
When the stars of hope are bright,
When my cup brims clear and high,
Smooth my path, and clear my sky,
        Son of God, remember me.

If my giddy feet would stray,
Chasing shadows that betray ;
Should my heart and will perverse
Covet dross that brings a curse,
        Son of God, remember me.

In temptation's struggle-hour,
When the flesh hath double power,
When the better nature sinks,
When resolve grows weak and shrinks,
        Son of God, remember me.

Wheresoe'er my pathway leads,
Whatsoe'er my nature needs,
Whensoe'er my courage fails,
Howsoe'er the fiend assails,
          Son of God, remember me.

When my day around me sets,
When the midnight glooms and frets,
When the sighing river foams,
When the death-cold shadow comes,
          Son of God, remember me.

Through the hour of densest night,
Through the whelm of Nature's blight,
Through the gloom and agony,
Thou Who sufferedst on the tree,
          Son of God, remember me.

Glad in sorrow's sweet surcease,
Wrapt in balms of changeless peace,
Borne on wings of ecstasy,
O'er the calm eternally,
          Bring me, Son of God, to Thee !

EPITAPH ON A BELOVED FRIEND.

WEARY one, rest from thy burden of care,
    All thy afflictions and sorrows are o'er,
Rest evermore in that paradise, where
    Earth's heavy-laden ones weep nevermore ;

Rough was thy pilgrimage, frail was thy form,
　　Nipped by disease like a flower in the blast,
Hot was the conflict, and fierce was the storm,
　　All the more sweet was thy triumph at last.

———

TO HARRIET IN HEAVEN.

EAR Harriet, and thou art no more,
　　No longer thy spirit is chained ;
Life's tempests and struggles are o'er,
　　The haven of rest is attained ;
Away from the troubles of life ;
　　Away from its sorrows and woes ;
Away from its pitiless strife,
　　Thy spirit has found its repose.

———

TO HANNAH.

AREWELL, beloved one, escaped from our keeping,
　　Gone home to thy crown and thy treasure at last,
Afflictions and sorrows, temptations and weeping,
　　Are fled with thy feverish dream of the past.

———

A LOCAL HISTORY.

 YOUNG man rose with a silvery tongue;
His eyes were bright, and his heart was strong,
And he vowed in the ears of the men of the world
He knew, and would sing them a marvellous song;
Whereat some laughed good humouredly;
The lips of many with scorn were curled;
" Go on, and be brave," said a few; but more
Were deaf to his voice as the stones could be.
But the youth of the cup of ambition sipped,
And his brow grew bold, though he trembled sore;
His looks went up a long patch in the sky,
Then sought the earth for a loving eye;
He touched a rude harp with meaning high.
And his voice rose clearly and broke among
The eddying people's, and rolled along.
For the cheers or the jeers he heeded naught;
His soul the scope of a burning thought;
The fire of his lofty theme had caught;
And he sang with never a stop or stay,
For his labouring breath and his pulses' play,
Till Fate stole up and the ballad ripped:
Then the singer faltered and stammered long,
And, last broke in the midst of his song,
To the pity and pain of a few in the throng,
And the proud content of the scornful lipped.
O woe! for the wings that so soon were clipped,
The wings that dreamed of the sun !
A grave deep down by the chapel wall,

But two feet wide and a fathom long—
A tiny dot of the earth holds all
That the earth could claim, from which he sprung,
Of the singer who deemed the great world too small
To hold the revealings that rose to his tongue—
Of the burden and bent of his soul and his song.

THE BELLS ON WATCHNIGHT.

LIST to the bells ! O list !
 Out on the upland there ;
Peals through the mirk and mist,
 Swing down the midnight air
Awfully, solemnly !
List what they say to thee.

" Kneel by the dying year—
 Wipe his lips, hold his hands—
Wearily lying here,
 Out on the waves and sands ;
Muse on the scath and crime
Wrought in his vanished time.

" Think of the destitute,
 Hungering, shivering ;
Plead for the dissolute,
 Cursing and quivering ;
Pray for the trouble-tossed ;
Pray for the anguish-crossed ;

" Feel for the desolate ;
    Pity the castaway ;
  Pray for the desperate,
    Sullied, and tossed astray,
  Tempted, tried, passion-strung—
  Mourn o'er the sin and wrong !

" Soothe to peace murder-mad
    Restless insanity ;
  Close up the wounds of sad,
    Bleeding humanity ;
  Give to *all* charity ;
  Human are all of ye.

" Widely o'er land and sea
    Scatter ye knowledge-light ;
  Girt with Philanthropy
    Wrestle with mental night ;
  Lift up the Truth divine—
  Lift—and the dark shall shine !

" Sigh o'er the premature
    Fading of faces, gone ;
  Weep for the good and pure
    From your embraces gone ;
  Tender ties broken, aye ;
  Bitter words spoken, aye.

" Weep o'er the moments fled.
    Bearing a record on,
  O'er opportunities dead,

And no more duty done ;
Plead for your frailties all ;
Let the dread curtain fall !

" Rouse from your somnolence !
Cometh another year ;
Shake off your indolence !
Arm ye in hope and fear ;
Look to the fore and fight,
Bury your dead from sight !"

THE POET'S MONUMENT.

AD are the shivering dank dead leaves,
To one who a lost love from his heart unweaves,
Who dreams he has gathered his life's last sheaves,
And must find a grave under wintry eaves.

Dead ! dead ! 'mongst the winter's dearth,
Gone where the shadows of all things go,
Stretch me full length in the folding earth,
Wind me up in the drifting snow ;

None of the people will heed it or say,
" He was a singer who fainted there,
One who could leaven with fire, or sway
Men's hearts to trembling unaware."

No one will think of the dream-days lost,
Of the ardours fierce that were damped too soon ;
Of the bud that was nipped by the morning's frost,
And shrivelled to dust in the sun ere noon.

No one will raise me a marble, wrought
  With meaning symbol, and apt device,
To link my name with a noble thought,
  A generous deed, or a new-found voice.

My life will go on to the limitless tides,
  Leaving no trace of its current-flow,
Like a stream that starts when the tempest rides,
  And is lost again in the evening's glow.

The glories will gather and change as of yore,
  And the human currents pass panting by,
The ages will gather their wrinkles more,
  And others will sing for a day and die.

But thou, who art dearer than words can say,
  My more than all other of earth could be;
Such a joy! that the Giver I thank alway
  With a glowing heart, that He gave me thee.

I shall want thee to dream me my dream all through,
  To think me the gifted, the Poet still,
To crown me, whatever the world may do,
  Though my songs die out upon air and hill.

And, Edith, come thou in the blooming time,
  Thy world will not miss thee for just one hour;
I'd like it best when the bells low chime,
  And the earth is full of the sunset's power;

And bend by the silently settling heap,
  While the Nature we loved, is a May all round,
While God broods low on the blue arched sweep,
  And the music-full air is a-thrill with sound.

And look in thy heart circled up in the past,
  And if I am perfectly graven there,
Unshaded by aught, save the anguish cast
  By the parting clasp, and the death despair.

Encirqued with the light of the pale regret,
  Of a " might have been " of a day-dream lent,
With a constant hope of a meeting yet,
  O ! I shall not want for a Monument.

A VALENTINE.

COME back to my bosom, Mary,
    Come back to your home at last ;
  Forget all the doubt and anguish,
    And the troubled and wasted past.

My heart has been longing, longing,
  For many a weary day ;
Come back to my arms, my Mary,
  And dwell in my sight alway.

How like a terrible vision
  The past with its pain has been ;
How many the groans unnoted,
  And the tears that have flowed unseen.

I wrestled for wealth and honour,
    To fill up the desolate void :
I won them ; but, oh ! my spirit
    Refused to be satisfied.

Ah ! those that around me fluttered,
    And envied my fortune so,
Should have weighed it 'gainst the sorrow
That ever lay gnawing below.

The years have lain heavily on me,
    And shadowed and seamed my brow ;
And the hot tears follow the wrinkles
    That traverse my wan cheek now.

I am weaker and feebler, Mary,
    I am lonely and growing old ;
And my home is so cheerless, Mary,
    And the world is so strange and cold.

And Mary, I loved you always,
    Through all those terrible years ;
But Heaven alone is witness,
    And the pillow that drank my tears.

The clamourous cry for affection
    Grew in me and would not be stilled,
With the sense that the one great purpose
    Of being was unfulfilled.

TO THE OCEAN.

H ! thou glorious, far-off ocean,
  Basking in thy realm of pride !
Matchless, all unrivalled monarch
  Of an empire vast and wide.

Oh ! I never yet beside thee,
 Stood, enchanted with the sight,
But the raptured tale has reached me
 Of thy grandeur and thy might ;

Of the myriad-handed commerce
 Which thy turbid wave affords,
Of thy gulphed and buried millions,
 Of thy glittering golden hoards !

And I oft in dreams behold thee,
 Hear thy voice's thundering bass,
See the mad, impassioned fury
 Of thy storm-distorted face,

And thy anger-pallid billows
 Lapsing widely o'er and o'er,
And, in calm, thy laughing wavelets
 Toying with the virgin shore.

Rimpling, twinkling 'neath the starlight,
 Shimmering in the moonlight streak ;
Then the noontide glory streaming
 O'er thy flushed and slumberous cheek,

And the distant white-robed vessels,
   Netted o'er with web-like strings ;
And the many sea-birds floating
   Round and round on wool-white wings.

And I long, O mighty ocean !
   Evermore thy face to see,
As the face of that bright maiden,
   Dear as is my life to me.

But I'm bound a weary prisoner,
   Mid these bleak and wintry hills ;
And a dusky stretch of landscape
   Evermore my vision fills.

But should Fate, just once, permit me
   On thy shore to stand one hour,
There enwrapt to gaze upon thee
   In thy wonder and thy power.

Watch the ever-changing aspect,
   Of thy bright but treacherous breast,
In the tempest of its passion,
   In the glamour of its rest.

O ! a holy satisfaction,
   And an awed and mystic joy ;
And a higher aspiration,
   And a loftier reach of eye,

And a wider range of feeling
Will wake to life in me,
With a grander wonder-worship
Of the hand that fashioned thee !

IMPROMPTU TO "DICKEY."

THOU hast sugar, and water, and seeds
Sufficient for all thy needs,
O birdie ! and sweet is thy song,
And grateful thy music to me ;
Yet I would, O I would thou wert free,
And dancing the glad world among ;
For 'tis sad as the seasons go by
To have never a glimpse of the sky,
And never a mate in the woods ;
Ne'er a sweet honey-sip of the flowers,
Ne'er a fling 'mongst the winds and the bowers,
And never a glance o'er the floods.
'Tis sad to be circled with bars,
Though gilded, whose narrowness mars
The lustrous spread of the wing.
I, too, am a captive as thou ;
Pain-prisoned and prison-bound now,
And all I can do is to sing.
Food, clothing, and all I may need
From the bounty of others proceed ;
Dependent and useless am I.

I may not go dance on the hills,
Or drink the wild gladness that trills
    The earth as the seasons go by.
Folk come to me, list to the flow
Of my carolings, pet me, and go
    Forgetting their words, and I sigh.
My life hath no depth and no mirth ;
I have not a place on the earth,
    And ne'er a love under the sky.

THE SAGACITY OF DUCKS.

RECOLLECT one sultry summer's day
    Reclining 'neath a sycamore to cool,
And watching listlessly some ducks at play,
    Across the road, upon a muddy pool.

And looking up, beheld the great M.Ð.
    Of Chillingworth come riding slowly down,
With pompous air, which shows (at least to me)
    If not a hollow heart, an empty crown.

His clothes were of that cut that marks the fop :
    A turban hat encased his meagre brains ;
His whiskers hung in style—a wondrous crop ;
    And on his neck reclined a *cold* watch chain.

A moustache graced his shrewish upper lip ;
    His eyes were small ; his cheeks were red and fat ;
His burly nose was crimson at the tip ;
    His brow, if such he had, was 'neath his hat.

And there he sat upright in awful state,
   As though the shameless egotist would say
Earth holds no other man so wise, so great—
   Ye simple, meaner ones, stand back, give way.

Of course, too proud to notice such as I,
   He passed in silence on his jaded hack ;
The ducks popped up their heads, and, looking sly,
   Bawled after him in chorus, Quack, quack, quack !

APRIL FOOLS.

HE sun has gone down, and the rose-light fades,
      And the cool night down from the mountain
      slips,
And swathes the chill earth in a garment of shades,
   And tenderly kisses the pale, parched lips.

The moon-lustre falls on a lone, deep lane,
   Bush-screened, bramble-grown, beech-shadowed, **and**
      Hist !
Step silently back in the shadow again,
   I hear a low sound—'tis the lovers' tryst !

Entwined like the shapes on an antique cup,
   Wrapt up in each other they come and go ;
Her features are white, for she gazes up ;
   And his are as dark, for he bendeth low.

'Mid the light and the shade of that rustic dell
   They lingering saunter to and fro !
They think not that life hath its shades as well,
   It seemeth all sunny—love paints it so.

He breathes honeyed words that are pure and fair,
   She answers with looks that are sweet as they ;
He buildeth bright fabrics in realms of air,
   She decks them with tendrils and flowers of May.

He praises her form and eyes' soft play,
   The glow of her lips, and her cheeks and brow ;
And much that, though once young and foolish as they,
   You'd pucker your features and sneer at now.

They pause in the moonlight, with fair heads bowed,
   And now to be faithful and loving and true ;
The moon hides its face in a small white cloud—
   And if he *did* kiss her, what is't to you ?

A feeling of mischief comes o'er the maid ;
   Averting her face with a vexed pretence
She utters one word of a doubtful shade,
   He, lover-like, instantly takes offence ;

And hot words are dealt with the force of prayer,
   Fierce tropes are like sods at each other cast ;
They stand for a moment irresolute there,
   And sullenly part without kissing at last.

The maiden trips this way, and he strides that
    For the breadth of a field and a half almost ;
Then suddenly turns, and compressing his hat,
    Darts back as if followed by vengeful ghost ;

And panting, and heated, and anxious, he
    Arrives at the wicket where late she bent—
On the door-step where she has paused to see
    If he *really* meant it, and would'nt repent.

" I could'nt go, Nelly, and leave you thus !"
    He bends and looks deep in the sad, blue eyes,
Then draws to his bosom the sly young puss—
    " Forgive me," says he, and the maiden cries.

The penitent head seeks its old soft place,
    While he kisses the long damp lashes dry—
The moon winks down with a sly old face,
    And the breeze on tip-toe steals tittering by.

ISN'T IT SO ?

NE kindred are we here,
    And each to each agrees,
    In mutual needs and aids,
    Supplies dependencies.

And some are made to bear,
    And some are made to cling ;
As mates the sapling vine
    With England's forest king.

And some are strong and brave,
   And some are faint and frail;
The lily maiden weds
   The warrior ribbed with mail.

And God to each hath given
   A something here of good;
A place for each to fill
   In human brotherhood.

The strong to toil and fight,
   Support, restrain, redress;
The weak to soothe and twine,
   To comfort and caress.

The great of brain to think,
   The iron of arm to toil,
The pure of heart to preach,
   The fair of lip to smile.

And some are made to rule,
   And some to serve the State;
And some to sit and eat,
   And some to stand and wait.

Not one, however low,
   But has a nook assigned
Within the busy mart,
   By God, the master-mind:

To ease the clamp of care,
  And oil the wheels of toil ;
Make anguish easier borne,
  And pleasure worth the while ;

To smooth the rugged edge
  Before the plodding feet ;
Make earth more pure and fair,
  And life more calm and sweet.

And each has got a charge,
  Something to cherish too ;
A little hand to lead,
  A prop to cling unto.

He is thy brother-man,
  However mean he be,
Who but his duty knows,
  And does it faithfully.

We cannot all be kings,
  Not all be grand and great ;
Why should we grasp and fret
  For things beyond our state ?

Why not take up our thread
  And weave it patiently,
Among the myriad threads
  That are but threads as we ?

Why should we blindly turn
   From kindred needs and aims ?
Why selfishly withhold
   What our own nature claims ?

How blessed the world would be
   If each would search his will ;
If each his work would do,
   And each his place would fill !

MELANCHOLY MOMENTS.

FAR up in the garret I dream of thee,
   O maiden, who dwellest by the far-off sea.
   Stretched out on my couch with my limbs at rest,
And my thin hands folded and still on my breast,
Shut out from the world and its care and strife,
I am lying becalmed on the ocean of life.
Behind the past with its pain and toil,
And the present lies still in the soft calm smile
Of the radiant future that dawns for me,
O'er the dim-seen hills of eternity.
The tempest is lulled, and the heavens are clear,
And the lights glimmer out from the arbour near ;
The fever of sickness burns low in my veins,
And silently wrestles and surely gains
A firmer hold on each vital part,
A surer grasp of the fluttering heart ;
A mightier power and a sterner sway

O'er this shadowing tenement day by day;
I know that a work in the churchyard waits,
And a messenger stands at the golden gates,
But lovingly pauses a moment, the while
I take a last look at the dim old stile;
My boat is half on and half off the shore,
Awaiting the tide that shall float us o'er;
From the horologue glideth the last few sands,
And quivers the balance in Time's worn hands;
The cable unravelleth coil after coil,
And the shadows grow long in the sunset smile.
I bask in the twilight of two dim shores,
With my head strained back, and my hands on the oars—
'Tis a moment ere I brave the dark stream,
So what can I do but be silent and dream;
'Tis the lull that precedes the last burst of the storm,
Ere the clouds break up and the sun shines warm.

BISSEXTILE: A LADY'S VALENTINE.

ONG years have trod the wake of years,
    And scores have wooed and mated,
    And friends and beaux have come and gone,
    And I have watched and waited,—
A woman with a woman's heart
    Still unappropriated!

You've danced attendance on my suit,
    You've given me smiles and sighing;
You've hinted, "Some folk would not care

If other folks were dying."
I've long discerned the prisoned love
   Your queerness underlying :

And yet you never spoke, although
   You gave me signs sufficient !
It might be diffidence ; perhaps
   You thought my love deficient ;
You may have deemed your home too mean,
   Your income inefficient.

I know not. Yet you might have seen
   How much I liked and prized you :
Sometimes I thought you faint of heart,
   And then I half despised you ;
Then blamed myself and bowed my heart,
   And—all but idolized you.

And this is all the reason why,
   I sometimes vexed and teased you,
Now slighted, tantalized, perplexed,
   Now hovered round and pleased you ;
Now touched your pride, and now your heart,
   First roused and then appeased you.

The reason why I carried on
   At times some mad flirtation,
Was just to draw from helpless love,
   To force from desperation,
To win, surprise, extract or squeeze
   The longed-for declaration.

And now the ladies' turn has come,
  And, if you will, I'll take you ;
I'll quit my airs and frippery,
  And do my best to make you
A little, earnest, homely wife,
  And love, and ne'er forsake you ;

I'll gladly yield the reins to you,
  And cease to plague and try you ;
I'll share your lot, be it weal or woe,
  And stand unchanging by you :
Ay, give ye all I am and have,
  If that will satisfy you !

ALL ALONE.

WO sisters, beautiful as twin sunbeams,
    Disported mid my childhood's realm of flowers,
  The blythe associates of my earliest dreams,
    The winsome sharers of my sunset hours.
  They sleep serenely 'neath the churchyard stone,
  And I am left alone, all, all alone !

THE MOTHER ON THE DEATH OF HER INFANT CHILD.

IKE the meteor's transient gleam,
    Like the stars at dawn of day,
  Like the music of a dream,
    Came our boy and passed away.

Gone to swell the snow-white throng,
  On the bright far-distant shore,
Where we'll meet again ere long,
  Angel-one, to part no more.

———

SONNET.

A LITTLE while ago these meads were fair
    And fresh, and flashing with a flood of green,
    And infant flowers with windle spray between
And gold-winged butteries and bees were there,
And lisping winds went o'er them like a prayer,
    And all was gay as though the dearth had been ;
    No shadow from the future marred the scene.
And now those very fields are crisp and bare,
Their glory severed, scorched, and withered dead,
    And gathered in the dust from thence it came
In tomb-like heaps, 'neath dusky thatch and shed ;
    And all the world around lives on the same ;
The sun shines brightly and the winds are rife ;
But they are faded, shorn.   And such is life.

———

SONNET.

WHEN twilight walks the earth with dewy feet,
    It steals from memory, haunted long-ago,
    That sweet, sad passion-dream I cherished so ;

A form with every charm and grace replete,
A tinkling fall of fairy footsteps fleet,
  A radiant face, with dimpling smiles aglow,
  A voice like rippling streamlet's murmuring flow,
Low words of hope, and love intensely sweet,
A whispered interchange of vows, one kiss,
  A crashing blow, of all the hopes the knell.
One brief half-hour of anguish-haunted bliss,
  One wild embrace, a long, a last farewell,
Darts like a vision through my brain, and then
My widowed soul grows calm and sad again.

SONNET.

INSCRIBED,

With feelings of sincere regard, to those who are dear to me at Mow
Cop; in remembrance of a very happy visit there—a few sunny days
spent amongst them.

THE glory of God appears to human eye,—
  Upon yon gold-shot bound of visual quest;
  Yon torrid sunset saddening in the west;
The glinting cliffs that commune with the sky;
The glowing clouds that, voiceless, ramble by:
  Upon yon tesselated hillock's crest:
  Amid the stillness, motion, and the rest.
Upon the shades that in the valleys lie;

The trees that whisper not but doze in peace ;
  The defluous fascination of the stream :
Where on the lake, the sunlight's fond surcase
  Plays, like the last faint promptings of a dream.
Thy glory, God, is round me, on my heart !—
Why do we sometimes wonder where Thou art ?

SONNET.

THE SABBATH.

! GLORIOUS day of rest ; sublime release
  From rankling care and all-absorbing toil ;
  The grinding wheels of commerce pause awhile,
And tumult, strife, and jarring factions cease,
And o'er the tired earth the angel Peace
  Spreads her soft wings, and 'neath thy hallowed smile,
  Anoints its festering wounds with holy oil ;
And hearts grow bright again, and hopes increase,
And from ten thousand thousand tongues and choirs
  The myriad songs of praise commingling, rise
Above the smoke-black tiles, the domes and spires ;
  Above the vapours and the calm blue skies,
To Him, whose word ordained the thrice-bless'd day
When Justice sleeps, and Mercy holds the sway.

DECEMBER.

UTSIDE the storm swayed
    In the palpable darkness,
      The lamp quivered faintly
        On the wan and drawn features,
The white breathing stillness
On a bosom of pillows :
Hands clasped in a tremour,
A fever of waiting,
While wandering, troubling,
The prisoned vitality
Talked down in its silence.
  " Cease, O my spirit,
Cease from thy travail,
Thy deep perturbation ;
The darkness is round thee ;
Thou art come to the silence,
The winter of nature.
The land of thy promise,
The goodly, the pleasant,
Is slipping and sliding
From under thy footsteps.
The strife of endeavour,
The tumult of peoples,
Lands, races, and cities,
In darklings and glowings,
Turbid forces, mysterious ;
Shard fragments of tempests
With pale, silent lightnings,

Are failing and fading,
Are dropping behind me.
  Ashore, dim and sorrowful,
Winding hither and thither,
Disconsolate, solitary,
Is around and beneath thee.
  A black fringe of waters,
 Laving ever—for ever
Mourning utterly, utterly,
Is nearing and nearing,
  And the new state of being,
The future, the unknown
Eternity of ocean,
Wrapt in duskings and dawnings,
Faintly lit by the glimmerings
Of Faith—the mysterious
And veiled conductor,
Is widening before thee.
The shreds of mortality,
The mistings and fadings
Of dreams that were precious
In life's day of dreaming,
Are trailing about thee.
  And Time, the unwearied,
Beats solemnly, slowly
In the distance—receding
And dying to silence,
As the faint, solemn sweepings,
The wonder-pulsations
Of the harp of Eternity

Swim soft in the borders
Of infinite distance,
And waken the spirit
To the new inspiration
Of marvel and motion.
  Oh, the panting, the panting,
The quiver of tension !
Be still and be patient,
Till the naked tree-stirrings,
The wailing of waters,
And the wind-sobbings fail
On the quick chords of being,
Till the frost-stars that glimmer
Through boundless abysses,
Take on them new meanings ;
Be patient, O spirit,
Be patient.
  The calmness
Grow calmer and calmer !
The widening æther
Hath warm palpitations,
And Life, in suspense
O'er the cold womb of Death.
Waits the new parturition—
In the far-off revealing.
The profluent surges,
Sweep inward and onward,
In a calm preterition,
Eternally, endlessly.
And beyond an horizon

Dimcast and uncertain,
Pale luminous lashes,
Like dawnings of sunlight
In eyes that are blinded,
Flush up the dead vapours,
And mystical breathings
Of an imminent waking
To a great revelation ;
Float fainter than whispers.

Soft ! Drifting and drifting,
The bright skirts of hazes
Revolving and folding,
Wrap golden about me.
While, thrilling, recumbent,
On ethereal wing-pulsings
Through thin waves of music,
'Neath gathering splendours
In breathless gradations
Borne glory-ward, floating,
For ever—for ever !

Lo ! death was upon him,
Till the grey of the morning
Broke cold on the moorlands,
And the storm had abated.
Then his features a moment
Flushed out a great radiance ;
Then died into blackness.
The blackness of ashes,
As the moon of the midnight
Pours light through a cloud-rift

And is suddenly darkened.
   All was done—and they placed him
In shape for his coffin,
And turned down the lamplight,
Let the few glowing embers
Die down into ashes ;
Drop the blind o'er the window
And leave him to darkness.

TIRED OUT.*

OFTLY float about me, Music,
      Wrap me up in soothing calms,
   Wile my spirit of its demon,
      With the magic of thy psalms ;
Wave the meadow's russet fruitage,
   Thrill the ivy's clasping bars,
Wake the mountain's bass intonings,
   Stir the lilac's bloom of stars ;
Loose the fountain of my being,
   Rouse my pulses' languid beat—
Let me lose the world a little,
   Find my wings and fold my feet.
I am tired of all the doing,
   Tired of all I've sung and wrought,
And my brow is damp with anguish,
   And my soul is sick with thought :

---

* The last Poem he wrote.

And the jar and incompleteness
  Of the things around oppress,
And the sense of baffled yearning,
  And the imploring tenderness,
And the hauntings of the vanished,
  And the sin and the regret.
That upon me lie so heavy,
  I would fain awhile forget.
Thrill around me, mystic music,
  Break in many a slumberous fall,
Charm me of my spirit's darkness,
  As of old the sullen Saul.
Let me taste Imagination's
  Sibyl-cup with Lethe blent;
Let my soul expand unfettered
  In her own wide element;
Let me drift along the twilight
  On the white aerial streams,
Starred with Fancy's constellations,
  Misted with the balm of dreams;
Let me feel the dew about me,
  Sunk on languorous asphodels,
Palm and laurel shadow-braided,
  Philter-charmed with opiate spells;
Let me feel the downy wafting
  Of innumerable wings,
Feel the touch, and gain warm glimpses
  Of the rarest fairy things;
Till a white Aurora gathers
  Up my starless arc of sky,

And a love-winged Iris beckons
  'Cross a summer realm of joy.
Wrap me from myself, O music,
  On thy surging sea of balms :—
Quiet—quiet—let me slumber
  On the lulling after-calms.

   *   *   *   *   *   *

And thereupon a dreamy dreaming came.
If I should wake no more ?—Oh, hope desired !
How will this body fare—will it repose
Untouched, unseen by one adventurous eye.
Until the storms have beat it into dust ?
Or will it sleep, in widely scattered
Where the fair winds of heaven excite the storms,
A fragment in the ambush of the fox ;
One in the sea-hunt of the cormorant ;
Another in the eagle's eyrie home ?
Where will their ashes sleep ? Oh ! wearisome
And long is life—bold, friendless, hopeless, bad !
How sweet is sleep, when one is wearied out !
How sweet is death when life is gone to aye !
Methinks that I could sleep upon the crest
Of any restless wave, as did my Master
Upon the raging sea of Galilee—
I am so tired ; come to me, gentle sleep !

THE NEWLY PUBLISHED PORTION OF
THE POEMS OF GEORGE HEATH.

THE INVALID POET.

SEPTEMBER o'er, the memoral hills had spread
. Their fan-like wings, and the wide expanse .
Smiled in luxury and opulence
Of wide abundance, and undiminished charms.—
A full-flushed matron in the prime of life,
With will unbroken, and serene of brow,
With spirit light, and flippant as a maid's,
With now and then a mood of soberness,
As dreaming of the future and the past.
The tinge of Autumn had not mellowed yet ;
The vision of the landscape, and red fruit
Still hung amid the clustering foliage ;
The fields along the slopes are wreathed with corn ;

The rivulets were shadow-haunted still ;
The sunset, like a holy Holocaust,
By myriad Nature offered to its God,
With hands uplifted, and adoring eyes
'Neath ocean brows of lofty lustrous calm,
Burned on the unhewn altar of the west,
And peer above huge coils of flossy clouds
Irradiate, with the all-pervading flame,
Like coloured wreaths of incense curled on haze.
The wrinkled hills, coeval with the sun,
The ocean and the stars, serene as when
Primeval forests sobbed around them, shone
Intensely bright, transfigured in the glory.
Long rafts of level lights stretched wide and far
From height to height along the Peniue hills ;
The valleys lay beneath them in a glow
Of softer radiance, and above the sky
Dozed in a calm of cherub slumberings ;
A little stir of humourous voiceless wind,
Enough to set the brooks a-tittering,
Involved the hills in trembling courtesings,
And stately rows of wigged and powdered trees,
And multiplied the thousand ripples on
The aftermath, and pounced with gay caress
On daises white, and shy-coquette of flowers
That, giggling, lowered and dipped their pretty heads,
As country maids when rifled of a kiss.
Beside a cottage roofed with homely thatch,
Beneath a canopy of sycamores ;—
A lordly row, that hung their shadow o'er

Across a patch, where, in the dawn of Spring,
A fairy family of snow-drops grew—
A young man sat upon a mossy stone,
Worn were his shoes and thread-bare were his robes ;
His puny limbs were thin and delicate ;
Upon the silence of his quiet brow
A shadow hung, and 'neath the widening eyes
The dark insignia of the sorrow-hand,
That never comes but leaves a mournful trace
Which no one may mistake, were charactered,
Around the chastened lips, a sensitive
Quick tremour ran, and 'neath the seedy vest
A hungry heart beat with a quickened pace ;
But triumph on the brow sat sunning now.
Tho' tears were in the eyes—the thirsty eyes—
That dwell upon the glory of the sunset,
And thitherward the hands were tightly clasp'd ;
Within the soul a calm exultant swell—
The consciousness of kinship with the grand,
The lofty, the sublime of earth and heaven ;
The spirit glorying o'er the power, the grasp
Of mind to feel and to appreciate
The glorious amid the beautiful of God.
And tears within the eyes—the shadow mist
That ever haunts the Summer bright of earth,
The weary droppings of despair o'er all
The futile struggles to expand the thoughts
That pant for utterance ; the impulses,
The mysteries of all we see and feel,
But never, never, never may express.

v

Anon the sun blaze sunk away and died,
And while the gloaming faded on the hills,
A change came o'er the form that sat amid
The shading of the sycamore.   The mind
Came back from wandering in the nature world,
And preyed upon itself; the yearning eyes
Turned from the outer to the inner world;
The tinkling sound of clogged and busy feet;
The clink of pans and pails, commingled with
The turning of a churn within the cot;
The gabble of the fowls, while fluttering
Away to roost; the herd-boy's shout; the sound
Of lowing kine, returning udder-eased
With empty duds, to dance the fields again.
The distant rumble of the homeward wain,
And all the hundred sounds of country life,
Rose with a chastened harmony upon
The lazy air, and played upon the ear,
And lightly touched his senses, but awoke
No perturbation, check, or dissonance
Within the mind: they were so usual:
And it, accustomed to their atmosphere,
Had grown impregnable: they had stripped off
Their individuality, and become
An element of silence; or more like
A soft accompaniment unto a song.
There while the glory sank and died; he dreamed :—
" A laden packman on the road at night
Pauses upon the summit of a hill,
And drops his load, and seats himself thereon,

And doffs his hat, and wipes his streaming brow,
And gazes back far down the dusty road :—
Afar the city nestles in the vale ;
The flashing lights are moving everywhere,
And double rows of lamps, like tiny stars,
Run blinking here and there ; and dreamily
The vision traces, long and listening,
The avenue of lights through which he came.
And nearer still, the dusky solemn trees
And blocks of cottages that rise
Dimseen, and mark the nearer torturous road—
And to his ear comes floating mellowly,
The mazy hum of many broken sounds
From the far city, inarticulate ;
No sounds defined—mixed—softened down
Into an indistinguishable, low
Dull monotone." I, like that traveller,
Pause on the rugged way, beneath the night,
And lower my load, and panting, gaze far back
And see the visions that I had before,
And mark them dusked and dimly ; as appear
Far distant objects in a morning fog ;
And hear soft shreds of sounds, all twin'd among,
But soft and beautiful, as some low strain
Waked from an organ in the twilight time
By fingers giving scope to spirit dreams
Within some vast, dimed, caverned emptyness
Whose every cavity gives back its voice.
How like a floating picture in a dream
That little cottage, where my memory

First caught a weak impression, seems.   The low
Long sunset light lies on it like a crown.
The cottage nest, whose low and broad'ning eaves
A man might almost reach with stretching up,
With battered chimney pot obliquely perched
Upon the gable, and a tutored plum
Stretching above the roof for higher hold ;
The doorway and the tiny avenue
O'er arched with tangled lobs of damson trees ;
The home-made patch ; the long and narrow lane ;
The gossiping streamlet straggling by its side ;
The variegated holly in the corner
Of the wee garden plot, where oft we lay,
Perdu, or played at cows with coloured shreds—
The flower-strewn, heart-shaped croft that lay below
Beneath the shadows of tremendous trees ;
The miry ditch behind, upon whose bank
The snowdrops come and then the primroses ;
The old gray Sunday-school, where the kind hand
Of him whose goodness through the many years
Has been my blessing, first conducted me.
These, with a thousand other features; rise
Before me, vaguely glimmering in the far
Dim mellowed mistiness.
                              Then comes the change.
The scenes rise up distinctly, nearer, fixed
In strange rays of light : a long, tall, gaunt,
And barefaced cottage, whitewashed outwardly,
A thin stark yew shoots up the front ;
Besides the door within the palisades

Behind, a nook of garden, nestling warm
Within a strong, high range of wall, or topped
With lolling rhododendrons, lilacs grey,
And long, lean slangs of ponds, o'ershadowed with
Dark clumps of hollies, running two above
And one below, besides an old bent road,
And everywhere are undulating slopes,
And belts of coppices, and meadow slips,
And pleasant lanes, and little serpent paths,
And humps of hills with face full of change—
These form a dingle, fixed for a time
Within my vision, changing constantly,
In light and hue, but featured still the same
While the wild panorama of the years—
The season's bannered dance; the stately face
Of queenly day; the night's stupendous march,
Sublime with nature's wonder-painting dews,
And hoary frosts and snows, and biting storms:
The rush and roar of winds; the tempest's surge;
The many shaped and many lustred clouds;
The thunder's awful talking, and the glimpse
Of lightnings issuing in forked shafts
From the black eaves of clouds; the calms,
The hushings, wastings, and the whisperings;
The glamours of great sunsets, and the wide
Unequalled splendours of the dawn. The awe
And erieness of spirit haunted twilight;
The floods of sunlight on the leys and lawns;
The marvellous night-shade weirdly alloyment;

With breathings of the many-languaged stars,
And all the manifold sublimity
Of the wide universe, grew on my soul.
A scene of wonderment and awfulness,
That filled my thought with silentness before
The unfathomable majesty, and wide
And vast stupendousness of visible things,
A feeling, or a reverence, or an awe
Dropped on my spirit, and my lips were dumb,
I wandered underneath all moods of skies,
And haunted nature in her every phrase,
And stood beneath the doming of the night
When o'er the orient the queen of heaven
Lay calm amid a sea of waveless film,
And all the vast still roof of blue, the white
Unnumbered multitude of panting stars
Intensely throbbed ; while mute around the earth
Lay slumbering, and trouble, pain and toil,
Grown dumb, bent o'er their wounds and died.
And up the vales the mists rose spectrally,
And on the hills the moon's magnificence
In webs of frosted silver, scattered lay.
I flung myself upon the earth and kissed
The hoary dews, and turned my face above
And watched the meteors gliding to and fro
And marked the shooting stars slip from their hold,
And glide with sheeny tails athwart the abyss,
And suddenly fade out and disappear.
And there I lay, and shuddering, deemed that these

Were worn out worlds whose sands of time had run,
Whom God had summoned to the judgment bar.
Unutterable thoughts rose on my soul.

The above terminates the poem to which the author has given the name of "Invalid Poet." The short life of affliction of George Heath, did not allow him to complete the undertaking, and consequently, like several of his other poems, it unfortunately remains a fragment. Amongst his manuscripts, however, are found lengthy passages which were evidently intended for the "Invalid Poet," with intervening suggestions for further poetic manipulation. These passages, in the order in which they appear, afford a good conception of what the poem if it had been finished, was designed to be, and as they comprise some of the finest thoughts he has anywhere penned, and indicate the opening of a fresh and much richer poetic vein, it would be doing an injustice alike to his memory and the public to withhold them from publication.

FRAGMENTS.

[Presentiment—Foreshadowings—A Dread—Foreknowledge of Sorrow—A Damp on the Spirits-—As the Thermometer will sink, tho' the approaching storm be days distant.]

[Secret Composition—Rhymes—A Wild and Ardent Love of Nature and Song—But feeling at first ashamed to own it.]

> Faded as fades the twilight into dark
> Or as the brook into the rivers rush.

When the first bright truthful dream is rudely broken, the flowery paradise of fancy vanishes and the real world looks so hollow and desolate—the mountains when seen from a distance and bathed in golden sunshine, look beautiful indeed, but when the cloud hangs upon their brow, and when seen nearer, look inaccessible, sterile and frowning.

Faded as fades the twilight into dark, as fades the sunbeam in the land.—There fell a shadow on her as a blank falls ᴐn the earth, when, noiselessly a cloud obscures the sun.

O realm of joy and love ! O land of light,
O home of peace eternal, infinite,
How longs the soul so press with untried wing,
The changeless glory of the noontide skies ;
To drink the nectar of thy taintless air ;
To lave its prisoned feet, so weary now.
Amid the calm, belustered land of
Thy ever smiling ocean crystalline ;
To wander o'er thy golden sanded shore ;
To bask amid thy living growths and blooms,
To revel 'mid the light and love of God.
O far off island in the monster sea ;
O longed for, hoped for, shadowed, unrevealed,
We gaze with longing, tearful eyes, into
The great dark silence of futurity
Wondering what pilot-star shall guide us there.
The spirit reaches out with yearning hands
To catch the floating weeds that speck the shore.
Wrestlings, upsoarings huge, unspeakable,
Feeling aye upward, blindly upward still
As gropes the tendril towards the larches top ;
As turns the blind his blank white eyes towards
The gorgeous beamings of the setting sun,
And reaches out and laves his withered hands
Amid the soft warm volume of his rays,
And feels within a pallid reflex of his light,*
And tho' he cannot see it, knows 'tis there.

---

*Correction by the Author (a lunar rainbow as it was).

Home of the beautiful, the good, the true,
How faints the immortal 'mid the realm of day,
Worn out with watching, yearning, heat and toil,
O'er shadowed with the constant cloud of sin;
How languishes, and grieves, and toils, and pants
To reach its native purity and rest.

O clime of tuneless tides, unshadowed skies,
Unfading blooms, untroubled hearts and brows,
How dear thou art : we clasp our hands and kneel.
Our tear-damp eyes strain upwards towards the stars
Which gaze unpitying down with sylph-like calm,
How dear thou art ! We love thee more even than
The home-sick exile loves his motherland :
We stand, like him, upon the shore and pierce
Far o'er the dusky glamour of the waves
Towards where we dream thou art, beloved home !

   *   *   *   *   *   *   *

Oh ! all we know of beautiful and good !
Oh ! all of fair that in our purer hours,
We dream might be—if other things might be—
If earth were pure, and sinless all could be—
Oh, all the holy whisperings of light,
Of glory and of purity that float
Into our souls in hours of calmer thought,
Are found, beloved, in thee—beloved, in thee !
Oh, all the lofty soul imagining,
The ideal world we revel in sometimes,
But dreamed of here, in thee are realized.
Oh ! all the spirit tides that surge and dash

With panting, articulate murmur, 'gainst
This shore of flesh, shall find an entrance there.
Sometimes we wander in the world of sense
And grow enamoured of its fading toys
And clasp the finite to the infinite.
And wonder why the weary void remains.
Sometimes its toils and care around us press
And clasp us close and cumber us about
And surge us from the living path afar.
Anon its trouble-times rescinds our faith
And then thou seem'st to be so far away.
We cannot realize thee—cannot feel
That thou art ever.   Clouds so dense, so close
Around thee cling: thou grow'st to be a dim
Strange shadowing of fair legend lore,
'And, oh ! our souls could weep, as one
Weeps o'er the funeral of his loftiest hope.

   And then some vision rises on our souls,
Some sense on which the seal of God is stamped
Distinct, complete and unmistakable.
It may be sunrise with her waking harp,
Her swell of song and dance of rosy dews ;
It may be sunset with her flowery flood
Of radiance down pouring from the hills ;
It may be midnight 'neath the awful stars,
And then we feel thee, O, so near, so near,
That we could almost grasp thee in our hands.
   Autumn.   The world was sad around : the change had
     come.
And Nature's face grew dim, and mute and sad—

Her gaudy weeds dropped fading round her form ;
Her rainbow tresses, glossy once and fresh,
Brushed back to wanton with the love-sick wind,
Hung round her features limp and lustrous.
Her face altered, yet we scarce knew where ;
Or looked the same, and yet a change had come
As when a fatal blight falls soft upon
A darling mother, who has seen old Time
Notch sixty marks upon the calendar
Of years, surrounded by the lives she got.
A change falls on her frame—a saddening blank—
They know 'tis so ; yet scarcely comprehend.
The sweet lips smile so sweet ; the lustrous eyes
Shine forth as light.   The voice, though weak, and low
Is still as full of kindliness and love.
And yet something is different,—something changed—
A stooping of the form, patter of the steps,
A fading of the crimson from the cheek ;
A weary sigh, perhaps they know not what,
And yet they feel she fadeth day by day,
And know her doom is fixed.   The leaves hang sere
Upon the silent tree.

*   *   *   *   *   *   *

The tearful sun wading through a hideous mass of
        inky cloud.

*   *   *   *   *   *   *

Arrived as 'twere unto a stand-still point in life—
Even as a weary and belated traveller in a strange
Land arrives at a place where two ways cross—

His feet are blistered; his heart is sad, and he longs
To reach some friendly shelter, and would fain
Start on that way which will soonest bring him
To it; but the thence untravelled ways stretch
Far o'er the desolate moor and out into the dreary
Night, and he, sorrowing, hesitates, knowing not
Which to choose.

*   *   *   *   *   *   *

Akin to nature building nests in imitation to birds.

*   *   *   *   *   *   *

And when the first green leaves came budding out
Upon the gooseberry and the currant trees,
We raised him, and he gazed a long wrapt look
Through the green windows o'er the daffodil beds,
Then smiled, and said, " Please, mother, go and bring
The one small twig with tiny leaves at top?"
I got him one, and then, and then a withy twig
With little yellow goslings dotted o'er,
He looked them round as if examining
Their web and thread—the marvel of their make,
Then, kissing them, look'd up, and softly said,
" Thank God! thank God, I've seen the leaves again.
I stand alone amid the human world—
No hands fall softly on my fevered brow;
No tender voice gives shape to pitying words,
That loving, lingering eyes are frequent with,
'Tis sad to have no friend, no love, and none
To feel a passing interest in one's dreams.
The western bard says, " none was ever yet

So utterly alone and desolate
But that some kindred heart responded to
The secret beatings of his own." But, ah !
I stand alone upon the senseless hills,
Outside the centre of all human ties;
I stand upon the hills where nothing grows
But shrivelled penury and stunted care,
And where the chill wind of adversity
Beats over on my white and stony brow.
I stand and gaze upon the jostling throng—
The surging sea of faces in the vale—
The scathing, struggling mass of life and strife ;
An ocean rocked and tossed by passion winds
Whose waves for evermore upsurge and sink,
Upon where crests, like ocean weeds and flowers,
Strange faces changing and commingling aye
Rise for one moment on the paly light   .
And gleam out spectral—fade and disappear,
While others rise—faces of morning hues—
Spring dawning faces,—beautiful and bright.
Touched into sunshine by the heart's delight ;
Limned into laughter by the tickling shams
And many-coloured shells that float around—
Sweet girlish faces soft and apple bloomed —
Chaste youth and maiden gleams—crisp dusky locks,
And long brown glittering tresses stuffed and twined—
Pure faces white and innocent, wrought into smiles,
By the congenial contact with their kind,
Bring out things that raptures, gazes upon and smiles.
To see the sheeny sea unconscious of

The mass of hideous life that writhes below—
Calm solemn faces—faces ribbed with care—
Wild—agonized, imploring, torture-twitched—
Weird, hideous, cunning, stony-staring ones,
Convulsed and passion-warped and writhen—
Long, wrinkled, shrivelled, mad and vacant eyed,
Sad, patient, suffering faces white as is
The snow upon the unflinching northern hills,
Whose placid summits kiss the icy clouds—
Brooding, despairing faces, mute and blanched
With swoon-like motion bellowing evermore—
Rise, fall, commingle, vanish, swell and sink.
I stand a statuary sentinel upon
The dimless hills that skirt the plain of life,
My vision like a waif of air floats o'er
The dismal scene.   I watch the constant whirl,
The eddying circle of the pied whirlpool
Deep in whose centre, ghastly horror-ribbed—
Enthroned amid the Sodom of his spoils,
Sits ghoul-eyed Death, in undisputed power
While round him float on black and putrid wing,
His goblin ministers, who do his will,
Impurpled crime, besotted ignorance,
And rabid lust and passion frenzy-fired.

  *   *   *   *   *   *   *

' Night's pallid sentinels—the sleepless stars.

  *   *   *   *   *   *   *

He watched the shooting stars slip from his hold,
And glide with sheeny trails athwart the abyss,
And suddenly fade out and disappear ;

And there his simple heart would, wondering, deem
Them worn out worlds, whose sands of time had ran,
Whom God had summon'd to the judgment seat.

* * * * * * *

It was a bitter, cold, and sterile Spring,
One of those spiteful Winter-ridden times
When surly March lays down the sceptre
With a scowl, and, clinging to the dropping skirts
Of maiden April, spits his withering spite,
O'er half her length.   The wind, day after day,
Howled fitfully among the pregnant trees
That waited patiently the cuckoo's chant
To hum their mass of heaving hidden life.
An almost constant rush of broken clouds
Swept o'er the wild and eerie looking sky.
Alternate storms of rain and hail poured down ;
Anon the sun flushed forth with glistening rays,
And all the blue would be a moment clear,
Save here and there huge bouldered heaps of clouds,
With smoke—like billows gorged and globular,
And wool-white, flossy, upper sides, sometimes
Lay black in the pale blue long sinuous seams,
Of bushy branching mare-tail straggled far—
Besides the window he would sit and watch
The blustering hail flush white upon the world,
And then the great big bellied cloud slide off
And form a black wall on the southern rim.
And then the sunshine and the radiant bow
Limned 'gainst the sullen black with apex lost
Amid the blue that stretch'd above ; or gaze

Along the windy, rock-bound passages
Of the auriferous clouds, which seemed to be
Long vistas opening into unknown lands.
Then he would sigh, " The parable of life,"
And still he lingered, and the time wore on
And came the south wind with the filtering showers,
The sultry air, and distant thunder-clap,
And all things seemed to surge with prisoned life.
The birds sang, and the fickle swallows came
To skim upon the surface of the pool ;
To build a nest upon the drooping shed,
To sit amid the sycamores and sing.

＊　　＊　.　＊　　＊ .　＊　　＊　　＊

Sorrow, like an eclipse hung upon his brow.

＊　　＊　　＊　　＊　　＊　　＊　　＊

　　The past seems far away, and all things changed,
Stand amid the present calm, and gaze far
Back and all the calm receding but fadeless past
Seems like a feverish-troubled dream.

＊　　＊　.　＊　　＊　　＊　　＊　　＊

As slips the moon into the bosom of a still white cloud.

＊　　＊　　＊　　＊　　＊　　＊　　＊

The earth holds up its sad pale face to the soothing kiss
　　　of night.
He watched them twittering past the window, glide,
And said, " Thank God, I've seen ye once again,"
And thereupon he sang a little song—
" Thrice welcome, fragile messengers of Spring,
Gay visitant of Summer's holiday—

　　　　　　　　　　　　　　　　　　　　　w

The most assiduous votary of mirth—
Glad herald nymph in Flora's fragrant train—
Wrapt worshipper at Phœbus' pageant shrine,—
Thrice welcome to our homely sea-girt isle,
And to thy tenant-right upon the beam,
And to our fields and bowers, our homes and loves.
I saw thee with thy tribe awhile ago,
Twittering a gay farewell, serenely glide
Into the gold of morning's misty realm.
I watched ye till ye faded from my sight.
And then I bowed my head and wept, for ah !
I never hoped to see ye birds again,
Unless, indeed, to watch ye from above,
Where never wing of yours may hope to soar.
I wondered often as the days went on
How far you were, if any friendly tale
Had chanced to chase your flight, if you had gained
The wished for port, all safe and well, and if
Your wings were very tired with winging o'er
So many hundred leagues of mottled waves.
All through the winter days I wondered oft
What spot of earth your restless wings had found—
If some gay tract amid unheard of lands—
If some rich island home 'mid virgin tear—
If some salubrious haunt 'mid unknown climes,
Where foot of man has never stamped its mould,
And never voice of mortal echoed 'mongst
The flowers festoon'd and forest-braided hills,
And not one sound disturbs its charmed sleep,
Save now and then the echoing roll of some

Enormous crumbling rocks o'ercome at last.

 * * * * * * *

What though the world should never hear my song,
Sings not the nightingale a tender song
Amid the forest shades, and 'neath the night,
Unto a slumbering world? And why? Because
God gave to it a song—and thus it sings,
Not unto man, but God, who blessed it so.

 * * * * * * *

 The night comes forth with sadness, leading on
The dusky gloom, swaithed hours thro' whose darkened
  realm
The hearsed clouds, with sad funeral pall,
And muffled step and slow, pass on and on,
Crape-plumed and draped, like mourners to a grave ;
Like sobbing women bending o'er their dead ;
Like languid ghosts with hands clasped 'cross the eyes ;
And e'en the day seems like a still white slab
Upon a tear-damp grave, on which one reads
The mournful legend of departed joy.

 * * * * * * *

 O Fate ! I only asked thee for a friend,
A tender, loving, sympathising friend :
I never hoped to win a dearer tie.
O Fame ! I only asked thee for a wreath,
A simple wreath, to please my friend withal.
O Life ! I only asked thee for a moderate lease,
A simple, quiet lot, ungilded by
The gloss of wealth and power, but blessed with health.
O Earth ! they have not deigned to heed my prayer ;

Thou wilt be kinder to me, mother earth.
And give me all I ask of thee, I know,
A quiet resting-place.

*   *   *   *   * '   *   *

I've seen the sun that through a Summer's day
Rode gloriously across a cloudless sky,
Sink 'mid the western mists with solemn face,
Kept off his beams, and all his power at night.

*   *   * .   *   *   *   *

  The noontide glory, twilight's mystic calm,
The morning's flush, and sunset's ardent glow,
Are marvellous ; are all Thy works, O God.

[*Describe some of the Works—Grand Scenes.*]

When he would pause in listening attitude,
And to his eye would spring the ready tear,
And he would softly sigh ; while round his soul
Association wove its mystic spell.

*   *   *   *   *   *   *

[*Songs of the Day—The Night—The Seasons—Songs of the
    Heavenly Bodies—A Perpetual Voluntary of Praise to
    God.*]

  My life is full of change, and hence of pain ;
A beauteous object rises on my sight,
And joins the current of its life with mine—
A tender object that my soul could love.
It blooms before me chaste and glorious ;
The tendrils of my heart entwine it round:
I glow to love it so, till I could kneel

And pray in piteous strains—Abide with me ;
Be true, and pure, and tender, as we dream
That life and love should be ; O share with me
The sadness and the dream of life ; and then
So I can bear the shadow and the storm,
And live and wrestle as a man should do :
Oh, do not leave me as the rest have done !
But ah ! just then it fades and leaves a pang,
A wailing bitterness within my soul,
A tomb amid the graveyard of the past ;
While others come to fill the vacant place,
But only come to fade when dearest loved ;
And thus my life is one long scene of change,
Until association, sighing, haunts
Sad memory's blotted page, and every scene
Reflects a shadow on the stream of life.

*   *   *   *   *   *   *

                    No sound was heard
But the simultaneous sobbings of the wind ;
And, far away amid the night somewhere,
The guttural mutterings of a cataract,
Like the dull murmur of approaching storms,
A distant clamour of awakening winds,
Or hollow murmurs of subsiding waves.

*   *   *   *   *   *   *

  By Time's resistless toil, huge piles that through
Unnumbered ages laughed his power to scorn ;
Or crush of giant tree, that years and years
Had stood up spectral, naked and decayed ;

Or wildly, frightful growl, or shriek of some
Fierce beast, or monster bird apocryphal;
And if ye sported o'er unfurrowed lakes
Unexhausted by the song of plashing oars,
Or rippling laugh of tourists on the shore;
Dull, stagnant lakes, besotted in their rest,
Half matted o'er with water, weeds, and flowers,—
Bestudded here and there with wooded isles,
Whose charming foliage braids their sombrous shores,-
Great strumpet sketches, swelling in the glamours
Of Sol's uxorious spell, whose amorous gaze
Flaps fulsomely and changelessly upon
Each pulseless breast, from day to day, or if
He wandered to the far-off orient,
Where flash the glittering spire and mineret,
And dome and mosque, and temple huge mooresque,
And floats the gay gondola dreamily;
O'er charmed lakes that drank the lustrous sky,
And azure bays that whisper of the sea,
No timorous rivulets, 'twixt banks of bloom,
And where the luminous firs thy dreams, 'mid
Great forest stretches of umbrageous palm,
And 'cross the gay festoons of creeping vines,
That span the still ravines and forest breaks,
And golden-plumaged birds with singings glide,
And 'mid the bosky vales a world of flowers,
A tropic growth of flowers luxuriates,
And virgin lilies bend o'er crystal streams,
And nod and kiss the ripples as they glide
Beneath the soft aroma-breathing breeze,

And airy groups in robes fantastical,
In all the gay romance of love and youth,
Make resonant with laughter-trills the heights,
Where glows an incandescent radiance still.

*   *   *   *   *   *   *

My life seems thus to me—a hay-day morn,
With sunshine fair and calm but dim with mists,
And cauled with clouds that bulged their black-ribbed
    shapes
Along the glory of Aurora's bower.
A dawning dimmed, and damped with shades at first,
But mid-day up the east a rift rose up,
And from the ether calm, and blue beyond,
The sun steals forth with wonder-making power,
And poured an evanescent glory out,
And wakes to life the music of the earth—
A rapturous song of happiness and love.
Anon a storm ferments adown the west,
And silently the great black clouds steal up
And gather round the foreheads of the hills.
The wind upsprings fitfully at first,
And chafes the elements to hideous war.
The lightning glares ; the thunder roars and rolls ;
The rain pours down, and darkness all the day :
Even so my life was calm, but dim at dawn.
Anon a glory burst upon my life,
And o'er my tranced and listening soul there stole
The wondrous echo of a raptured song.
Anon affliction's cloud closed o'er my soul,
And Sorrow's tempest bursts around my head,

And all of joy seemed hustled out of life ;
But ever, 'mid the pulses of the storm,
The echo of that song comes back to me,
And fills my life with charity and love,
And gives me fortitude to live and hope—
The one sweet drop of nectar in my cup.
   *   *   *   *   *   *   *

A long black shoal of clouds lay in the still
Blue ocean, like rock bow'd shore of some
Chaotic island waste, huge blocks on blocks,
Vast oblong heaps of parti-coloured shade,
And isolated lumps of gleaming quartz
Unshaped, auburn, like tufts of yellow broom,
In strange confusion tumbled everywhere.
   *   *   *   *   *   *   *

Rich honey falls, like dew, had drizzled on
The sheeny leaves of the old oaks and elms,
And glistened there, exhaling nectar's scents :
Each tree a posey fragrant, and a busy mart
Where myriad bees awoke a constant hum.
 *   *   *   *   *   *   *

                    Be mine
To sow the country with a plenteous stock
Of noble deeds ; to simplify great thoughts ;
Digest great truths, and soften down harsh shapes
For lesser minds to grasp ; to say sweet things,
And throw them broadcast to the winds ; to heal
Sad wounds that ache, and purify the font
Of inner thought ; to think for those who toil
And suffer silently, and have not time

To think the life they feel ; to be the voice
That utters all the panting heart of still
Blind, patient, labour-life, throbs audibly
To dream ; to raise the standard of example
Worthy of life ; to soothe, with kindred hand,
With tender, pitying hand, the weak, the wronged,
The erring, suffering ones, and to the bad
Be evermore a conscience of reproach.

*   *   *   *   *   *   *

The floods far up the valley blustered white
Amid the dark moon-mingled scowl of night ;
The hills around them rose black-bowed and stark ;
The clouds above them swayed in densest mist ;
The torrents hissed and surged, and sobbed the wind,
Like the vast heavings of a deathless mind
Gone mad with agony—strong, furious, shrill ;
Anon, exhausted, calm and stony still.
The tempest fiends, with fearful shriek and bark,
Lashed into madness, wrestled 'mid the dark,
Low cringing, crouched the black wind within trees
And bushes stooped, as men sunk on their knees
In awful prayer—stern, ghoul-like eyes afraid
Gleamed pitifully amid the shifting shade.
Storm demons, vapour-draped and icy-faced,
Hurl'd headlong torrents o'er the shuddering waste ;
Anon the slopes precipitately tore
Horse wreaths of cataracts, whose thundering roar
Clashed with the trumpet blarings overhead,
Dimmed to the shuddering soul in shadow dread.
Beyond the hills the huge volcanic blaze

Of belching furnaces, a ghastly haze
Of lurid sallowness, now dark, now bright,
Hung on the clouds amid the western night,
An awful scoffing of sardonic spleen ;
A fearful laughing of a devilish dream.

   *   *   *   *   *   *   *

Noon-day, and dark and drear : the tempest lowers ;
Loud round the heights the wild Boreas roars ;
Anon the murk breaks up ; the sun bursts forth,
While foaming storm-steeds rear far up the north,
And great white bulks athwart the azure sweeps, ;
And on the circling hills the snow lies deep.
Then the grey steed dust thickens on the air,
And long grim shadows gather, gape and stare,
And o'er the landscape bursts the torrent fray,
And gloom and desolation rule the day.
Vast night hath vanished, and the quiet stars
Have passed into obscurity of light,
And o'er the wintry landscape big paunched clouds
Glout sullenly ; the light is scarcely light ;
A damp all-clasping gloom is everywhere.
My temples ache and throb, and sickness burns
Silently within me.
              All my hopes and dreams
Have pressed into the shadows for a time,
And with the day—the melancholy day—
My darkened spirit holds a gloom-brow'd vigil.
How very small our little objects seem !
How very trivial our pursuits and plans !
When viewed in retrospect.

And hunger still the mouthing vapours rolled
About the dark, dumb mountains, and the trees
Grew awe smit, standing spectre still : at times
A shuddering brake about the upper leaves,
And all the body of waters waiting long
In awful calm, and durst not utter voice.
Anon ! South-east the clouds upsprung above
The gaunt horizon, and an arc of pale,
White, misty light spread upwards, widened out,
And all the earth-pearl sown from east and south,
And shadow-darkened from the west and north,
Lay wondrous still and eerie underneath ;
And, lo ! an angel with a mist-wreathing brow
Rose, faintly-shadowed, 'mongst the snowy steam,
And grew, and grew in grand proportions, while
The upper light upon his inner robe
Of radiance dimly, subdued, down-poured.

    *   *   *   *   *   *   *

  Existence is a child's race for the cup,
The golden cup, that 'neath the rainbow lies.
The more his.

    *   *   *   *   *   *   *

The darkness was rift with a noise like a cataract's fate,
And earthward swept, blinding a radiance as awful, as
       bright ;
The island bent fear-struck, the forest, the fen, and the
       night.
            The reef and the ocean were all
A-quiver, a-glamour, a-glimmer with light.

    *   *   *   *   *   *   *

[*Second Daughter.*]

She sang sweet songs in her young girlhood's days,
Around the lanes and around our lowly cot ;
And she could sing—O how my lass could sing !
Youth passed among the fields o' Summer night,
And bent their heads to listen to her song.

*   *   *   *   *   *   *

A dense disordered march of vapour-rack
Shot through with mists of lights, dividing wide,
Stirred o'er the mountains 'neath the southern sun.
The trees, like lank, impassioned hands outstretched,
With mute imploring gestures, rose distinct
The deadly gloom ; as when some new waked soul
Lifts up strong, agonising hands for light.

*   *   *   *   *   *   *

Emblems of a rushing noise.
The drowsy sibilence
Of wind-swept oaks whose robe of withered leaves
Have struck through all the blasts of winter fierce.

*   *   *   *   *   *   *

[*Grandmother.*]

I've one withered leaf hangs on an oak
Through all the change of Autumn, and the blasts
And sterile loneliness of Winter; while
The frail companions of her Summer's day
Have dropped away and mouldered into dust.
I've seen it hang a shrivelled thing amid
The fructuous opulence of young maid Spring,

Until another generation burst around
And hid it 'mid the tincture of her charms,
Until the first brown tinge had spoiled the green,
Then slip away in silence, as if 'twas
The first fruits of another Winter dearth.
So I am now a withered thing, alone ;
A waif of other days—all things are changed ;
I long to slip away unseen, unheard,
To those I loved, that long have left me lone.

   *   *   *   *   *   *   *

They tell me that the more the vine is pruned,
The deeper, richer is her wealth of fruit ;
They tell me that the more her roots are pressed
And prisoned low, the stronger and the higher
The palm lifts up her head unto the heavens.
I know that more the creeping camomile
Is trodden on, the more luxuriantly
It grows ; the richer fragrance flings around.
So be it with my life ; the more the scythe
'Of death lops off the dear ones from my stem,
The greater growth of tenderness, the fruit
Of truer, wider sympathies for all.
The loved, the sorrow-thirsty round me cluster.
The more affliction grindeth on the roots
Of my existence, still the more my soul
Wings upward towards the atmosphere of heaven,
Where vision hath a grander, wider zone,
And where the air is purer ; and the more
Misfortune stampeth on the bud
Of my out-going hopes, the greater be

The calm luxuriance of my flowing thoughts ;
The richer fragrance of my words and deeds.

*   *   *   *   *   *   *

[*Thoughts for a Prayer.*]

And thou, O Virtue, with the brow benign,
O Virtue, purest spirit of the earth,
And rarest, whether in the garret high
Above the grossness of the city's sin,
Or in the valley 'mongst the villages,
Or on the mountain's brow, where pastoral toil
Makes beautiful the landscape, where dwellest thou ?
O come and dwell with me, and calm and curb
Impulses, headstrong waywardness, and bring
My passions underneath thy sway benign !
O come and be my prompter—be my friend,
And travel with me under every sky,
And lead me up the path of innocence
Unto the home where holy honour sits
Enthroned, and communes with calm-browed peace.

*   *   *   *   *   *   *

And I was conversant
With all the moods of nature, and to me
They seemed the shadowings of things beyond.
I thought that, may be, in this visible,
The shape, the pattern, the unravelling
Of the invisible was charactered,
If but the puny mind of puny man
Could rise above itself and comprehend
The mighty hieroglyphs.   I loved the stir,
The throb, and heaving of the Spring ; and then

The wide magnificence of Summer, with
The glow of suns ; the wave of woods and chant
Of animation ; then the mournful roll
Of mist-surpliced, and wind-wielded Autumn, borne
Athwart the hecatom of leaves full low,
And silent-like funeral ; and then
The dearth and dissonance of Winter : Death
Awaiting resurrection life.

    *   *   *   *   *   *   *

I looked Death firmly in the face, and ceased
To start and tremble at the thought of him.
I reasoned with my coward faculties,
And quivered at the name, and conjured up
Before in array the figure Death,
In every possible shape, and drew a line
Round all his terrors and his properties,
And analysed, and pondered deep, and viewed
Them o'er in every aspect, till my mind,
Accustomed to their seeming, ceased to fear.
I chose the fearfullest of shapes, and reasoned thus :
" The worst, if it should come, is only so.
I'll steel my soul to meet the most severe.
A thousand things may hap to soothe the blow,
Or may be change the current for a time.
There are full many chances in the lap
Of Providence : 'tis probable that I
Shall draw a blank ; and yet 'tis possible
That I may draw a prize ; I cannot tell :
I know not, but at least Death will but be
A visitor once ; why should I die and die

A hundred deaths a week?   I thought, I'll work,
And do the little I may do while I can.

*   *   *   *   *   *   *

The clouds lay all along the mountains, where
The night marched like the tide from sea to sea,
And mists in ragged fringes hung upon
The edge of darkness.

*   *   *   *   *   *   *

Sometimes when we have sped the downward course
With headlong foot, a sadder pause falls on
The fever of our spirits ; e'en as one
Who wanders in the darkness ; comes at length
Unto a chasm's edge and knows it not,
But feels a sudden dread within his soul,
The presence of a danger which compels
The shuddering sense to check the giddy foot
Before the last, the fatal step is taken.

FOUND DEAD.

THERE she sat beside the window,
    With the curtains drawn away,
  Looking out into the glory,
    Of the fast declining day ;
Over blocks of busy factories,
  Over vast and grinning tiles,
Over stacks of belching chimnies,
  Over tiers of sooty tiles,
Far athwart the pale horizon,
  Where the sunbeams, lingering still,
Wrought a crown of transient glory
  On each dim far distant hill ;
Swept the dreamy eyes the welkin,
  While the milky sun-lit hue
Slowly melted from the grandeur
  Of the deeper, darker blue ;
Watched the fleecy cloud-wraiths floating
  Calm and spirit-like to rest,

In their white and shining raiment,
  In the haven of the west,
Up into the quiet chamber
  From the wide and busy street,
Sounds of rumbling wheels, commingling
  With the tramp of hasty feet ;
And the hum of many voices,
  And the vacant laugh uprose
From the throng of hardy toilers
  Hastening home to court repose.
But she heard them not, and scarcely
  Saw the radiant cloudlets glide,
Like the angel, Hope, for ever
  Pointing towards the shining side.
She was dreaming, fondly dreaming,
  Dreams of beauty, one by one,
Scenes embalmed by weeping memory
  Faded with the past and gone,
She was far from noisy cities,
  Free as Fancy's airy wing,
Roaming 'mid the blossomed woodlands
  Such a wild and elfish thing ;
Or with golden head uncovered
  Basking in the shady nook ;
Weaving crowns of ferns and foxgloves,
  Throwing pebbles in the brook,
Tossing hay in bleaching meadows,
  Pulling Hero's shaggy locks,
Culling flowers from mossy ruins,
  Climbing ledges of the rocks,

Darting through the sloping garden,
　Chasing pussy here and there,
Stealing like the radiant sunbeam,
　Bright and smiling everywhere ;
Sitting on the beach at sunset
　On a loving father's knee,
Listening to his tales of fairies
　And the wonders of the sea.
She was in her little chamber,
　Kneeling by the bedside there,
With a fond face bending o'er her
　Listening to her evening prayer ;
And she felt again the pressure
　And the thrill of long ago,
When that tender mother laid her
　On her pillow, white as snow—
Drew the curtains closely round her,
　Shutting out the fading light,
Pressed a kiss upon her forehead,
　Softly breathed a fond good-night.
But those days of love and sunshine
　Waxed to weeks, and months, and years,
And a cloud of blackest sorrow
　Rose at last, surcharged with tears.
For that pure and gentle mother
　Laid her loving sway aside,
Sank, when Autumn leaves were falling,
　'Neath affliction's hand and died
And the world became so dreary
　When that wasted form was laid

In her snow-white robe to slumber
  'Neath the yew tree's dusky shade.
But the cold and sombre Winter
  Slowly, slowly passed away,
And sweet Spring, with shower and sunshine,
  Lengthened out the transient day.
Then she wandered, sad and listless,
  Through the blushing fields and bowers,
Courting Nature's smiles and kisses,
  While she stole her fairest flowers.
Wandered to the silent graveyard,
  Knelt beside the naked mound,
Dropped a tear or two, and scattered
  Nature's treasures all around ;
Darker, darker, fell the shadow,
  For her father grew less kind,
And another claimed the title
  Which the noble dead resigned.
And she did not treat her kindly,
  As the sainted one had done ;
So the cloud fell darker—denser,
  As the months and years rolled on.
Then at twilight oft she rambled
  Where the larch and willow wave ;
Sat beneath the shady yew tree
  On a lone and silent grave ;
Not alone, for oft another
  Came that lowly seat to share—
Came to gaze upon those features
  Which he thought divinely fair ;

Left the gambols of the village,
   Stole away from scenes of toil,
Came to cheer the grieving maiden,
   Came to win a grateful smile.
He was one of Nature's nobles,
   Though his face was bronzed and flecked ;
Though his form was not in gaudy
   Or in costly robes bedecked ;
And his heart was brave and tender,
   Free from sorrow, free from guile ;
She could read it in the sun-light
   Of a broad and happy smile ;
In the flashing and the glowing
   Of those deep, magnetic eyes,
Never shrinking, never flinching,
   Clear as Summer's liquid skies,
Strength and energy and daring
   In that stalwart form were met ;
Truth and honour on that forehead,
   Like the seal of God, were set.
Yes ! he often came at twilight,
   Came at first with timid feet,
Ever longing for her presence,
   Dreading still her form to meet ;
And whene'er his eyes i' th' distance
   Caught the gleam of snowy dress,
Or the waving of a ribbon,
   Or the flutter of a tress.
Ah ! his feet would pause a moment,
   And his heart would throb again,

And the soul that laughed at danger
  Owned itself a coward then ;
And his face would glow with blushes
  If she only looked or smiled,
And the hero in her presence
  Was as docile as a child.
But as time went on, the blushes
  And the shyness wore away,
For she grew to be the sunshine
  And the glory of his day.
And if aught his footsteps hindered
  She would grieve and wonder why,
For his presence filled her bosom
  With a strange and secret joy,
For to him she told her troubles,
  All the shadows that were cast
O'er the Spring-time of her being
  From the present and the past ;
And he strove to soothe and cheer her,
  Spoke so fondly—tenderly ;
Satisfied her spirit's yearning
  With his honest sympathy ;
Till they closer sat together
  On that grassy grave alone ;
Till the small white hand lay prisoned
  Still and passive in his own ;
Till his arm stole softly round her,
  And his breath was on her cheek ;
Till she felt the stout frame quiver,
  But she could not—dared not speak,—

While he poured with strange vehemence
    All his passion in her ears,
All his hopings and his yearnings,
    All his doubtings, cares, and fears;
Till he sued to be the pilot
    That should guide her through the strife;
Asked to have within his keeping
    All her being, all her life;
Till her heart grew mutely happy,
    And her spirit owned the spell,
For she knew his words were truthful,
    And she felt she loved him well,
Till she could but creep more closely
    To the haven of his breast;
Till her fair head graced his shoulder,
    And his lips to hers were pressed;
And she listened while he builded
    Fairy castles in the air,
Bright with sunbeams, gay with flow'rets,
    Which together they would share;
While he 'alked of home and comfort,
    Of the altar and the throne,
Of a shady vine-roofed cottage
    When she came to be his own.
Sat they there till o'er them slowly,
    Strange and sweet, an influence stole,
Till their tongues grew mute with rapture,
    And they spoke but soul to soul;
Sat until the sunlight faded
    And the shadows longer grew,

Till the night let fall her curtain,
   And the stars came peeping through.
Homeward then beneath the larches,
   Hand in hand they went their way,
Heeding not the darkness round them,
   Dreaming only of the day,
Ah! how oft, in pensive twilight,
   Through those blooming fields they roam,
Far adown the verdant valley,
   Where the mimic cat'racts foam ;
Followed joyously the windings
   Of that shade becheckered stream,
Gathered flowers from dim recesses,
   Watched the wavelets dance and gleam,
Or beneath a willow seated,
   With her hand in his, he sang
(While weird echo wildly mocking
   From each nook and cranny rang) :

THE LOVER'S SONG.

"Oh! ye barren-hearted mortals,
   Ye who breast the waves alone,
With no sunny smile to cheer you,
   And no hand to clasp your own :
Ye, who sad and single-handed,
   O'er life's pathway tread,
Scorning flowers of rarest beauty,
   Culling bitter weeds instead.
Oh! the barren waste grows fruitful,
   And the desert blooms with flowers,

And the shadow yields to sunshine
   'Neath a love as true as ours.
Oh! ye moping ones, who ever
   Kneel at Mara's bitter shrine,
Ever sit in fancied darkness,
   Ever murmur and repine;
Ye who say the world is dreary,
   Bounded by a stormy tide,
Ever gaze beyond the brightness
   To the dark and gloomy side;
Oh! the barren waste grows fruitful,
   And the desert blooms with flowers,
And the shadow yields to sunshine
   'Neath a love as true as ours.
O! beneath a spreading chestnut,
   In a shady, quiet spot,
Close beside a sparkling brooklet
   Stands a vine-embowered cot;
And we'll make it bright, my darling,
   With the halo of our love;
O! we'll make this earth a foretaste
   Of the Paradise above.
For the barren waste grows fruitful,
   And the desert blooms with flowers,
And the shadow yields to sunshine
   'Neath a love as true as ours."

Ah ! 'tis ever thine, " Life's Spring-time,"
 Ever thine, immortal youth,
To imagine scenes of beauty,
 And to dream them fairest truth :
Thine to gaze adown life's pathway,
 O'er the rough and thorny part ;
In the glow of light reflected
 From the sunshine in thy heart,
Dreaming not of Summer's fever,
 Or of Winter's chilly gust,
Gazing steadfastly right onward,
 Meeting all with perfect trust.
O ! thou ever blooming goddess,
 Wherefore cheat thy subjects so ;
Wherefore strew the path with blossoms
 That will wither ere they blow ?
Wherefore hide the darksome pitfalls,
 Wherefore gild the hollow fruit,
Ever gleaming in the distance,
 Mocking aye the vain pursuit ?
Is it sweet to thee to see them
 Fighting, groping blindly on,
With the darkness thick'ning round them,
 All their dreams of beauty gone ?
Is it sweet to see them yielding,
 Own with many a bitter tear,
That their hopes were but delusions,
 And their joys but transient here ?
Ah, perchance thou lov'st to see them
 Gazing, ever gazing back.

With a look so sad—so wistful—
  To thy smooth and shining track.
Ah ! thou know'st they will not hate thee
  For thy bright—too brief deceit,
For the illusion, while it lasted,
  O ! 'twas sweet—intensely sweet !
Sitting there beside the window
  She was beautiful to see,
Turning aye the gleaming circlet
  Round her finger absently.
From the calm and classic forehead
  O'er the shoulders white and bare,
Like a shower of golden sunlight
  Fell the wavy, fluttering hair.
And her robe of snowy muslin
  Plain in style, but pure and neat,
Fitting loosely to her figure
  Closed around the fairy feet.
And her features, O ! her features
  Strangely beautiful were they,
For the flush of youthful vigour
  And the smile had passed away.
And a still and marble whiteness
  Overspread the saintly face
Where her hand of thought was slowly
  Working many a silent trace,
And the calm sad eyes, so thrilling,
  Still were inward, gazing back
Through the cloud-rack and the shadow
  To " the smooth and shining track."
" Ah !" she murmured, " all have fallen

Faded swiftly, one by one ;
E'en my girlhood's love has withered
    And its object vanished—gone !
Though we thought, alas ! that sooner
    Than our love should change or pall
Sooner should the sun grow rayless,
    Sooner should the heavens fall.
We who stood alone together
    Mingling sweetly soul with soul,
Now are severed wide asunder—
    Far apart as pole from pole.
Presently a brighter influence
    Crossed the dream track of her life ;
Up before her stole an object
    Whisp'ring softly, " Darling wife."
Manly arms were twined around her,
    Tender lips to hers were pressed,
Quick the mists broke up and vanished
    And she felt supremely blest,
As she whispered, " O my husband !
    Welcome to my home and heart,"
While he stroked her hair and echoed,
    " Never, never more to part,"
And her inmost soul exultant,
    Low, re-echoed " Never more."
Came a tap, and then a footstep,
    And a maiden cross'd the floor,
Bowing, " Here's a letter, madam :
    'Twas for you the postman said."
All at once the happy vision
    Folded up its scroll and fled,

And she tore the missive open
  Read it by the waning light,
"I am coming, Annie; meet me
  By the river-side to-night."
Not another word or token,
  Not a sign, a mark, a name;
But she needed none, she knew it,
  Knew from whom and whence it came.
"He is coming, O, " she murmur'd,
  "Coming! coming home at last,"
And the weary weeping, waiting,
  All will vanish with the past,
All those days and nights of watching,
  With a sinking heart and frame,
List'ning for a well-known footstep,
  And a form that never came—
As a dream will be forgotten
  When his arms are round me flung
When he tells in honey'd accents
  Why he stayed away so long,—
Calls me, once more, wife and darling,
  (O! how sweet the title now,)"
Then she mused, while blushes faintly
  Dyed the smooth, transparent brow.
Fell to strange and nervous musings
  Looking o'er the dusky hill
Far into the future, dreaming
  Of a title dearer still.
"Then," she thought, "he'll never leave me
  Save from dawn to evenfall,
And his home will be the circle

Which contains his all in all."
Day-dreams, O ! ye mystic day-dreams,
  How ye lead the soul away
From the turmoil of the present
  To a calmer, brighter day,
O ! what light, what glowing lustre
  O'er the tiréd spirit streams
When the fair, but frail, enchantress
  Wafts us through her realm of dreams.
O ! we feel the tender presence
  Of a hand in days of gone ;
Hear again the voice's music
  Of a dear departed one.
Comes the sound of rain distilling
  Through the verdant beechen trees,
Or the whispering hush at starlight,
  Or the lull of sunset seas ;
Or the straggling brooklet's ripples
  Or the twitter of a bird,
Heard with some sublime confession
  Some intensely thrilling word ;
Strangely sweet associations
  Of a life for ever fled !
Scenes we thought we long had buried
  With the unremembered dead !
Looks the young man gaily forward,
  Picturing scenes of radiant bliss,
And the old man, glancing backward,
  Blushes 'neath his love's first kiss.
And the crime-empurpled exile

On a strange far distant shore
Lying 'neath the broad banana
  Is a sinless child once more,
Playing by the low thatched cottage,
  On his head a mother's hand;
Ah ! he sheds a tear while dreaming
  Of the dear old native land !
And the sailor on the mast-head
  While around him pants the wave,
And the soldier wounded—bleeding—
  While beneath him yawns the grave ;
Each forgets his toil and danger,
  Skips the lapse of seathing foam,
Feels the joyous thrill of contact
  With the loved ones of his home.
And the hearts that groan in travail
  For their brother's sins and woes,
And the grieved and weary-hearted—
  They who languish for repose—
And the worn-thin arms stretched forward
  Grappling fiercely with the night,
And the tear-stained eyes, intensely
  Piercing forward towards the light ;
And the restless, yearning spirit,
  Panting with immortal quest,
Gain a brief glimpse of that higher,
  Holier, purier life, the best.
Blessed day-dreams ! happy visions !
  Gilded fancies, dearly prized !
Scents of summer flowers, long faded,

Gleams of bliss unrealized !
Ah ! dream on, unhappy women ;
   Thick around thee falls the gloom ;
Go, as goes the lamb to slaughter,
   Blythe and gay to meet thy doom.
On she donned her boots and bonnet
   Round her shoulders pinn'd a shawl ;
Fluttered down the dusky staircase !
   Stood a moment in the hall ;
Hurried out into the twilight,
   Down the grim and dusky street,
Far away into the suburbs
   Where the town and country meet.
Onward, onward through the valley,
   While the keen and bracing air,
Raised a flush upon the wan cheeks,
   Fluttered lightly 'mongst her hair ;
Onward, till the river's murmur,
   Deepened to a thundering roar ;
Till she saw the foam-wreathed wavelets
   Lick the steep and sandy shore ;
Onward, 'neath the sloping alders,
   Till her distant piercing eye
Caught the outline of a figure
   Limn'd against the dark-blue sky.
And a joyous thrill came o'er her,
   For she knew that form—that gait !
And she hurried swiftly onward,
   Full of hope, to meet her fate !
With a glowing smile she met him

Hid her face upon his breast,
Feeling like the storm-tossed sailor
  When he hails a port of rest ;
But no sweet responsive pressure
  Met the pure and chaste advance ;
No fond kisses thrilled her being ;
  Not a tender word or glance !
Only once his stern lips, coldly
  Touched the forehead, snowy white,
When the pale, grieved face looked upward,
  Beaming with the old love light.
Stepping lightly back, he muttered,
  " It were better for our peace
If this foolish, childish folly,
  All this mummery should cease.
I am tired to death of acting,
  And my heart is sated quite,
So 'twere better far to tell you—
  Tell you all the truth to-night.
Ah ! the time I well remember,
  In the evening's golden glow,
When I first beheld you, seated
  'Neath a yew tree bending low ;
And your fresh and glorious beauty,
  Bursting full upon my view,
Struck me,—thrilled me with a feeling
  Strong and wild, as strange and new.
Oft I came, but found that only
  From the altar's sacred shrine
Could the fairest child of nature

Y

And the wond'rous charms be mine.
Strange to say my frenzied fancy
    Led my fickle heart astray,
Reason fled with calm reflection,
    And mad passion ruled the day.
And you ! you knew me high born,
    Knew how low your own estate ;
Knew that only with an equal
    Could the heir of thousands mate !
Yet you yielded ; evil moment !
    Causing years of mad regret ;
It were better, doubly better
    Had we never, never met !
For beneath these quiet alders,
    Ere the rays of morning start
With yon speechless stars as witness,
    We must part—for ever part !
Go your way, and 'mid the lowly
    May you find a braver arm,
And a nobler heart to value
    And your virtues shield from harm !"
Then he held his hand towards her,
    Looked, and saw with grim surprise
O'er her face a death-like pallor,
    But defiance in her eyes.
Ah ! your marriage ! prove it, Annie,
    Trumpet to the world my name ;
It was but a sham—a fiction !
    'Twill but load your own with shame.
Suddenly the arms were outstretched "

Madly, pleadingly, until
Sank the wide distended eye-balls,
   And the leaping pulse grew still,
And the white-lips only quivered
   Ere all sense and reason left.
And she fell, as falls the tendril
   When the sturdy larch is reft ;
Standing there, a craven whiteness
   O'er his fine, dark features spread ;
O'er his frame a creeping terror,
   In his breast an awful dread.
" Crushed and ruined ! noble Annie !
   Pure as is the font of day !
Cursed be the hour when passion
   Led my better sense astray."
For awhile he bent above her,
   Cursing fate, when on his ear
Fell the distant sound of footsteps,
   And he fled in haste and fear,
Softly sighed and moaned the breezes,
   And the rivers thunder'd low !
And she lay there, white and rigid
   Like a figure carved in snow.

(End of Part First.)

PART SECOND.

IS a building in a city
    Modern, angular, and bare;
    Cross with me the whitened doorstep
  And ascend the ample stair;
Tread with silent steps the passage;
  Let the weary-hearted rest;
Enter noiselessly the chamber
  Looking out towards the west.
All is silent as the graveyard;
  Gloom and darkness brood o'er all,
Save the first faint rays of dawning,
  Struggling through the windows small,
On a plain but snowy pallet
  Lies a prone and wasted form,
Bent and broken like a lily
  In the thickness of the storm,
Through the long night, since the watchman
  Found it lying still and low,
Where the alders bend in silence
  And the river thunders low,
It had lain there mad with anguish
  Tossing wildly to and fro,
Suffering nature's sternest measures
  And affliction's recent throe!
Now it lies so still and peaceful
  In the dawning, dim and grey,
That we scarce can deem it human,
  Scarce believe it breathless clay,

But that now and then a spasm
　　Wrenches from the heart a moan ;
Now and then she mutters something
　　In a wildly pleading tone,
Sunken are the cheeks, erst roses,
　　And the lips are bloodless-white,
And the forehead looks like marble
　　In the morning's dusty light.
And the eyes so large, half open,
　　Gleam a wildly vacant stare
And the dusk of grey is blended
　　With the golden in her hair !
Is it ? can it be the being
　　That we saw but yesterday ?
Building gay and airy castles,
　　In the evening, calm and gay !
O ! unyielding fate ; how cruel
　　And how absolute thy power !
O ! the foot how hard, how ruthless
　　That could crush so fair a flower !
By her side an old man seated
　　Still as figure cut in stone,
Touched her pulses with his fingers,
　　Held her hand within his own ;
Bent his form, and worn and storm-wrapped
　　While as flaxen is his hair,
And his wan and furrowed features
　　Tell of sorrow and of care ;
At his right, upon a table,
　　Lies a burly silver watch

Dealing time with calm precision,
   Tick by tick, and notch by notch,
And a box, a spoon, a tea-cup,
   Specs and nicknacks half a score,
And a case of labelled phials
   At his left upon the floor.
And he sits there calm and silent,
   And his eyes are dim with tears,
For his soul is mid the labyrinths
   Of the sadly vanished years,
When another form and figure,
   Crushed like this, before him lay,
One whose mortal long has mingled
   With corruption, worms and clay !
Ah ! he once was boyant hearted ;
   Once was happy, fair and young ;
Once had been the village hero,
   And the envied of the throng ;
Master of a noble science ;
   Husband of a sweet, pure wife ;
Earth to him was like an Eden ;
   Like a cloudless dream of life.
Years flew on and not a shadow
   Damped their Summer's day of love.
O ! they almost had forgotten
   Him who rules and reigns above,
He who gave those cherub beings
   Crowding gayly round the hearth,
He who clothed them all with beauty,
   Gave them innocence and mirth;

Time sped on, till lithesome Effie,
Fairest of the joyous band,
First sweet Spring of their union
Once the Queen of Baby-Land.

Finis.